Jeremy Tucker

before a canyon

A Story About Victor and Me

bright sky press
HOUSTON, TEXAS

2365 Rice Boulevard, Suite 202,
Houston, Texas 77005

10 9 8 7 6 5 4 3 2 1

Library of Congress Cataloging-in-Publication Data on file with publisher.
Printed in Canada.

before a canyon

A Story About Victor and Me

JEREMY TUCKER

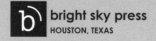

bright sky press
HOUSTON, TEXAS

Dedicated to
Mom and Dad

Both have anointed me with unconditional love

TABLE OF CONTENTS

Introduction by Samuel E. Karff

Periodically a teacher will encounter a student with extraordinary promise. Such a student may be gifted with an unusually nimble mind, a passion for learning, and an insatiable curiosity. If we are truly blessed, he will also manifest a robust idealism and a deeply formed social conscience.

About thirty years ago, I encountered such a student. My relationship with Jeremy Tucker began when he was about five, and I had the good fortune to be his rabbi. I first experienced his independent judgment when he was approaching thirteen but decided not to become a Bar Mitzvah. His parents insisted that he, after several years of Hebrew School, discuss the decision with me. Jeremy explained that for him it would be primarily a social event—not a spiritual rite of passage. He seemed surprised and delighted when I supported his decision. I explained that not becoming Bar Mitzvah at this time would not affect his Jewish identity.

Some years later, during his college years, he came to see me. Over a sandwich, he declared he was an atheist. When I probed, Jeremy expressed his belief that we each have a calling on this earth. He felt his derived from a special love of children and a passion to use his knowledge and skills to help the most vulnerable and marginalized among them to live a better life. I responded that, regardless of his declared belief, I could not regard him as an atheist. This pleased him greatly, and our bond deepened. Whenever he was in town, he called, and we met.

I was hardly surprised that he was a prize student at Yale University or that he distinguished himself at Harvard Medical School. And it seemed fully in character when Jeremy spent two years between Yale and Harvard in a Phoenix barrio working as a Teach For America corps member.

Jeremy was born into a comfortable world. His parents loved him deeply and wisely. They implanted and reinforced a strong self-respect, supported his intellectual and artistic interests, and took pride in his deep concern for the welfare of others. They also provided for Jeremy to be educated in the finest schools, to travel widely, to indulge his curious mind, and to follow the dictates of his compassionate heart.

Even as a youth, Jeremy was troubled by the vast disparity between his own life experience and the world of those who lived on the other side of town. The Teach For America program enabled him to reach out to the underserved, marginalized segment of our society. It gratified both his love of children and his social conscience.

No doubt those who dedicate several years of their life to this program contribute to one of our nation's most crucial tasks. No less is at stake here than the future of America in a competitive global economy. The difference between success and failure in a classroom becomes the difference between empowering the youth of our growing "under class" to aspire and qualify for the jobs of tomorrow, and consigning them to alienation, street corner loitering, and crime.

But even within Teach For America, there are different levels of engagement. Many teachers in the corps, understandably spent by a day in the classroom, will make a clear distinction between work hours and recreation hours. Jeremy's goals, however, were more ambitious. He cultivated a relationship with a student outside the classroom. The student fortunate enough to receive this level of commitment from Jeremy was a boy named Victor. Readers of this book will get to know both teacher and student, not primarily against the backdrop of a school day, but in Victor's home and in other venues to which Jeremy took his friend—culminating in a trek through the Grand Canyon and the American Southwest. We experience vicariously the formidable, painfully frustrating, but ultimately inspiring dimensions of bridging the distance between a comfortable life in Houston and the barrio in Phoenix. We also discover the fruits of giving a troubled teenager an honest, all-encompassing relationship of genuine caring, steadfastness, and tough love.

This is a book about a teacher who engaged a teenager 24/7 as they trekked through a majestic and forbidding canyon. It is a story that includes moments of angry confrontation, disappointment, exasperation, and regret—and it is a story with tender moments of connecting, understanding, and restoring hope.

In the story, the teacher and the student take turns instructing each other. There is a poignant sequel to this narrative which, in time, may become the basis of Jeremy's next book. The event on which it would be based was life-transforming for Jeremy, and it also changed our relationship from teacher/student to a deep, mutually nourishing friendship.

Six years ago, at the conclusion of Jeremy's first year in a pediatric residency at Texas Children's Hospital, I received a shocking phone call from the chief of pediatrics, the man who had fervently recruited Jeremy to his program. He told me that Jeremy had been assaulted by a cancerous brain tumor and had undergone surgery that left him cognitively whole, but physically disabled.

The trekker through the Grand Canyon was now dependent on a wheelchair. He who had written a stirring account of his relationship to a child who was handicapped by life's circumstances beyond his making was now himself a conspicuous member of the handicapped community. He who had helped this child struggle for a new life was now embarking on a similar journey. One cannot overstate the magnitude and depth of Jeremy's loss. In the wake of this trauma, he came perilously close to losing his will to live. The reader should know that the story of his struggle is a different story. Know that in his emerging role as a counselor for under-resourced children in a charter school, Jeremy bears witness to being one of them. He insists that we are all handicapped; only the nature of our disability distinguishes us from one another.

A profound continuity between Jeremy before and Jeremy after that fateful surgery remains. He has not lost his passion to befriend and empower marginalized youth. His love for and commitment to children remains; his special rapport with children is as strong as ever. That sense of a calling, which he spoke of to me many years ago, remains undimmed.

Victor Villanueva
Sixth Period
Creative Writing Class

About Me

Hi, my name is Victor. My hair is black and I'm brown.
I got brown eyes. I'm twelve years old, I almost got
thirteen. My favorite foods are pizza and vanilla and
my favorite thing to do is going to Disneyland with my
family. We went when I was six. Also I like to race in
the bikes in the mountain. My bike is a half. I like
motorcycles and I like going to overnight camps. I been
to one in fifth grade for a week. Plus my best thing is
laughing with all my friends. My favorite sports are
soccer and football. And I like when my mom tries to
teach me how to drive.

by Victor

before a canyon

PART I
the way you see

Public Speaking

He doesn't enter the classroom with my other sixth graders, and he doesn't say why he's there. He slouches on the cement pathway outside the classroom door and looks blankly into space. He doesn't have a backpack or parent with him, nothing to explain his presence except a folded pink carbon copy paper gripped tightly against his tan uniform pants. According to the pink paper, his name is Victor Villanueva, he'll be turning thirteen next month, he comes from Che Guevara Elementary, and he's transferring to Basil M. Hatfield into my homeroom class. The pink paper has the name LAVERNE VILLANUEVA in dark block letters beside the word Parents. The line beside Guardians has been left blank. This bodes well for the boy, I imagine, compared to many of my other students. At least he has a mother.

The pink paper doesn't say that his mother waited to enroll him in school until the second week of class, because she was working too many shifts cleaning motels. It also doesn't mention that his family used to live in one of Phoenix's most violent neighborhoods where there seemed to be murders almost every week and where members of Wetback Power, a gang also known as Doble (doh blay), were known to shoot anyone wearing rival colors on their street. Nor does the paper say that Victor's father lives ten hours away and sees his son only on major holidays.

As I finish reading over the pink paper, I unlock my door. The line of students files into the classroom while Victor stands alone outside, leaning against the wall. "Are you sure you're in my homeroom?" I ask him, naively wondering if the principal realizes that I already have thirty students.

"I don't know," he grunts as he enters the room.

I smile at him gently while I write his name in my grade book. "Good," I say as I show him to his seat. "I'll figure out your schedule in a few minutes." But he doesn't respond. I wonder if Victor is normally shy.

After completing my attendance roster, I stand at the front corner of the room, my back pressed up against the large teacher-desk.

"I've got a new idea," I say to my class with an enthusiastic grin.

"We're going to report current events every morning during homeroom. It'll be fun, like show and tell, except it'll be about world affairs."

I feel energized. This is going to be great, I think to myself, something they will really love. My students smile as I tell them what I mean by current events and describe how I imagine the first thirty minutes of each day will run.

"You all will get to be each other's teachers," I explain. "And you'll learn about public speaking, too."

By the middle of my explanation, I notice that their smiles seem to have grown: a couple of students are chuckling while others are turning red or even covering their faces. They appear to be more than enthusiastic. I wonder if something I am doing or saying isn't quite right.

I pause, check my shoes as well as the zipper on my pants, and then glance over my shoulders. That's when I first notice Victor, the boy who has just joined my homeroom, standing beside me. He grins up at me politely and then, as if to help me understand what he's doing, begins to gesture his arms in a rhythm similar to my own. Although I'm a bit surprised by the fact that he's standing next to me when he should be sitting at his desk, I have trouble getting angry. He's two feet away and looks somewhat useless, like a small bug drowning itself in a big smoothie. I guess he's not as shy as I thought.

I glare at Victor. He's about five feet tall, a good foot shorter than I am; has black hair, longer and less curly than mine; and has dark tan skin, much darker than my own pale skin. His white-collar shirt has come untucked, but his pink paper is sticking out of his uniform pants pocket.

Perhaps because my body freezes when I see him, he stops moving and without saying a word quickly tucks his hands behind his back and looks at me with ready eyes. He continues to stand where he is, making no effort to return to his desk. I wonder if somehow he's trying to help me. I also wonder if he meant to make me feel embarrassed by his circular hand gestures. I interpret them as misguided and funny rather than insulting or mocking, and I'm somewhat surprised that he'd stand in front of the entire class on his first day at a new school. I assume that he must have a reasonable degree of self-confidence.

As I look at him, all that occurs to me is that maybe he'd be willing to help me create a schedule for our current events presentations. What does not occur to me as I watch Victor watching me, and what I do not understand until well into the school year, when I finally figure out how to teach, is that sixth grade students should not be allowed for any reason to get out of their seats, impromptu, to play teacher. Nor do I realize that even on his first day of school, Victor already knows that.

After I smile politely at him, he returns to his desk. I ask for volunteers for our first week of public speaking. None of the children raises a hand. What's going on? I think to myself. I was sure they'd be fighting to do this. Don't they love talking about things they find important? "Okay now, everyone's going to have to participate, so someone might as well offer to start us off." Still, no hands.

One girl, named Shamika, a physically-mature, forceful girl, who reads fast and who earned a hundred percent on all of her diagnostics last week, mumbles loud enough for me and all the other children to hear. "Shoot, I'm not standing in fronta all them. That's cheesy." Cheesy? What's she talking about?

Next thing I know, a barrage of children are shouting out, "Mr. Tucker, Mr. Tucker, I don't want to do this neither. Mr. Tucker, Shamika ain't doing it. That's not fair. This sucks." Here I had thought this would be similar to a drummed up version of show and tell, but it's turning my class into a mob of angry children.

"Y'all not being mature," Victor stands up suddenly. Everyone stops talking and looks at him. "It's gonna be fun. Like being a news reporter. Except nobody's gonna say nothing bad to no one."

I smile. Thank God for this new boy.

"I'll go first, Mr. T," he says. "I'll do mine on porn."

■ ■ ■ ■ ■ ■ ■ ■ ■ ■ ■ ■ ■

Finding Phoenix

Before going to Phoenix, while I was in college, I taught creative writing to fifth graders several times a week as a volunteer. My entrance into the school each day was the same. Usually about five minutes late, I would speedwalk to get there, over the freeway, through the gray snow, and into the school. I would storm through the front door, wave at the secretary in the main office, and hurry through the empty hallway to the fifth grade classroom to be greeted by a collective shush. The thirty children would be sitting at their desks with a blank sheet of paper and a box full of pencils.

"Jermy, Jermy, Jermy. Please stay this time, Jermy," the kids would scream out. "Are you going to juggle today? Are we making more board games today? Can we listen to TLC again? Can I work on my mystery?" The kids were always excited to see me, and that was one of the reasons I went as often as I did.

That was also the reason why I decided to apply to Teach For America. My plan was to continue to teach the same kinds of lessons to the same kinds of kids, but not as a part-time volunteer and not anywhere near the northeast. My dream job after college was to work for a couple of years in sunny California teaching fifth graders at an urban public school near a beach.

When I told my plan to the fifth graders, they cheered gleefully in response to the news. "I wanna be in his class! Can I? Can I, Mrs. Sessum?" Mrs. Sessum, their veteran teacher, smiled patiently. A few of the children tested name possibilities. "You'll be Mr. Jeremy. No, he gotta be Mr. Tucker. I know, I know. Mr. T!"

"No, no, I'll just be Jeremy," I replied, pronouncing my name as "germy."

But things didn't go as planned. I was assigned to teach 120 sixth grade students in Phoenix, Arizona and told that I'd have to go by Mr. Tucker. It seemed like it would be the death of my spirit, not to mention the death of my informality. And so I did the only mature thing I knew how to do: call my mother.

As was often the case, she didn't feel as sorry for me as I felt for myself. She told me I should accept the assignment and go where Teach

For America said I was needed.

"But how will I survive this?" I begged. "It's bad enough that I don't have my own class, that I'm not teaching fifth graders, and that I'm being sent to a city I've never been to that's nowhere near a beach. But they won't even let me go by my name. Can you believe I have to be called Mr. Tucker? I refuse! I won't do it. I'm Jeremy. What are they going to do? Fire me?"

"Jer," she said, "Jer, they're right." She paused. "You aren't the volunteer anymore. You're the teacher. You'll be spending more time with a lot of these children than their parents do. These kids need you to be an adult for them, not another kid. You need to get used to them seeing you as Mr. Tucker, even if that's not how you see yourself."

"But, but…" I said, trying to protest. It didn't matter to me what she or anybody else told me. I thought it was wrong. I would always just be Jeremy.

Even when I was packing my bags, becoming a teacher in Phoenix wasn't easy. I was running a full hour late for an eighteen-hour road trip from Houston to Phoenix with a caravan of cars. When I heard multiple horns blowing as the caravan arrived in front of my house, I jumped up and hurried out of my bedroom, dragging two suitcases behind me. I didn't stop when the wheel on one of the bags broke off, nor did I remember to carry with me the unpacked items lined up on the floor beside my bookshelf: my tennis racket, tape player, blanket, and pillow.

My mother, father, and sister were sitting on the front steps of the house waiting to say goodbye to me. "Are you okay, Jer?" my mother asked, scooting out of my way. "And what happened to your bag?"

I heard her but didn't stop to answer. I thought the caravan would leave without me, that I'd be driving to Phoenix by myself. I shoved the giant suitcases into the car without taking a minute to hug my mother, or father, or sister, and I forgot to go back into the house to get the rest of my things. I left without pillows. I left without blankets. I left without a hug goodbye. And so, in my daze of lateness and confusion, the summer didn't really end; it simply ran out of time.

The caravan stopped at White Sands National Monument just after a giant thunderstorm had passed, so clouds were emptying out of the sky as dusk approached. I sat on wet sand with the wind at my back and wrapped a borrowed maroon blanket around my shoulders. I tried to write something deep about sunsets and journeys. The wet sand was soaking my pants, though, so even my underwear grew damp. I stopped writing and stood up to give my behind a chance to dry.

The storms had cleared and left behind cirrus clouds wisping through the sky and water drops molding out the sand. The light of the setting sun over the white grains made the ground appear glossy and serene, shadowed and layered. I wondered if I was seeing sands and storms, white and black, or if the landscape was simply a reflection of sunrays, projections of light, and contours of shadow. I couldn't tell how much of what I was seeing was actually me.

The next day, our caravan arrived in Phoenix. We decided to drive around the neighborhoods where the school assignments were located to see what they were like. As we explored the streets, I got the feeling that everything was as straight as it was quiet. The land was flat and empty. Open lots sprawled across the ground. There were a few scattered palm trees, but most front yards contained little green—mostly dirt, cement driveways, and occasionally a picnic table. The houses were light shades of pink and yellow and looked fairly new but small. Thin wire fences surrounded most yards, and metal rods covered most windows. The sidewalks and driveways of South Phoenix seemed entirely deserted. After I had lived in Phoenix for two or three months, I was told that it always seems this way, except late in the afternoon when the ice-cream truck comes by and children pour out of their houses to buy ice-cold Sprites and Flaming Hot Cheetos.

After several days of orientation and apartment shopping, the school year began. I knew I'd be teaching 120 sixth grade children at a school called B. M. Hatfield, which was for fourth to eighth graders. I wasn't well prepared. When I first saw my list of students, I noticed that many of them were twelve or thirteen years old. This surprised me. I had thought that sixth graders are usually eleven. It wasn't until later that I learned the kids were older than average sixth graders because they usually started school a year or two late.

During the first week of class, I tried to learn as much as I could about the specific tastes of the students. I led "get to know you" games with toilet paper. I gave out questionnaires about movie tastes and boy or girlfriend personality preferences. And I tried to talk to kids as much as I could between classes and after school.

Several students told me they liked writing plays and making up stories. Others said their favorite parts of school were the math games and science fair projects. And when asked, almost all of them said they would love to learn to solve mysteries.

In talking to the students, I also realized that very few of them lived with both their mother and father and that every one of them received a government-subsidized free lunch. I was surprised they didn't complain about the school cafeteria food. I asked why they didn't, and they said it was because they were always hungry and liked the burritos and corn dogs. One student told me that school lunch was his biggest and best meal of the day.

■ ■ ■ ■ ■ ■ ■ ■ ■ ■ ■ ■

Victor Villanueva
Sixth Period
Creative Writing Class

My Neighborhood

My neighborhood is right here. It's crazy and wacked.
Everyone goes to the street to play if you look outside.
They're smoking or drinking and driving fast and they all
have children that almost get runned over. In my house we
don't go nowhere. We stay home to watch TV. And I stay to
fix my bike. In my neighborhood in the day it is quiet and at
night it is loud.

by Victor

Child Protection

During our math period today, while I'm standing in front of the chalkboard explaining an assignment, a woman I've never seen opens the door to my classroom. "Victor, venga aquí," she says in a sturdy voice. She's a tall woman with a broad face and long, dark, wavy hair. I look at Victor. From the sour expression on his face, I can tell that this is his mother.

Victor gets out of his chair. As he moseys over to the doorway, he glances back at several boys in the room with a mischievous grin. I tell the class to get started with their work, and then I walk over to the woman to find out what's going on. Victor faces me but doesn't smile or say a word. "Señora Villanueva?" I ask, since no one's telling me.

"Sí," she says.

I go through my routine. "Soy el maestro, Mr. Tucker," I say, and then try to shake her hand. She holds my hand weakly, barely touching the palm. I notice the skin on her face, that it's freckled, that there are sharply indented shapes on her cheeks. She explains something to me in Spanish, but she speaks more quickly than I'm prepared for, so I lose track of what she's saying almost immediately.

"Sí," I say. "Victor puede decirme." I look at Victor. He has not moved from beside his mother's leg. "What's going on, Victor? I don't understand."

"She said I gotta go with her to the house. She said I be back in a few minutes, like an hour."

"Okay, I guess so," I say. I'm not sure what the school policies are about students leaving directly from their classrooms, but as Victor stands there with his mother, it seems I have no choice but to let him go.

About an hour later, while my students are outside playing soccer during gym class, Victor and his mother return to my room. I am sitting at the oversized teacher-desk when I see Mrs. Villanueva standing in the doorway, her shoulders nearly filling it.

"Victor," she shouts without moving. He squeezes around her to enter the room.

"Thank you," I say. "Gracias," I wave, but she doesn't smile. She shuts the door hard as she leaves. Victor slowly walks to his desk without saying a word. He puts his head between the bends of his elbows as his body drops into his chair. He's breathing quickly and making a strange noise, so rather than talking across the room, I walk over to him. He seems to be slightly faint, but I can't see his face.

"What's going on?" I ask.

He doesn't say a word at first. He turns his head into one of his hands so that he's facing away from me.

"Nothing," he says, and then pauses. "It's 'cause I had my brother's pants on. It was by accident, but she don't believe nothing." He speaks in a tiny voice and looks like he's woozy.

"Are you okay?" I ask, not knowing what else to say. There's something dripping off his nose and over his chin. I put my hand on his shoulder.

He doesn't move. "That's why she be hitting me," he talks into his elbows. "She had a belt, and she be hitting it on me."

"Where did she hit you?" I bend down closer as I hold my fingers over my eyelids.

He breathes out and wipes his nose on his sleeve. "Everywhere," he mumbles, turned away from me.

I slow down my breathing. "Where does it hurt?"

He takes his hand and slowly puts it onto his back, pauses, and then moves it to his leg. He makes another noise under his arms and says something that I cannot understand, because he's faced away from me and his face is covered. He then moves his hand again to reach around to the other side of his head and touches his ear. My hands are on both of his shoulders now. I try to stop him from shaking, to hold him still.

"How did—" I start, but don't get all the words out.

In one swift motion, with a heave of his shoulders and a soft, high-pitched sound, he falls out of my hands, out of his chair, and onto the floor. I feel as though he's jumping from somewhere high, and I want to catch him, but I don't move, don't touch him, just stand there and watch him fall. He wraps his body around the metal leg of the desk. He curls up in his khaki pants and covers his knees with his white collared shirt. He is panting now, shielding his body with the uniform, continuing to breathe in small grunts. I stand motionless above him, unable to speak. I look at him with his nose pressed into the classroom carpet. The carpet looks wet.

I stand, silent. I can't see his face.

Five or ten minutes later, Victor is sitting in his chair again. He holds a textbook straight up in front of him, but isn't moving at all. The class has several more minutes outside on the soccer field.

"Victor, why don't we go down to the nurse?" I say gently. He puts down the book without saying a word, and we go.

The nurse is a kind, soft-spoken woman, whom students often request to see.

"Hi there, sweetie," she says to Victor as we enter her area behind the main office. She is leaning over a filing drawer.

"Victor was showing me some new bruises," I start off slowly. "He was just with his mother when—" The nurse stops what she's doing as she interrupts my sentence midway.

"I think Victor and I will talk in private in one of the examining rooms," she says. "I'll send him back in a little while. Everything's going to be fine." Her calmness is reassuring. I leave Victor with her and hurry back to meet my students as they finish their game.

The next day the nurse tells me that when she examined Victor, she found red and purple stripes across his back, as well as blotchy bruises on his neck and the side of his leg. Some of the marks look new, but the rest seemed to have been there for a while. She called Child Protective Services (CPS) to inform them of the situation. Apparently they went to Victor's house later in the afternoon to speak to his mother. They did an assessment and then afterward suggested "alternative parenting strategies." This is very lucky, the nurse tells me. Usually when they get a call, CPS just fills out a report and files it. That's all she or anybody else says about this incident. We never have another interaction, although students often ask to see her for small physical maladies.

Before Victor goes home, I ask him how he's doing. We are standing outside on the paved sidewalk. I've already dismissed my class, and there aren't other kids around.

"What happened yesterday was pretty bad," I say. "How are you feeling now?"

"Fine," he says in a low flat voice. He appears to want to say more, but needs a moment. I wait. "You know, Mr. Tucker, I hate my mother. She be hitting me too much." He rubs his eyes with the bottom of his shirt. "Sometimes, I wish I could be with my dad. He live on a ranch in Utah, but he said I could be with him someday. That's why someday I'm gonna be with my dad." Victor touches his leg.

"I hope you'll be with your dad someday too," I say.

■ ■ ■ ■ ■ ■ ■ ■ ■ ■ ■ ■ ■

Purple

From the doorway of my classroom, if I wear my glasses and stand on my toes, I just barely can see Victor's house on the other side of the teacher parking lot. His is the small pink one, the one with a broken picket fence, a brown Chevy in the driveway, and an old blue Buick in the front yard. It takes Victor about three minutes to walk from his house to my classroom. And ever since the third week of school, when I first met his mother, he's been doing just that between three o'clock and five o'clock almost every other day.

"Hey, Mr. Tucker. We got tutorial today?"

The door to my classroom is open but Victor stands outside. School let out at three, and I wasn't planning on working with any kids this afternoon. I was hoping to leave school on time to catch up on my grading at home. Plus, Joe, another Teach For America corps member, the less talkative of my two roommates, was going to teach me how to rollerblade. It was going to be a celebration of quiet.

"How are you, Victor?" I use my Mr. Tucker voice as Victor drops his backpack onto the ground outside. I'm adding up my evening hours while we talk.

He pokes his head inside. "Hey, Mr. Tucker, do I have to go to T.O.R. tomorrow?" T.O.R. is the time-out room, where students go when they need more than a detention.

"Of course you do. You were out of control today," I say in an apologetic tone. His behavior's been getting worse this week. Unsure if I should invite him in, I walk over to the doorway.

"Come on, Mr. Tucker. That's not fair. I didn't do nothing," he moans as his face contorts to look like an angry Muppet.

"Fifteen No's in less than four weeks? Three No's today? You've been getting No's almost every day." In the system I inherited, a "No" is a detention. It means that a child must stay after school to sit silently for an hour.

Victor shifts his hips but keeps his arms flexed and tense at the elbows. "That's 'cause Mrs. Pass gives No's for nothing. She be an ugly, fat-ass bitch." Mrs. Pass is a first-year teacher like me. Her social studies class thus far consists mostly of copying state capitals off the board. During class time, she shrieks if children touch their hair and gives detention to children if they drop their pencils. Her classroom is next to mine.

"Mrs. Pass has been very clear about how she expects you to behave," I say. "And please don't talk about her that way. I know you don't like her, but you're going to have to learn to get along with her." This is what my mother used to tell me when I complained that my teachers were unfair. She also usually added, "You have to learn not to feel sorry for yourself," but I decide to save this for another day.

"Everybody hate her. She be yelling at everybody." Victor droops against the wall outside my classroom.

"It seems to me she's been pretty fair," I respond quickly. "If she gave you a 'No,' you must have done something." I step into the doorway.

"I didn't do nothing," he says monotonously as he stares into space. His mind is somewhere else.

"Don't tell me that. I see how you act in my class." My sympathy has waned, despite the fact that Victor may be right. Meanwhile, he continues to stare.

"Hey, Mr. Tucker, guess what?" His tone changes as he grabs his bag and squeezes past me to enter the room. "Me and Miguel rode our bikes to Peter Pan Pizza yesterday and we saw these niggas and they started messing with us." He begins to giggle as he talks faster. "So I be like 'Yo niggas, wassup? Get the fuck away from us' and they be like 'Oh yeah, watchu gonna do, wetback?' and I be like, 'Who you callin' a wetback, bitch?' and I jump off my bike and start throwing rocks, and them dumb niggas start getting all scared and they got away from us. You shoulda seen me and Miguel. We was laughing so hard."

I say nothing about his swearing. I don't give detentions after school.

I try to think of the phrases I was taught during my Teach For America six-week teacher-training course this past summer: high expectations, racial tolerance, alternatives to violence, conflict resolution, self-control, imminent physical danger. A three-hour lecture fast-forwards through my head.

"Wow, Victor." My words run together. "I'm glad you didn't get hurt."

He puts his backpack onto a desk, unzips it, and takes out a twice-folded and partially ripped paper. It's his math homework. He unfolds it, walks to the blackboard, and sees a half piece of purple chalk lying among five white ones. I give up on going home early as he picks up the purple chalk enthusiastically to copy the first homework question onto the board: 467 x 864 = _____.

He looks at me and smiles. "I forgot how to do it, Mr. Tucker."

■■■■■■■■■■■■■

Macking and Jacking

"Hey, Mr. T, I drew my maze real good," Victor comments.

"You did, but your math essay wasn't too great. It looked like you were rushing."

Victor, Nayeli, Jairo, and Amelia have stayed after school today to help me finish putting student work onto the wall. As we redecorate the classroom, I think about the first time I ever visited the school. Hatfield's right in the middle of South Phoenix and was named after a once-famous war general. When I arrived, I felt swallowed up by the one-story, brown-brick fortress, surrounded by a black ten-foot bar fence, and enclosed by a building with no front windows and no front entrance, at least none that's visible from the road. I walked through the halls of the school until I found the vice-principal in her office and introduced myself.

"I see," she said with a cool nod as she repeated my name.

She led me outside to a group of small individual classrooms, called temporaries, which despite their name, had apparently been there for more than ten years. My classroom, she told me, would be the temporary beside the school field.

"It's the farthest one from the main building," she pointed out with a laugh. "I'm sure you'll do fine."

As we approached the classroom, I was able to see that the walls were windowless and dim yellow, matching the color of the number fourteen painted on the classroom door. Wishing me luck, she opened up the room, handed me a copy of the classroom key, and left. I walked around the room for about an hour and formulated a plan for how I was going to set it up. I saw desks. I saw clusters. I saw problem-solving corners and art stations and game tables. I also saw hundreds of oversized mismatching math rules, vibrant, shiny, dizzying, disconcerting, covering every square inch of wall.

After three weeks with the two-hundred multicolored math rules decorating my room, I decided to take them down. That's why the children came this afternoon, to help me remove them. One of my youngest students, Nayeli, is helping to staple students' drawings and stories onto a newly cleared wall.

"Mr. Tucker, Mr. Tucker, look at mine's. Mine's is baddest!" she screams out when she sees her maze. Today we applied fractions to the Greek myth about the Minotaur and the labyrinth. As she attaches her drawing and essay to the wall, she uses twice the normal number of staples.

"Everybody liked your class today. You're our best teacher," Victor says. Yesterday he said I was the most boring. Two days ago I was too hard, and the day before that I was too easy. I've learned that student feedback, especially when it's from Victor, isn't the best measure of my success.

After we finish stripping down the explosion of math rules and after we finish covering the walls back up with essays and mazes, the kids decide to play outside. They run over to the swing set, and I watch them as they push each other on the swings, grabbing at each other's waists, pushing and swinging. There is a broken rhythm to the way they move, a clumsiness to their motions, how they want to swing high and want to be pushed, how they want to push but don't want to be kicked.

After a while on the swings, they tell me they are going to "jack" drinks from the snack bar. In order to earn their trust, I've decided that I won't get students in trouble for breaking school rules when they come after school voluntarily. But today, the kids ask me to come along. I'm flattered by their trust and interest in having me, but I turn them down. As it did before, I expect that eventually this trust will pay off and allow me to help children when they most need it. But when the children tell me their plan for right now, I shake my head.

"I can't believe y'all are going to steal." I explain why I think stealing their school's food is selfish and rude, not to mention immoral.

One or two students and a teacher normally work at the snack bar each day during lunch. Students form a long line in front of the window counter where the sales are made. I wonder if the door to the shack has been left open or if one of the kids has worked in the snack bar before and learned a trick for getting inside. When they come back to where I'm waiting, they've each got a bottle of fruit juice. No candy or chips. No soda. Just juice.

We sit on the cement steps outside and chat while they tip back their cold drinks. They ask me why I didn't get something. I say I didn't want to. I don't like to steal, I explain again. Victor asks me if I've ever stolen anything in my life, so I give him an honest answer.

"You really never jacked anything before, Mr. Tucker?" he asks again as if he misheard me the first time.

"Not really," I say, feeling almost a little disappointed in myself. He looks back at his bottle of apple juice, puts it to his lips, and turns his head up to face the sky. He chugs it all within seconds and lets out a big "ahhhhh." Then he looks at me again and burps out a huge guffaw.

"Mr. Tucker, Mr. T," Victor's friend Jairo shouts out, although I'm sitting beside him, "Has you ever kissed a girl before?" Where is this question coming from, I wonder. I look at Jairo. He's a skinny kid with a giant gold chain and a tight-ribbed, white tank top, neither of which matches his red bike and boyish smile.

I try to give another honest answer. "I'm twenty-two years old. I kissed a girl for the first time when I was—"

"No, no," he interrupts, "I mean on the mouth, like this." He makes a sucking noise, and all thirteen years of his body twitch and shake. The kids and I laugh. Jairo glows.

"I've had a few girlfriends," I decide to be vague. But he says nothing;

he doesn't seem satisfied with my answer. Either he doesn't understand it, or doesn't really care.

But Victor does. "Eww, Mr. Tucker was getting his groove on."

"I don't know if that's how I'd put it." I sense I'm not doing a very good job of playing teacher. I then think of my other roommate, Clayton, also a first-year Teach For America corps-member, who seems to be fitting into the shoes of kindergarten teacher rather well. He's a Trader Joe's enthusiast, eats only vegan foods, and sings loudly as he strums his guitar.

"My kids are magical," he told me the night before as he described classroom sing-a-longs and rainbow drawings. When I mentioned that I was having some difficulties, he jumped in quickly. "I know what you mean," he said with a sigh, and then told me a story about a student of his who's homeless, another who's afraid of the toilet, and a third who doesn't tie his own shoelaces. "One child never even has dinner," he ended with another sigh.

Thinking of Clayton, I look at the children sitting beside me on the stairs and try to think of something important to say. "You guys have to see things from lots of perspectives. That's what your Language Arts teacher, Ms. Immaho, always says, right?"

"Do you want to fuck Miss Immaho, huh Mr. Tucker?" Amelia asks.

Nope, I think to myself, I'm not doing well at this teacher thing at all. Amelia has a proud smirk on her face. She is obese, the most obese of all my students, and her voice is loud, deep, and confident. Perhaps she is blunt with her sexual interrogation because she fears no one would want to interrogate her.

"Amelia!" I stare at her. "I don't want to hear you talk like that," I say.

"What? I'm a good girl." I try to keep from laughing but cannot help it. For an obese teenager to seem cool, she really cannot be a 'good girl' at all.

"You like Ms. Immaho, huh Mr. Tucker?" Victor asks.

"No, she's just a teacher on our team. That's it," I say.

I can't tell the kids that I find Ms. Immaho unattractive and rude. After my first week of teaching, when I went to her for help as my mentor teacher, her advice to me was to get used to failure.

"Mr. Tucker, I think the best way for you to learn how to teach is to experience failure first," she said. "Then you'll never forget what it feels like, and you'll use anger and fear to your advantage in controlling the students in your class."

Victor keeps staring at me. "You don't like Ms. Immaho?" he asks.

"No, I do, she's a good teacher," I say.

"Mr. Tucker likes Ms. Immaho. Ah!" Victor shrieks as he turns red in the face and points at me.

I smile but say nothing. Anger and fear are the words of my mentor teacher. I almost wish she were more like my roommate and suggested rainbows and sing-a-longs.

■ ■ ■ ■ ■ ■ ■ ■ ■ ■ ■ ■ ■

Testing

In the middle of a fraction quiz in math class, Victor raises his hand to ask me if I'll tutor him after school and let him redo his paper. Before answering him, I look over his work. Unfortunately, he has no idea what he's doing. Many of his answers make no sense; he isn't even doing the problems the right way. So I agree to help. After school Victor waits for me to get back from my fifteen-minute, after-school bus duty.

He knows that in the afternoon I often have bus duty, which consists of watching children climb onto buses while listening to teachers blow their whistles and yell "no running" loud enough for the principal to hear.

He sits patiently on the cement stoop outside my classroom. He jumps up when he sees me and never asks what took so long. As I unlock the classroom door, another student runs over with a note written in dark cursive pencil:

Mr. Tucker, please send Victor here. He has detention. I gave him a 'No' today.

—Pass

Victor and I walk together to Mrs. Pass's room. I want to see if he can stay with me to get tutored instead of going to detention. Rows of desks fill her classroom, the walls are bare, and colorful construction paper figures dangle from the ceiling in straight lines over the aisles. About thirty students sit silently in the room. Today is her day to hold the after-school detention for all sixth-grade classes.

I walk across the room and quietly ask Mrs. Pass why Victor got in trouble. I tell her I'm hoping Victor can spend his time in tutorial with me rather than in detention with her. Staring back, she stands rigidly and moves her large body stiffly toward me. She holds her record book tightly and smacks it against her thigh. "Mr. Tucker, do you know what he did?" she asks in a sharp voice that seems to use up all her air. "He spit on another student's lunch in the cafeteria. He is a disgusting child."

"He did what?" I say stupidly.

"Fine." She continues, "Take him out. I do not want to look at him. Anyway, I'm going to write a referral to the office. "

This is a serious offense Victor has committed. I groan. I grunt. I try to put an angry look on my face. "Victor, that's not good," I say. "Victor, that's disgusting," I add.

"Victor, that's kind of horrible."

"You should talk to him about this behavior," she says.

"Trust me, Mrs. Pass, we are going to have a long talk about this one. That behavior is unacceptable." I look Victor in the eyes and frown. I make a loud humph, but he holds his face steady. Even though he appears worried, he says nothing. We exit Mrs. Pass's classroom and head back to mine.

As we walk, I try to scold him, "What'd you do that for? That's messed up. You know you can't do stuff like that."

"I didn't do nothing, but the fool got all crazy." Victor tells me all about this other student.

When we return to my classroom, we discover that my student Jamal wants to be tutored as well, and I think it's a good idea. "We'll do math first and talk about behavior second," I say intently. "Let's do some practice problems on the board to make sure you guys know what you're doing before you retake the quizzes."

Jamal's problems in school include much more than math. He normally doesn't get a single question right on any of his reading tests, and he sleeps during recess. His hair is greasy, his eyes are bloodshot, and often it looks as if his clothes haven't been washed for weeks. All that said, Jamal is a good kid. After school he likes to follow me around while I go back and forth between the office and my classroom, emptying out papers from my box and making photocopies. He begs me to tell him what we'll be doing in my class the next day and he loves to look at my teaching materials ahead of time. Usually he asks me to help him find a book in the school library. And when we sit down and flip through library books together, he usually pulls his chair beside mine and rests his arm on my shoulder. "I sure like reading," he'll say.

I give the kids a fraction addition problem to do on the board. As I walk the boys through the problem step by step, Victor keeps popping up with right answers. Not only does he know the steps, but he also knows them quickly, and he's able to get the final answer to the question right, too. "How did you know all that, Victor?" I ask. "Let's do another question." I give the boys a question to do on their own.

Victor writes out all the steps onto the board as quickly as he did last time. He steps back from the chalkboard to show me his answer. He has this one right as well, and his method is exactly what I've been teaching. I smile.

I watch him carefully as he easily gets a third question right. "Victor, I need to talk to you outside for a minute," I say nonchalantly. I don't want Jamal to hear us. We go outside and stand on the grass beside the wall of my classroom.

I look Victor in the face and grin. I'm happy to know my teaching is working and even happier to think that I'm starting to be able to read this kid. "I see your game, Victor. You knew what you were doing all along, and I fell for it. You outsmarted me and Mrs. Pass."

Victor looks at me, but appears confused. Am I giving him too much credit?

I bluff, pretending to be sure. "Victor, you don't have to play me anymore. You got me. I won't send you back to detention."

Victor squints. I shake my head and smile, but he says nothing. I wonder if I've made a wrong assumption. I stand silently, the smile falling off my face, and Victor still looks confused. I take a breath.

Maybe these practice questions were easier than the ones on the quiz. Maybe he was having trouble concentrating during math class and is able to think straight now. Maybe he does better with chalk.

But before I get out my apology, Victor's face turns red, and he bends at the knees. He looks to his side at the dull yellow wall and then looks back at me. Tilting his head and giggling, he pats the side of my shoulder. "I'm good, huh. I'm smarter than my teachers."

I'm relieved. "You may be," I say. "You definitely outsmarted me." As I think about this twelve-year-old kid and my college diploma, I start to laugh. When Victor got in trouble at lunchtime, he knew that after school he was going to get it from Mrs. Pass. He figured that during math he'd mess up his quiz, hoping he could convince me to pull him from detention to tutor him after school. He banked on the fact that he'd be allowed to redo his quiz. It was a perfect plan.

When we go back inside to resume the math tutoring with Jamal, I can't keep a straight face. Every time Victor says something correct, I chuckle. That makes Victor giggle, and soon Jamal is laughing too.

Strangely, I'm not angry at Victor at all.

■ ■ ■ ■ ■ ■ ■ ■ ■ ■ ■ ■

Fight

Right before math class, a fight breaks out in front of my classroom. Shouts resound, and students push each other trying to get a better view. I don't know what's happening until I make my way to the front. Apparently, Jamal shoved Victor, and then Victor shoved Jamal, but now all I see is Jamal punching Victor in the face, over and over in his face. Fists fly left and right, at Victor's cheeks and he stumbles and can't keep his balance. He's swinging his arms trying to defend himself, but he doesn't have good enough footing to aim a proper blow. Jamal's fists move fast and hard. It's the fastest I've ever seen Jamal move. His mouth is open, and he's clenching his teeth. His face is pulled down at the sides. He grunts out swear words too fast for me to follow. I'm worried for Victor—he appears to be ducking and hasn't thrown a single punch. Quickly, against school recommendations, I put my body between the boys.

I stop the fight and hold onto the boys' bodies, wrapping my arms tightly around their shoulders. After a moment they stop jerking. We stand very still. I calmly tell one of the students in my room to ask Mrs. Pass, whose classroom is adjacent to mine, to watch the class. Remaining between the two boys, I walk them to the office, my arms still loosely hugging their shoulders to make sure they can't run off or hit each other again. I explain the situation to the principal's secretary and then rush back to my class. Later that day, I learn that Jamal has been suspended for ten days, and Victor for seven.

The following afternoon, Victor comes to find out what work he's missing in school. After a while, he notices I have a mini-tape recorder in my classroom and begs me to let him use it. I'm curious to see what he'll say, so I agree. He grasps the recorder like a microphone between both of his hands and paces deliberately around the classroom perimeter. As he speaks into it, he changes his tone of voice:

"Hey, yo, people, it's me, Victor. You know what happened yesterday? I got in a fight with this big ugly black ass bitch. Do you know what's a bitch? It's a black ass fool. I was just kickin' back by the door with my ladies, see, and that dumb nigger Jamal. I was sitting down. He said I was talking shit. He came and pushed me. I pushed him back. And then he jumped on me and socked me once. I was so mad, I went to kill the motherfucker. But when I was going to hit him back, Mr. Tucker got me. The same day after school, they suspended us. They suspended us that same day. And then, after school, I went over to his house and got in a fight and beat the living shit out of that black ass fool. All right, y'all. Laters."

After finishing, he looks over at me with a gleam. "Mr. Tucker, did you hear how I said that? That was funny, dude. I sounded bad!"

"You certainly sounded mad," I say, frowning.

He rewinds the tape and then listens to himself. 'Do you know what's a bitch? It's a black ass fool' he hears himself say. "Dang, Mr. T, I'm funny. I'm like a stand-up or something. You was laughing too, when you heard me say that."

"I'm not sure," I say. Although Jamal is black and Victor is Mexican, I had not realized until he made this tape that there was any racial tension between them.

The tape continues. 'I was so mad, I went to kill the motherfucker.' "That's the best part. How do you reverse it so I can hear that again?"

I want him to hear me say 'rewind.'

"How do you rewind it? Just push this button here," I say, pointing at the backwards arrow on the machine.

After listening to himself say 'beat the living shit out of that black ass fool,' Victor rewinds the tape and listens to himself again. He snorts with laughter.

"You lucky I like you," he says. "'Cause if you was some other teacher, I wouldn't have stopped punching at Jamal when you got between us. I wouldn't care who I was punching." I don't remember Victor doing much punching when I held Jamal off him, but I say nothing.

As I listen to him, I wonder which Victor is the real Victor, the gangster-wannabe on the tape or the child standing here talking to me now, snorting, showing off, unclear about the word or method for rewinding.

The second quarter of the school year begins next week, and I decide to switch Victor into Mrs. Pass's homeroom. I took a difficult student from her homeroom earlier in the year, and she says she wants to return the favor by taking Victor from me now. I accept the offer happily, but part of me hopes that Victor will be harder for her to handle than she expects.

■■■■■■■■■■■■

Funny

Victor, Miguel, and Jamal come to my classroom after my regular tutoring session today. It's strange to see Victor and Jamal together again after their fight a few weeks ago, but they are getting along as though it has all been forgotten. The third boy, Miguel, is Victor's best friend.

He is generally quiet and pleasant, has a big smile and a rapid blink, and enjoys watching Victor's antics as well as playing soccer with him. He speaks relatively little English. I've been working with him on his spelling lately, and Victor and Jamal have asked to join in. I call out words for the kids to write onto the board as I look through their old papers for misspellings. One of the words Victor has wrong in several of his stories is the word 'funny.' He has it written "fony." When I call out this word, the boys think it's too easy. They ask me sarcastically what it means. Then they get sidetracked. They start telling stories about the 'funny' things they have done over the past few years. Jacking stuff. Skipping stuff. Talking stuff. Taking stuff. Getting injured. Getting girls. Failing classes. Failing school.

"Failing school?" I ask.

"It seems bad at first, but when you look back at it, it's pretty funny," Jamal explains. He stands beside the blackboard with a piece of white chalk in his hand, running the chalk up and down his jawbone.

"You mean, if you get bad grades now, that's funny?" I ask.

"Yeah, pretty much," Jamal responds.

"Okay, well, how 'bout if you get bad grades at the end of eighth grade? That's still funny, right?"

"Yeah."

"How about in ninth grade, if you fail out of high school, is that funny?"

"Yeah. I'd just go to another school." Jamal swings his chalk back and forth until it finds its way into his nose.

"Jamal!" I say. He removes the chalk. "Okay, so suppose the first eight years of school have been so funny that you haven't learned enough to pass any class at any high school with any teacher worth anything. Is that funny?"

"No, I guess not," he says.

Then Victor pipes in, "I think it'd be fun. I'd just sleep and eat and shit and watch TV."

I have no response, and Victor smiles triumphantly. He skirts over to the board and runs his hand along the entire length of the metal chalk bin, pushing dust onto the floor. Miguel continues to sit in silence.

His face is blank and his mouth maintains a steady gape. Victor looks over his shoulder at Miguel and says something in Spanish. Miguel nods and laughs.

After a moment, Victor stops moving and tells me another 'funny' story, giving me his usual hesitant look of half-pride.

"Okay, how 'bout this one, Mr. Tucker. So there was this little ugly old lady going down the street. She was cruising in her little fifty-something year old Chevrolet. She was talking all this shit." Victor looks at me and grins. I shake my head and grimace. He knows I don't apply rules after school. He's got an eraser in his hand now and is cleaning off the chalkboard as he speaks in his stage voice.

"So she was this old ugly lady driving in her junky old car," he says. "Well, you know how old people talk too much shit? Me and Miguel started throwing rocks at her car, and we broke her window. She was so mad, she tried to chase us, but we was too fast. You know how it is." Old people talk too much shit? Is this some sort of a cultural thing or is Victor just making this up?

I tell the three boys that last night I was at a meeting when some punk, probably someone a little like Victor, broke into one of the cars in the lot where all the teachers had parked.

"The teacher whose car got broken into is a nice woman," I add. "The damage is going to be very expensive for her to fix." I tell them she's a friend of mine. I ask Victor if he thinks that's funny.

"I would have jacked all the stuff from the car," Victor giggles.

"Jesus," I say, and he laughs some more.

Victor, Jamal, and Miguel decide to scoot their three desks around mine. One by one they turn the desks and twist their bodies. The four of us now form a circle, or at least some sort of trapezoid.

"Look," I say, "You've gotta be able to see the difference between what's funny and what's not. You and your friend ruin some woman's car after the woman cusses at you, and that's funny, right?"

"Yeah," Victor and Jamal agree.

"How about if there's someone else in the car with the woman and that person takes out a gun and shoots at your friend. Is that funny?"

Jamal responds, "One time these four cholos in the park started shooting a gun at me—it was really funny."

A cholo is a Latino who dresses as if he's in a gang. Jamal is black. I think again of the fight between Victor and Jamal the other day. It's strange to be having this conversation with these two boys while they are sitting so calmly beside each other.

"Okay, really, well," I stumble, trying not to think about Jamal getting shot. "What if your friend got shot and killed, would that be funny?"

Victor interjects, "If someone killed me, would you come to my—what's it called—my funeral?" He seems half-serious.

"Of course," I say. Now I've got a picture in my mind of Victor in one gang and Jamal in another, racist trash-talk between their gangs, a drive-by shooting, and Victor getting killed.

"You'd probably be laughing at me two years later," Victor says casually.

But I don't feel casual. "No, I wouldn't. I'd be really sad, and your mother would be really really sad," I say.

Somehow I have forgotten everything I know about Victor and his mother. He says nothing, but his face freezes.

Jamal seems to sense that the tone of the conversation has changed. After a few moments of silence, he says in a whispering voice, "If I got shot, but I didn't die, my mother would ground me for months."

No one knows what to say. The corners of our desks are touching.

Lost in thought, Victor stares at the chalkboard while Miguel reads over his list of words. "Funny."

Victor barely replies, "Funny. F-U-N-N-I."

■ ■ ■ ■ ■ ■ ■ ■ ■ ■ ■ ■ ■

before a canyon

Victor Villanueva
Sixth Period
Creative Writing Class

Thanksgiving

I went with my cousin to his house and we help them and
then I didn't know where we were going. I left to my friend's
house and I didn't do the thing that they did and the other
things. Then we went back home and they were doing the
turkey. Then I went to my room. I fell asleep and I dream I
was the turkey and they were eating me and I didn't know
what to do. Then I woke up and the food was ready.

by Victor

Brave or Dumb

The only times I sit behind my desk are when I'm organizing student papers and when a guest speaker comes to my class who bores me more than grading. The abstinence speaker is teaching my homeroom today. It's the last period of school, and I sit behind my desk.

Until the speaker gets to the interactive part of the lesson, I am in my own world, looking at math journals and writing progress reports. After a while, I notice some students standing and look up. Adrianna and Victor are passing out papers to all the students in the class.

"What about me?" I say with a grin, not knowing what I'm getting myself into.

Victor hears me and comes right over to my desk. "You gonna do the D.A.R.E. sheets too, Mr. T?" he asks. "I wanna do mine with you."

Before I can say I'd rather not, he gives me one of the papers in his stack and then shouts out, "Adrianna, Mr. T needs one of your sheets, too." I find it impossible to reject him when he's enthusiastic like this. "First we do them alone, Mr. T, and then we see what we got." Victor returns to his assigned desk at the front corner of the room.

Skimming the two handout pages from the guest speaker, I'm relieved to see that the "Dares" have nothing to do with sex or abstinence. They are lists of "Would-you-do" questions, each followed by a large "YES" or "NO." I wonder how this questionnaire fits into the lesson.

Victor works intensely and quickly, with his head down, never pausing to consider an answer. He's using a blue mapping pencil, which he probably carried off from another class, since he never has anything of his own to write with. He moves it rhythmically down the page.

While I'm working, my mind begins to drift. I wonder why it is that Victor, out of all his classmates, is the one who wants to pair himself with me. Why not any other children? Why always Victor? And why do I always cave in and say yes? These are questions I should have asked several months ago, but for some reason I didn't.

I have only answered five of the ten "Would you" questions when Victor jumps out of his seat and runs over to me, bursting out "I'm fast, huh? You're only on number five?"

"Hold it, boy, I'm hurrying," I say, staring at the page.

"Go on, Mr. T, hurry, hurry, hurry," he says.

I pause, look up from the paper, fix my eyes on him, and hold a frozen grimace. He can see my hidden smile. He laughs, and then he stops talking. I look back down at the paper and try to finish quickly, regrettably going with my first instincts and not taking time to think about having to share my answers.

Immediately after I circle my last answer, as if we're in a relay race, Victor quickly jumps to reading the first question aloud. "Ride a bike without a bike helmet?" He looks at me. "Yes," he laughs, "Would you?"

"Me, too, yes. We're both stupid."

"My bike got stolen. I don't got a bike," he replies. "Okay, number two," he says, before I can say anything else. "Get in a car with a drunk or stoned driver?"

"No," I answer assuredly.

"Yes," he giggles.

I look at him with a frown but say nothing. For the first seven "Would You?" answers, sometimes he says 'Yes' when I say 'No,' but never the reverse. I never say I would do something risky that he wouldn't do. I remain very teacherly.

"Number eight. Smoke cigarettes or chew tobacco? I said no," he says.

"Um, well," I falter.

"You wrote 'Yes.' You said 'Yes.' Dang, Mr. T, didn't they teach you that's bad for your body?"

"Well, yeah, I mean, I just tried it, and anyway, the question says 'would' you, not 'have' you or 'should' you, and you never really know what you would do." I'm speaking quickly.

Victor doesn't respond. He continues with number nine. Meanwhile, I'm just as glad not to discuss our answers. I think of all the times he's answered my questions when he's come to visit me after school. I bet there have been times he wished we didn't discuss those answers either.

After we finish the first page, we decide to answer the second-page questions immediately as we read them. "Would you give a class report on something unusual?" I read.

"No," Victor says.

"Yes for me," I say smugly as I circle my answer and press my lips together. I hurry onto the next question, trying to maintain Victor's pace. "Ask a clerk where to find something in a store?"

"Yes, I do that a lot," he says.

"Yeah, me too," I reply.

"It's smart, huh Mr. T?"

I agree as I read on. "Tell your parents you did something wrong, knowing you might get in trouble?"

"No," I say.

"Yes," Victor says as he circles it. "Sometimes I like to tell."

Ignoring the part of the question about parents, I say, "I've never understood that, Victor. Why do you tell me so much?"

Pausing from checking over the handout, I look at him.

"It's 'cause you're my first boy teacher," he replies with a sheepish smile. "I'm always telling you. I tell you all my secrets."

"I know. It's really weird," I say.

"'Cause what if I never told you? It'd be less fun that way."

What if he never told me?

■ ■ ■ ■ ■ ■ ■ ■ ■ ■ ■ ■

Victor Villanueva
Sixth Period
Creative Writing Class

My Family

I got seven brothers and sisters. I got my mom, my big sister,
and my smaller sister, who's six. I got a five year old brother,
a seven year old brother, and a seventeen year old brother
as well. I just hang with my big brother. Also I got my oldest
sister in Mexico with my grandmom.

My family argues too much. They won't let you do nothing
bad. When I want to go somewhere, they make me talk
to my brothers first. And they always make me throw the
garbage away and I can't play wrestle in the house.
It's 'cause my cousins is gang bangers and my mom don't
want me to be like them.

by Victor

Party

It is now the last week before Christmas. The children have been somewhat rambunctious, but they're very excited about the class party we've been planning. We've decided to have a Christmas celebration at the end of the week—I'm getting a bunch of pizzas, and the kids are bringing in cookies, cakes, and soda. We have a tree already. Adrianna told me her mother didn't have enough money to afford one, so I decided to buy the whole class a tree. It's against school policy, and I haven't asked if it's okay. Adrianna and several other children have been bringing lights to decorate it and all sorts of cardboard cutouts to put onto the walls.

Victor has been spending more and more time with my homeroom class. After I switched him out of my homeroom into Mrs. Pass's, he's begged me nearly every day to switch him back. He promises he'll be better, so I tell him that during the last week before Christmas, I'll allow him to rejoin our homeroom in the afternoons. Mrs. Pass is happy to let him leave.

The afternoon before our party, I suddenly get a sharp pain in my stomach during the homeroom period. I have to go to use the bathroom, and I cannot wait. I go to ask the teacher next door, Mrs. Pass, to keep her eyes on my class, but when I open up the fire door between our rooms, she and her class aren't there. They've gone outside without telling me. I look around at my students.

"Kids," I tell them, "Guys, I've got to run out for a moment. Seriously, we're having a huge party tomorrow, so please, behave yourselves. There's no reason to fight or mess things up. We're going to have a great day tomorrow. Please be good, and I'll be back in just a minute."

Oh God, I think to myself as I rush out of the room. This is a terrible idea. I am breaking every rule I've learned this year. I am leaving thirty teenage children in my room without any adult supervision. This isn't legal or wise. But I have to go to the bathroom. I have a terrible pain in my stomach, and there is no one I can think of quickly enough who could watch my class. So I run down the hall and search out the bathroom in the nurse's office. Once there, I briefly forget about the children and think only about myself.

As I'm leaving the nurse's office, feeling much better, it occurs to me that something may have happened while I was gone. I'm hopeful that everything is fine, but I begin to feel a little nervous. The children will keep themselves under control, I think optimistically. I'm sure they don't want to lose their party.

As I walk back down the hall inside the building and prepare to exit through the double doors that lead out to the temporary buildings, Victor and Adrianna come running toward me. "Mr. Tucker, Mr. Tucker," Victor shouts, "Mr. Tucker, everybody started fighting and throwing things."

"They were all throwing things, and the tree got knocked over," says Adrianna, a little more calmly than Victor. "We were trying to pick it up."

"Then Mrs. Pass came, and then the vice principal, and they all be in there," Victor adds. "And Mrs. Pass, she be saying it weren't right for you to leave us, and the Vice Principal couldn't get around the tree, and then she was going through your desk 'cause it's too messy."

"It's 'cause they were being bad, Mr. Tucker," Adrianna says. "The boys were all throwing things."

"Not me," Victor says. "But Jairo and Jamal started fighting, and then even Miguel, he got real mad, and I be trying to break them up, so I push Jamal real hard. Then Shamika started yelling at the kids too, and they started hitting her."

"It wasn't Victor's fault," Adrianna says. "That's why they sent him and me to find you."

"Mrs. Pass took over the class," Victor frowns. "You better hurry. She's crazy, and the kids are still fighting, and they're throwing things. Blocks and papers. And your stapler, too."

"Hurry, Mr. Tucker, hurry!" Adrianna tries to shout. I race after the children and run back to my classroom. The kids stop on the steps as I push past them.

I open the door. The children are all sitting. They see me. Everyone stares. I have no idea what's going on.

"Surprise! Merry Christmas!" they yell out.

"We cleaned the room, Mr. Tucker," Shamika says.

"I picked up the trash," adds Nayeli.

"We fooled you, Mr. Tucker," says Jamal.

Miguel stands by the door with a huge grin.

"Ah, Mr. Tucker, surprise!" repeats Victor. "We got you bad. It was my idea, too. Ask Adrianna. You looked real surprised, Mr. Tucker. You were scared, especially when I said about us throwing things and about the vice-principal."

"We cleaned up everything. The shelves, the desks, the floor. We made the room look real good," says Adrianna proudly.

"And the tree looks good too," says Victor. "We fixed it up."

"Victor, you were just watching. It was the girls," says Adrianna.

"Yeah, I know," Victor shrugs. "But everybody was nice, and your room got nice, too. The girls did it mostly, but it was me a little bit." Victor pats me on the back and smiles. "Merry Christmas, Mr. Tucker."

■ ■ ■ ■ ■ ■ ■ ■ ■ ■ ■ ■

Victor Villanueva

Sixth Period

Creative Writing Class

What I Would Like To Do During Winter Break

What I would like to do during winter break is go to Mexico
or Disneyland or down to my cousin's house or to Utah to my
dad's house. What I want to do in Christmas is get presents
and play around like a baby and I will eat all sorts of food
and all sorts of junk and I will eat some animal meat and I
will be going to the mountains on bikes and going to the top
of the mountain and going to the house of the mountain.
Then I will play a lot of video games and drive my mom's
car if she lets me and I will go to my sister's house and I
will be going everywhere. I will be going to California if
my mom goes to California. I will be going to Mexico.
Maybe with my cousin.

by Victor

A Christmas Story

We're beginning a new semester at Hatfield. Mrs. Pass wants me to transfer Victor back into my homeroom. As I guessed, his behavior last quarter was beyond Mrs. Pass's control. She called him a "horrible child."

"Mr. Tucker, am I in your homeroom now?" he asks on the first day of school after Christmas break, before the eight o'clock bell. Victor finds me in the hall inside the building, as I'm walking from the office back to my classroom to unlock the door.

"Yes, I think so, Victor. But first you'll need to sign a few things. You know, like I told you before, a behavior contract, a homework paper, and a 'Pursuit of Excellence' sheet for you to bring to all your classes. That's what you'll have to do if you want to return."

"Okay, hombre, very good," he says in a strangely agreeable tone. "Oh, Mr. Tucker, guess what, my father was killed the day before Christmas."

We walk through another set of doors.

Wait. "What?" I say, still focused on my plans.

"They shot him in Utah the day before Christmas."

"Jesus, Victor, Jesus, I don't understand."

"It's true. I didn't understand at first either, 'cause nobody told me nothing," he says. "But I heard them talking when he didn't show up for Christmas. Somebody killed my dad while he was sleeping in his trailer."

Quietly, Victor walks beside me staring into space. He doesn't say another word. Seconds later we arrive at my classroom. Victor stands at the back of the line and doesn't speak to anyone. I greet the kids and wish each one a happy new year. I give them new seat assignments, now in groups, except for Victor, whose assigned seat I had already decided would be at a desk by himself on my side of the classroom.

Victor's behavior in class is awful. He sets a bad example and is able to influence many students with his great charisma. If he fails to turn them, then he distracts them so they can't learn. I find myself explaining this to him and telling him that as his homeroom teacher, I will make it my business that he "strive for excellence" in all his classes this semester. I don't acknowledge his news about his father.

At lunchtime, the day finally pauses. I call Victor aside while we're waiting outside the cafeteria. I ask him again about his dad. I think maybe I was confused this morning about what he said. But he tells me the same thing. His father was shot the day before Christmas.

I drop off my class at the cafeteria, pick up my welcome back corn dog lunch, and go to the school office. The principal, Joe Baker, is on lunch duty. I go into his office and close the door. I stare at his new floral design.

At that moment, I am not a teacher. I need to call home. I need a space to sit alone. Not my own space, but someone else's, somewhere I can feel like a visitor. I look around the office and sit behind the desk. I call my mom. She isn't home. I call my dad. He's out at lunch. I put down the phone, feeling helpless and stupid. I cry behind the principal's desk. Like I'm the principal, but I'm crying. A crying principal. Me.

■ ■ ■ ■ ■ ■ ■ ■ ■ ■ ■ ■ ■

News

That day right after school I find Ms. Immaho, my mentor teacher. "Hey, Ms. Immaho, can I talk to you for a second? I have some news to tell you about. It's pretty bad."

"Sure, but I'm on my way out."

"Okay, I'll try to make it fast. The thing is that Victor's father was killed during Christmas break."

"Really? Who killed him?"

"I'm not sure."

"I wonder if he's trying to take advantage of you again. Are you sure it's true?"

"I think so. I'm pretty sure Victor was being honest. I don't think he'd lie to me about something like this. He told me a couple different times."

"Hmm. It's probably true. I wonder what his father did to get killed."

"I don't know. I'm worried about Victor, though. He isn't showing much emotion about the whole thing. He actually did really well in class today. I'm not sure what I should do to help him."

"You know, he might be fine. Did he know his father?"

"Yeah, I think so. I mean, I don't think he knew him well, but, I mean, this is his father. I'm sure he loved him."

"He may have loved him, but this kind of thing happens around here all the time. He's probably not that upset."

"I don't know. When a child loses his father, it's a really upsetting thing."

"For you and me, that's true. But you're assuming that these kids are like us, Mr. Tucker. These kids are very different from us. They see people get killed all the time. A lot of them stop feeling it or just get a little angry."

"Even when it's their father?"

"Victor is probably less upset than you are. He's used to this kind of stuff. He doesn't have to mourn the way you or I would. It's really sad, but that's the way it is around here."

■ ■ ■ ■ ■ ■ ■ ■ ■ ■ ■ ■ ■

Victor Villanueva
Sixth Period
Creative Writing Class

"Take the day Christian punched…"

Take the day Christian punched his Dad in the jaw and then he got an attitude and then his Dad said watch I will hit you in the jaw with the belt and the kid said you fool I am gonna destroy you for hitting me in my cute face you are gonna suffer. Then he took off to get a knife and killed him. Then he went to jail. He died with the death penalty.

by Victor

There

It's three-thirty on Monday afternoon. I've just come back from talking to Ms. Immaho when I hear the familiar knock on my door that I'd missed during winter vacation. This is earlier than usual for Victor, but I can tell from the muffled taps that it's him.

When I open my door he doesn't ask for M & M's or Dr. Pepper. He doesn't ask me to tutor him in math or work with him on spelling, and he doesn't bring a friend. He drops his bike outside my door, walks inside, and sits at a front-row desk. I walk around, nervously organizing things in my room and trying to make conversation while he slouches at a desk almost entirely still. I mention that I was surprised how well he did in school today. I was impressed by the careful way he wrote out every step for the word problems, I add.

We change topics several times while I pace, until finally I ask him about his father. He tells me again what he told me twice during school already, that his father was murdered in his trailer in Utah. That's when I sit down.

Not knowing what else to say, I ask Victor when his father moved to Utah.

"He stopped living in Phoenix last year," Victor answers.

"How come?"

"He was always drinking and smoking."

"Why'd he leave?"

"He always came home all drunk and stuff, and be all yelling at my mom. I think they got separated." Victor speaks in a matter-of-fact tone. He picks up a scrap of paper off the floor.

"He was probably sad to leave his kids, though," I say.

"He didn't want his kids to see him like that. I think he left 'cause he didn't want us to see him all drunk and smoking." Victor pauses.

I think of the stories he's been telling me all year about his neighborhood. "You see that anyway, don't you?" I ask.

"Yeah, I guess so."

"What did your father do after he left Phoenix?"

"He was in Utah. He was a cowboy. He lived there."

"What sort of cowboy?"

"I don't know. He worked on ranches and did stuff with horses. I was gonna go there too," Victor says. I remember his telling me about his father's ranch, and I regret that I never asked him more about it.

"I remember you told me you wanted to live with your father. You really loved him a lot."

Victor doesn't reply. He stares at the desk and twists the scrap of paper in his fingers. He wraps it tightly and flicks it with his thumb. He then looks back at me.

"The two men that killed him are here."

"What do you mean here? Here where?"

"The cops saw them here in Phoenix. They were driving around my neighborhood."

"You mean here?"

"Yeah, 'cause when they busted into my dad's trailer in Utah, they found a bunch of letters and stuff from his brother. Now they're after his brother."

"Where's his brother?"

"He's living in my house right now. He's my tío, my uncle."

"My God."

"My tío sleeps right by the door to our house. He keeps a gun by him all the time." I can't imagine my uncle sleeping by the front door to my house. I also can't imagine him with a gun. Uncle Rick's a dentist in Connecticut, who loves Broadway and the Yankees.

"What does your mom think?"

"She's scared, I think," Victor pauses. "She's going to Mexico tomorrow."

"She's leaving you guys here?"

"She's bringing my dad's body back to Mexico. That's where they're going to bury him."

"So she's leaving you on your own? Alone? Here?"

"Yeah, I mean, my uncle's here." I look at Victor. I'm about to ask again if she's leaving him here, but this time I don't.

"I wonder why these guys are chasing after your uncle," I say.

"They're Mafia, dude. They're Mexican Mafia."

Mexican Mafia? My mouth gapes open. I try to imagine what my family would do. "Are there police guarding your house?"

"Nah," Victor replies casually, as if I've been watching too many movies.

I don't get it. "You mean nobody's watching to make sure these guys don't get near your family?"

Victor doesn't respond to my question. "They saw them drive around our neighborhood," he says. "There's a warrant out. They're gonna go to jail. I hope I see them first, though. I'll blow their brains out. I'll get José's gun and kill their ass."

"I know you want to do that, but then you'd have to go to jail."

"I don't care if I get locked up. I'm gonna kill them."

"I know you want to. I would too. But it'd be better if the cops find them first."

Thinking about tonight, I don't feel good about sending Victor home. "Look, I'm going to give you my phone number. Just in case you need something, even if it's the middle of the night, call me. You know what I mean, like if there's any emergency."

"Oh, okay. I probably won't call, though," he says.

When we leave my classroom, we walk in separate directions. I head out toward the parking lot while Victor jumps on his bike and rides toward the big field where kids are playing soccer. As I approach my car, I hear his voice calling out from behind me.

"Tucker. Mr. Tucker. Sorry about reading." I turn around. Victor is riding back over to me on his bicycle.

"Why? What'd you do? You were good today," I say, unsure what he's talking about.

Victor races up to me and jumps off his bike. I stop walking.

"No, remember, I said 'Move out of my way, nigga' right in the middle of class."

Victor and I walk through the parking lot side by side. I'm trying to balance fifty yellow and red math folders in my arms while Victor walks his bike. When we get to my car, he puts his bike on the ground, helps me open the trunk, and put the folders inside. He then teases me. I tell him to be careful, and he waves as he rides down the block back to his house.

As I think about Victor's apology, at first I wonder how I managed to ignore his comment during class in the first place. I wonder if I was even listening, although I do vaguely recall hearing something of that sort now that Victor has mentioned it. I remember accidentally standing in a place that was blocking the assignment written on the chalkboard. Victor probably asked me to move so quickly and lightly that I didn't give it much thought. Maybe his father's death excused almost anything today. Maybe I didn't want to discourage him: he was doing his work and trying to follow directions. Maybe when he said "Move, nigga," I only heard him say "Move" and didn't hear the "nigga" part at all. Or maybe the reason was that he seemed almost embarrassed as the words came out, as if he knew he shouldn't have said them.

But then, regardless of what happened, there he was, like that, chasing after me, apologizing, asking me for nothing, going out of his way to show me respect.

When I get into my car, I picture Victor in his bed, and then I picture the uncle with the gun sleeping beside the front door. I can't leave things like this. I decide to go over to the main building to talk to the school police officer before I drive home.

The officer is an attractive blond woman in her late twenties with a thick Boston accent. I find her sitting at her desk doing paperwork. I ask if she could tell me what she knows about the Utah men coming to Phoenix and explain that I'm worried about some kids from our school in the house alone and unprotected.

"Apparently these guys called Phoenix last Wednesday and drove here on Thursday," she explains. "It appears they killed six other people in Utah besides your student's father. They were spotted in Phoenix yesterday driving a red Camaro with Utah plates. However, nobody can verify that these are the right guys for sure. Mrs. Villanueva has got the cop's name in Utah who's been on the case, but I myself haven't talked to any police officer to get an official report. At this time, most of what we know is what the mother, Mrs. Villanueva, told her daughter Vanessa to tell us."

She goes on to tell me that these guys have a pattern of breaking into houses, killing the person they're after, and then stealing the person's things. Mrs. Villanueva has said she's leaving here on the tenth of this month to bring her husband's body to Mexico and returning on the thirteenth.

"What I really need is the name and phone number of the cop in

Utah," she adds. "If you could help procure that, then I could find out exactly what's going on." I wonder why the school security officer hasn't been able to get the name and phone number, but I agree to help.

That night I call Victor's house several times, but no one answers the phone. The next day Victor comes to school. Apparently, the two suspects have been apprehended in Phoenix, and no one has been able to reach anybody in Utah who knows about the murder. Even though I'm happy and very relieved, part of me was hoping to be a hero. That night, I watch "Jeopardy" and eat my nightly chicken curry.

■ ■ ■ ■ ■ ■ ■ ■ ■ ■ ■ ■

Victor Villanueva
Sixth Period
Creative Writing Class

Who Is Your Hero?

My dad is my hero but he died he used to take me to his
ranch and I want to be a cowboy like my dad and I wanna
travel everywhere like my dad and I wanna learn how to ride
horses like my dad and I will like that I flew an airplane like
my dad and I learned how to make big tortiyas and I will be
my dad and I will do all of his dreams and I will take over
the ranch when I grow up. My mom is doing that but
then I will.

by Victor

Candyman

I walk across the street after school to talk to Victor's family. Over the past several weeks, he's been racking up more detentions than usual and often for easily avoidable things like shouting out curse words. To me, it seems almost intentional. I realize that I haven't yet spoken to his mother in the aftermath of his father's death. My singing roommate will be home early, if I'm remembering correctly, so I decide today's a good day to visit, talk about Victor, and offer my condolences.

A single bush leans against Victor's house, and an old blue car is parked on the dirt in the front yard. I rehearse my introduction as I walk up the smooth cement driveway: Hi, I don't know if you remember, but my name is—, I'm Victor's teacher; it's good finally to—, Victor's acting a little—, I think Victor needs—, I'm so sorry for—, I'm worried that—, Victor's not—, why isn't Victor staying after school—? Victor has stopped coming after school, and it seems as though his behavior has become more uncontrollable than before.

I stand in the driveway and stare at his house. It is stucco with black bars over the windows. The siding is flamingo; the garage, papaya; and the roof, beef. I feel overwhelmed by pink.

After a few seconds, I knock. A full-size girl who looks older than a teenager answers the door.

"Oh, you're Victor's teacher," she says in a high, quiet voice. "I'm his sister, Celia. You want to sit down over here?"

Two small children scramble off the couch as she sits on the other. Celia walks slowly. She seems fairly self-assured except for her childlike voice. The inside of the house is much darker than its exterior. The shades are drawn, and the television is the only source of light in the room. Several children sit frozen on the stringy brown carpet and say nothing. I notice they aren't looking at the television. Unsure what they are looking at, I smile. My hands rest in my lap.

"My mom will be home in about five minutes. Do you want to wait?" Celia asks politely.

"Yes, if that'd be all right," I reply. We sit quietly.

I can't tell how old Celia is, probably in her mid-twenties. She has a round baby-face that belies her mature manner. She appears comfortable handling the small children, whom I assume to be her younger siblings. The only toy I see is a white plastic rattle, lying beneath a glass coffee table. On the wall behind me, I notice framed baby portraits, wedding photos, and several Mexican figurines on a glass shelf, plus many glass and porcelain angels. There's a brown rectangular table where the TV room and kitchen join, but there's no wall between them, so from the couch I can see clearly into the kitchen. A new microwave sits on a counter, and everything is immaculately clean. Glancing around the house, I wonder why Victor so rarely has his own writing utensil. I somehow imagined his home would be disorganized. Right now, it mostly seems dark.

While we wait, several more kids emerge from the stark white hall-way. Celia gently yells "Cállete" at them as they run into the TV room and sit on the floor. She tells me that her mother works during the day as well as at night cleaning two different motels and usually is home from about four-thirty to five-thirty in the afternoon.

I ask Celia how she thinks Victor has been doing lately.

"We're very worried about him," she says. "He cusses at my mom a lot, and he's always hitting the kids."

I mention to her that last week was the first time since the beginning of the year that Victor did not come even once to talk to me after school. I also tell her that I've signed him up for an after-school college tutor program, and that he's been refusing to go. At first, Victor said that he was forgetting to stay, but by the end of the week, he changed his story. He said that he wasn't staying after school for the college-tutor program, or even to visit me, because he had found his own Teenager Program. I tell Celia that during this time, I also have noticed his behavior growing much worse. I ask her what she knows about this new program.

She explains the Teenager Program to me. Apparently he gets picked up in a white van at about four or five every afternoon, is given several bags of candy, and is dropped off in a neighborhood similar to this one, but on the west side of Phoenix. He walks from door to door and tries to sell candy. The same van that picks him up returns him home around ten o'clock at night. Usually no one sees him when he returns home, because everyone is already asleep. Victor's Teenager Program does not sound like a program meant to help teenagers.

Celia explains that the candy company pays him at the end of the week with cash, movie passes, and video game tokens. He has told her that he's making a lot of money, but she doesn't know how much. When I ask about weekends, she says that he's with the people in his Teenager Program either selling candy, in an arcade, or at a movie theater.

After I've waited about thirty minutes, Victor's mother arrives. I am aware of her strong chin and thick arms, which I recall from the time we met during Victor's first week of school. Mrs. Villanueva is a large woman, not overweight, but big. Her hair is long, black, and wavy, and she smiles a lot, but it's only a half-smile. I can't tell if she's grinning to be polite or if she's nervous. After I re-introduce myself in Spanish, Mrs. Villanueva tells me she's concerned about Victor. She says he has seemed different ever since winter break. She doesn't mention her husband's death. Apparently, Victor's been arguing with her a lot and refusing to listen to what she says. She says she doesn't know why.

"What's your opinion of Victor's Teenager Program?" I ask.

"I like it because it keeps him off the streets."

"True."

"It keeps him away from gangs if he's not on the streets," she adds, sounding exasperated.

"Yeah, that's good that he's not in any gangs." I pause for a moment. "But he's also learning that school isn't too important for making money."

"I hope he'll stay in school." She grins sheepishly, "I hope he'll graduate from high school and get a lot of money."

"That would be great. Someday he'll get to that. But there are other sixth-grade issues besides his after-school program and his present behavior that I feel we should address," I say. "But for now I don't want to complicate things. We have to think a bit more about what's causing him to act the way he has been lately."

She nods. I mention to her that I'm particularly concerned with how he's been dealing with his father's death. She replies that she'll talk to him about his father, his program, and his recent behavior the next time she sees him. I wonder when that will be.

Unfair

For the second time this week, I've gone to Victor's house. School's only been out for a few minutes, so we have about an hour before the Teenager Program sends its white van to his house. Victor and I sit on the concrete driveway, facing the side yard, with our legs stretched out into the grass. Although his house is on a street corner, a tall wooden fence standing between the side yard and the street keeps us from feeling exposed to the people walking by. While we talk, my eyes fix on the dark wood of the fence. I'm not looking at Victor, but I can tell he's popping a pimple on his face. He tells me it's the first he's ever had.

"Victor, the thing is that in school, I can't give you attention all the time. You want me to come to you before you start every math problem and to check each one as you finish. But I can't do it. There are all these other kids in class who need me as well. You can't jump out of your seat or yell across the room every time you get impatient or frustrated."

"It's 'cause you never come to me. I have my hand up for thirty minutes, and I don't know, you always doing something else."

"What do you think I'm doing? I'm helping all the other people in the class. Have you ever seen me just sitting behind my desk doing nothing? No, and you know it, Victor. I can't have you acting like this anymore."

"You be unfair to me, so I be unfair to you."

"What do you mean, me 'unfair to you?'"

"You give me all this extra work that nobody else has to do. I just want to be normal like everyone else."

"Well, you're not normal."

"Yes I am."

"No, Victor, we tried that. Everything was normal for you at the beginning of the year. And you know what? You didn't act like everybody else."

"So? You be giving me a "No" when I didn't do nothing."

"Didn't do anything? You? Come on. Who do you think mocked me in the beginning of the year?"

"Everybody."

"But who most of everybody? Huh Victor? And who do you think cussed the most in my class?"

"Everybody."

"But who the most, Victor?" Pause. No answer. I stare down at the driveway. I look up.

"Not me."

"Yes, you, Victor. How about hitting girls? Who do you think did that the most?"

"Everybody does."

"But who the most? You, Victor. So stop thinking you were so good."

"But they be messing with me. They talk shit to me, and you don't do nothing. So I go mess with them."

"I don't know. I think you talk a lot of stuff to them as well. I hear you start things. Boy, I even see you start things. To tell you the truth, Victor, I think you're where most of the problems start. You need to stop seeing yourself as a victim." I pick up a handful of dirt beside the driveway and watch it run through my fingers. My words feel empty.

Victor's volume builds. "If they be messing with me, I'm gonna be messing with them."

"When people are messing with you, you have to tell me, not make the problem worse," I say calmly.

"You wouldn't believe me if I did."

"What? You know that's not true. I believe everything you tell me. I've never called you a liar."

"Yeah, how 'bout that time I tricked you and Mrs. Pass?"

"How about it? I didn't call you a liar, although you were. Plus, afterward, I laughed. You didn't get in trouble for that. If anything, I'm unfair because I'm too nice to you. Look, I know you like trouble; you've told me all about it after school. You even said it was because I was your first male teacher and what if you never told me. So why are we arguing about that?"

"It's not fair for you to go and get me in trouble all the time when I tell you things."

"What? When did you ever get in trouble for things you told me? You only got in trouble for things I saw you do. Things you told me about, you never got in trouble for. Like ditching school. You told me you had ditched school one time with Miguel, and you never got in any trouble for that. I never told anyone."

Victor pauses and then looks directly at me. His eyebrows are pulled down and he's biting his lip. "You told everybody what I told you about my dad. You told Mrs. Pass and Mr. Johnson and Ms. Immaho and everyone."

My fingers grip the edge of the cement driveway. I lean back briefly, but I'm not able to hold myself up. I speak slowly and gently. "We're your teachers, Victor. You weren't getting in trouble. I wanted them to be able to help you. I wanted them to know what had happened and where you were coming from."

"Yeah, well, now all the kids know, and they be laughing at me behind my back. They be saying my dad was a stupid wetback, anyway."

I lean forward again and touch Victor on the back. "I'm sorry, V, I'm really sorry. That's awful what they're saying."

"Ms. Immaho told some kids, and now everybody knows. You were the only one I told."

"I'm sorry. I screwed up. I thought your teachers could help you, but I should have asked you before I told them. I'm sorry."

"I just want to help you." I stare at the grass between my feet, unable to look Victor in the eyes. "You're dealing with difficult stuff here, and I just want to help you. But something needs to change. What can we do?"

"I don't know."

"Well, I tried to think of something the first time, and it didn't work out, so you're gonna have to help me this time."

"I don't care. Do whatever you want."

"No. You have to agree as well. I mean, I know you like talking to older people, so what's the problem with the tutors from Arizona State University?"

"I already told you, I don't like that after-school program. I'm not going to it anymore. I went once, okay, and it was boring and there were all these little kids and I'm not going again." Victor sounds more demanding than usual.

"All right, all right, I didn't know that. You don't have to do it. But we've got to find you something. You need someone older, and your mom and I don't think the Teenager Program is enough. The way you've been acting just isn't right."

I stare again at the wooden fence behind Victor. I can't see the street. I can't see anything except little black holes in the wood.

Then, breaking the silence, Victor says, "Fine, I'm wrong. Okay? I'm wrong. Do whatever you want." He's speaking flatly as if he has no voice.

"What? You don't mean that. Tell me the truth."

"No, fine, I'm wrong."

"Don't lie to me. You don't think you're wrong." I pause. "Fine, look me in the eye and tell me again,"

"I can't," he says softly, still with almost no voice.

I have run out of things to say when we hear the muffled clangs of the big band music on the ice cream truck. Victor asks me if he can go inside to get money, and I nod.

When he disappears inside the house, his other older sister, Vanessa, comes to the door. She looks and sounds a lot like Celia, even though her face is more oval and she seems more rebellious. Vanessa is an eighth grader at Hatfield, and although I've heard about her a number of times, this is the first time we've met. She seems mature like Celia, but somewhat less soft and vulnerable. There is a bit of a bounce to her walk. She is only fourteen and Celia, much to my surprise, is only sixteen.

We stand on the driveway and chat while Victor and his younger siblings run out of the house and down the street to buy Hot Cheetos from the ice cream man.

I decide to tell Vanessa how I feel. "I just don't know what to do with him. It seems like we aren't connecting anymore."

"Victor has changed a lot," she says.

"What do you think I should do?" I ask.

"I don't know. We trust you. Whatever you think." I am flattered by Vanessa's trust. I wonder if Victor has told her about me.

"Do you think all of this is going on because of your dad?"

"He's been very upset since our dad died," she says, "I think that might be why he's acting so different."

Even though Vanessa speaks with the voice of a small child, when we talk I feel as though she's my age. I don't notice until much later that she and I talk about Victor's problems and never about her own. I forget about the fact that she's just fourteen years old and that Victor's father is her father, too.

I say to her, "I know Victor's upset about his dad, but I'm not sure how much. What do you think? He doesn't ever talk about it at school."

"I'm going to tell you something, but you have to promise to keep it a secret." I nod. "Every night, when Victor goes to bed, he cries and cries and bangs his head against the wall. Sometimes I go in his room and sit with him on his bed, and he hugs me. We listen to the Tupac song 'Dear Mama' and talk about our dad and cry together."

As Vanessa talks, I think to myself how hard Victor must have to work to hold back his tears every time someone at school mentions his dad. Maybe this is why he didn't want anyone to know. My body hurts.

As I'm getting ready to leave, Victor's mom pulls into the driveway. She gets out of her car and gently shakes my hand. I tell her that Victor's "comportamiento" isn't improving. She suggests that as a punishment we move him back into Mrs. Pass's homeroom where he was before winter break, but I know that Mrs. Pass wouldn't agree to take him back. Besides, I don't think it's a good solution, anyway. I explain in non-ideal Spanish that he's in a lot of pain right now because of losing his dad, and that's why he's acting the way he is. I make a suggestion, "Tenemos que buscar un modo de dar a Victor y no continuar a quitar cosas de él." (We have to find a way to give to Victor and not keep taking things away.)

She smiles at me and goes inside.

■ ■ ■ ■ ■ ■ ■ ■ ■ ■ ■ ■

before a canyon

Victor Villanueva
Sixth Period
Creative Writing Class

Juanito

Once upon a time Juanito got mad at his mom then she went after him he went where they put the whales she called the cops then he said I belong with the whales and he sang with them then he fell down and tried to swim but he didn't know how then he said I belong with all the mammals and they will not get down but he jumped again and fell down and then they went to the house but he didn't want to go then he said I am going to the sea then he started swimming with them and he was happy and went too far and drown. The End.

by Victor

Snickers

I first discover my two Snickers bags are empty late in the afternoon right before I'm about to go home. As I look at the bags, I feel a knot form in my stomach. Resting limply inside my backpack, the bags have been cleaned out. My students probably find this funny. I can almost see them laughing, calling me names, calling me stupid, calling me easy.

"God damn the world," I shout. I grab a desk and throw it, with a grunt and a lift and a push and a shot. It's like pulling a trigger. I then yank an already broken clock off the wall and hurl it across the room. Finally, I rip the "Pizza Par_ _" sign off the wall, ball it up, and leave it on the coffee table in the middle of my classroom. I put the two empty Snickers bags next to it.

How dare they? I think. Bastards.

When I get home, I call my mother in a rage. I'm ready to quit my job. I want to leave Phoenix. She listens to me rant for a while, and then responds.

"Jer, you forgot why you're there. You're not there for yourself," she says. "You're there for the kids. You can't just quit on them like that. So pull yourself together and do what you have to do to turn this into a learning experience for everyone."

Sometimes I hate my mother.

At eight o'clock the following morning, I find my students huddled around the door to my classroom waiting for me to open it. I look at them.

"I need everyone to get in line now," I say in a deep, controlled voice, "I'm angry today, class, so don't try anything. Trust me, you don't want lunch detention with me today."

Within seconds, my students form a line. Nobody makes a noise. Nobody speaks. This is the first time I've ever greeted my homeroom class like this. They look afraid.

I don't try to project my voice. "Class, when you enter the room, go directly to your assigned seats, take out only a pencil and paper, and answer the two questions I've written on the board," I order. "Do not ask me questions, do not leave your seats, and don't you dare open a mouth. I'm very angry this morning."

As the children sit, I see them reading the questions on the board trying to figure out what happened. After they finish writing, I pick up their answers and immediately read them.

Question 1: What do you see on the front table?

-Two bags of snickers empty and a big piece of white paper that said Pizza Par. I think it is there 'cause somebody tore it off the wall and people were stealing all Mr. Tucker's snickers.

-What I see is empty snicker bags and a crumbled up piece of paper that almost said pizza party. I think it is there because the bags are empty and we are not going to have a pizza party. Mr. Tucker is very angry.

Question 2: Why is your teacher angry?

-It makes him very angry 'cause his mom send those candy for his whole homeroom for Valentines but not just for some people. The big white paper said Pizza Par_ _ 'cause we were trying to earn a pizza party. I know who were stealing those snickers from behind your desk. It was Victor and Pedro. I think Jairo, too.

-My frind tock some my techer candy. I know hu did it but he said not to tell and if I do he goin to kick my but.

By lunchtime, I get the four guilty students—Victor, Jairo, Pedro and José—to confess to their crime. I then speak to each student's mother on the phone. At the end of the day, I give candy from a new bag of Snickers to all the students in the class, except for the ones who stole from me. I thank the students for being honest. We then discuss plans for a pizza party at the end of the week.

Victor comes alone to my classroom after school. He punches a desk and says it isn't fair. He complains that he got in trouble even though everyone else in the class was stealing as well.

"They told me to do it," he whines. "Everyone was doing it."

I don't respond. I am more angry at him than at the other three students despite his pathetic demeanor. As he talks, he keeps his head toward the floor. I wonder what he was trying to prove when he stole candy, candy which I would have given him after school had he asked.

I know he is mourning the death of his father, and I know this has been a hard time for him, but still, of all his teachers, I don't understand why he stole from me.

By coincidence, it happens that I have an appointment to call my college mentor, Professor Marans, this afternoon. I was planning to tell him how well things are going in Phoenix, but instead, all I focus on is my Snickers.

"All I could think about was how stupid I was," I tell him. "I'm too incompetent even to protect my own candy. I feel really stupid and humiliated."

"So you were stupid. It's not about being stupid," Professor Marans says. "It's about how sad it is that what's in these kids' pockets for ten minutes is more reliable and less risky than a relationship with you, the best relationship some of them may have ever had. The problems you're having are because of their limitations, not yours."

"Their limitations, not yours," I say back. Theirs, not yours. I repeat this over and over to myself for the rest of the night.

■■■■■■■■■■■

Victor Villanueva

Sixth Period

Creative Writing Class

I Dream I Was An Angel

The picture of I have a dream is something I dream. Once I dream that I got some powers and I flew up to the sky and I became an angel and I told him that I was a devil and he got mad and he said I don't want to hear that word again or you will be with him. I got mad and I said devil and he drop them and then he took my wings and I fell down and I didn't do what I wanted. The end.

by Victor

Revisiting

It's a little after five o'clock, and I've been working in my classroom all after-noon when I hear two light knocks on my door.

"Mrs. Turkey!" The voice giggles an octave higher than usual. I know the sound of the scuffles on the concrete walk leading up to my classroom, so I wait for a series of knocks before I answer the door.

"Who is it? Go away!" I say before I open the door. As I swing it open, I say "Hey guys" in a tone I use with anyone who comes after school, a what-can-I-do-for-you-today voice.

Pedro will start out, "Whatchoo doing?" while Alma will say, on behalf of herself, Elizabeth, and Rebecca, in a cracking voice, "Oh, hello, Mr. Tucker." And Jamal will ask, "Mr. T, can I put my backpack in here?" with a goofy smile and a scrunched face. But "Mrs. Turkey" is Victor's way of greeting me in the afternoon, always trying to convince me that he's the one in charge, especially when he comes with his friend Miguel.

Victor pokes his head past the doorway and sees the green writing folders out on my desk.

"You're reading our stories?" he says, "I bet you read mine first."

"No," I lie. "Why do you say that?" I feel embarrassed.

He walks past me and into the room. Miguel follows silently behind.

"Good. It's 'cause I wrote three stories, so it'd take you too long."

"I know, you wrote a lot. I don't know how you write so fast."

"I just sort of think something up and then it all comes out," he says. He is looking behind my desk, probably hoping to find candy.

"I believe it," I say. "You're faster than I am."

"Nuh uh, Mr. Tucker. You be lying to me." He's trying to speak this way.

"Well, you wrote three stories this afternoon. I barely wrote three sentences."

Then, without a pause, he sits in my chair and swivels away from my desk and slides it toward me. "Mr. Tucker, let's get a pizza," he says.

I walk from the doorway back into my classroom. "I don't know. This after-school food thing is getting expensive." I lean against my desk as I motion at Victor to get away.

"Come on, Mr. Tucker. You got money. You're rich. You're a teacher," he says, looking through the sticks of chalk by the blackboard. "I was good all day. I did my work in your class. I finished everything in reading. I was even helping Miguel, huh Miguel? I'm the bomb. I been getting smart, Mr. Tucker."

Miguel stays silent.

"True, although sometimes I think you're too smart."

"You started to yell at me in Math. You're like, 'Victor, finish your work. Get to it now.' I'm like, 'Hey homie, check it out, I already finish.'"

"You were good today," I say.

"That's 'cause we was doing fun stuff, so I did all my work. I like algebra. I'm the smartest at algebra." Victor writes on the board with purple chalk $5x + 7 = 20$.

"Hey, why aren't you at work now?" I ask. "You should be out selling candy, right?"

"Nah, I retired."

"Retired?" I try not to laugh. "What happened?"

"I don't know, Mr. Tucker. Come on, let's get the pizza," Victor begs.

After much debate and discussion with Victor and Miguel, I finally agree. While I go out to pick up the food, the kids hide in my room. I know it's against school policy, but I don't want to make them stand outside in the hundred degree weather waiting for me to return. And at this point in the year, after all the time we've spent together hanging out, I trust they won't steal from me or mess up my room. There isn't anyone to show off for.

When I return, I find the boys cleaning the room and rearranging the desks. They are talking about new assigned seats as we gather around the low square table at the front of my classroom where we put the pizza and crushed peppers.

"Let's have an afternoon discussion," I suggest.

"Okay. Let's talk about sex," Victor says as he dips his hands into the box and drops half the melted cheese off his pizza. "You like pussy, Mr. Tucker?"

This isn't quite what I had in mind for our afternoon discussion.

"Well, we can talk about that. Do you know what doctors and smart people call that part of a woman's body?"

"Pussy!"

Miguel stops eating.

"It's called a vagina. That's the medical word."

"It's kinda shaped like this," Victor says as he puts down his pizza and holds up his hands, "and it's got some stuff in it, and that's where I put my thing when I get horny." He giggles while cheese and red sauce seep through his teeth.

"Yes, that is what a woman has sex with," I answer him as best I can.

"How does it work?" he asks as he stuffs a crust into his mouth. "I mean, I heard that semen comes out of women like it comes out of men."

"Not really. Women definitely don't have semen. Only men have that. But watery stuff does come out of a vagina."

"Their eggs," he says confidently.

"Well, not that either, but women do have eggs, and those sort of come out when they're having their period. But that looks more like blood. When women have sex, their vagina lets out watery fluid." I realize I don't really know how to explain this.

"Where do the eggs come from?" Victor asks.

"Women's eggs? They come from a body part called ovaries. That's where they're made."

"Men have sperm that come from their balls."

"That's about right."

"I heard of a man one time that had a baby."

"That'd be pretty hard for a man, because the cells that grow into a baby do all that in an organ called a uterus, right around here," I say as I stand up and point at my lower belly. "Men don't have a uterus."

"They don't?" His voice squeaks as he asks.

"No, that's a big difference between men and women. Women have a whole big organ that men don't have."

"How come men don't have a uterus?"

"Well, I'm not sure how come exactly, but it has to do with hormones and whether you're a boy or a girl. For example, you heard of testosterone?" The boys nod.

"That's the main man hormone. That's what makes your voice get deep and your body get hairy as you grow up."

"I got a lot of that one. I got big this year, Mr. Tucker. I got a lot of testosterone. That's why all the ladies be wanting to bone me," Victor says.

I decide I need to shift the conversation. "So let me ask you guys, why do you think some kids have sex when they're so young?"

"They be watching too much porno," Victor smiles.

"I don't know, 'cause a lot of kids watch porno, but they're not having sex. You know, there're a lot of other things a person can do who watches porno besides having sex with someone."

Miguel looks at me and smiles. He says nothing as he chomps down the end of his crust.

Victor redirects the conversation again as he is going for his third slice.

"My mom has a new boyfriend. I'm going to have a step-dad soon."

"Really? Didn't she just lose your father?" I realize I shouldn't have said this, so I say more, not wanting to be rude or to embarrass Victor in front of Miguel. "What do you think of the guy?"

"He's thirty-six. I like him. I jacked money from him."

I can't tell which came first, liking the boyfriend or stealing his money.

"Oh, so he's a little bit older."

"Yeah, it'd be like if I was with a third grader."

"That's gross," I say.

"Not if she's fine. I'd freak her."

"You'd have sex with a third grader? Dude."

"Hell yeah," he says. There's a pause.

Miguel sees that neither of us is smiling.

Victor lifts his chair and turns it around so that he's sitting in it backwards, straddling the metal backrest. "You just don't see it," he adds.

I'm not aware that last year, as a fifth grader, his girlfriend was a third grader. Also, I don't get that the mother's new boyfriend is three years older than she is.

Victor turns his head to the side and speaks in a quiet voice. "I wonder how your eyes work," he says.

I don't understand where this question is coming from. "What do you mean?" I ask, still thinking about him with a third-grade girl. I look hard at his face. He stopped eating, but there are pizza crumbs on his chin.

"Like, if I was in your body and you were in mine, things wouldn't look the same. 'cause how our eyes work is different." He wipes off his chin and sits without moving.

I look over at Miguel. He's choosing another slice of pizza. I wonder if he understands Victor's comment. "You mean our perspectives are different?" I say.

"Nah, I mean, how come you can see?" Victor says. "You can feel yourself, right? And I can feel you." He touches his leg with his hand and then reaches across the table and touches my arm. "That's how you feel me. But how do you see me? I mean, what if you were me? If you had my eyes to see me, maybe you'd think I look the same as you now see you."

I look at him but say nothing.

"Like, let's say you think Miguel looks brown. Well, maybe that's what I call it too so I say he looks brown. But to me he looks brown the way you see someone you call white. We're seeing different things. We just call it the same."

"You know, I used to think that too," I say. "I sorta still do. I started thinking that when I was about your age. We were in the back of a truck and driving out to somebody's ranch. I was trying to explain to my favorite counselor, Sheri, why people might have different favorite colors." I remember being a teenager at overnight camp, sitting in the back of a truck with my horseback riding group, and Sheri. That night we watched Arnold Schwarzenegger in "The Running Man."

"Yeah, like, let's say you like blue the best and your homie's favorite is red. Maybe what your eyes see as blue your homie sees as red, like Crips and Bloods. Maybe your favorite color is the same one, it's just the way you see things and what your teacher told you they're called."

"I think it may work that way too." I say.

Now he starts talking faster than before, as if he's trying to get to something. "It all starts with cells, right? That's where everything starts."

"True."

Miguel sinks a little.

"And cells make your skin and your skin makes your body and your body makes, you know, a person. But where do the cells come from? There was a big explosion, right?

"You mean The Big Bang?"

"Yup, the Big Bang. It killed all the dinosaurs and that's how we got cells."

"Maybe, but dinosaurs were made of cells, too."

"They were?" He doesn't sound frustrated that I've broken his momentum, so I explain what I mean.

"Cells make up everything that's alive. Even the animals before dinosaurs."

"Birds came before dinosaurs," he says.

"Birds and dinosaurs came at about the same time," I explain. "But a long time before that, there were all kinds of really little animals."

"Like ants?"

"Like there were these animals called amoebas, and they were just one cell big, not even as big as one of the little pizza crumbs on Miguel's face." Miguel smiles sheepishly as he wipes his cheeks.

Victor asks, "But where did the amoebas come from? My teacher said the sun exploded and that's what made the earth."

"Maybe. It could have been the Big Bang. It definitely could have been."

"All right then, but what started all that?"

"I don't really know," I answer, trying to remember what the Big Bang is supposed to be.

"The world was just nothing. And then one day the nothing became something. I guess God did that."

"Maybe," I say.

"Do you believe in God, Mr. Tucker?"

Miguel stops.

This is not a question I want to answer in front of Victor or Miguel. I don't like preaching my beliefs, especially to impressionable teenagers.

"I don't think so. I mean, I don't really know. How 'bout you?"

"You don't? 'Cause you can't see nothing?"

I've gone too far for a teacher, but I decide to stay honest. "Because I don't feel anything," I say.

"You don't feel it's right?" he asks. Miguel blinks a lot.

"It's not about right and wrong for me. It's more like hot and cold. Like you might say you feel hot, and that's just how you feel. It's not that you think it is hot and everybody should think it's hot. You just personally don't feel cold. Well, sometimes I personally don't feel God. Just like I don't feel cold right now."

"I don't know. I'm not sure about God," Victor says. "Sometimes I believe in God, because how else did all this get here, but sometimes it doesn't make sense to me with all the things that happen. I believe in Jesus, though. And hell. What do you think happens when you die?"

I don't know what Miguel's family says about afterlife and I don't want to confuse him, but answering Victor honestly remains my priority.

"I think that's it. After you die, I don't think you feel anything anymore." I say, speaking in a low tone.

"I'm scared of dying," Victor says. "It probably hurts a lot after you die."

"Probably. I don't know. Maybe not," I say.

"But think about it. If it hurts a little to get a scrape and a lot to get a big cut, it probably hurts real bad when you die."

Victor sort of makes sense. "But maybe it happens so fast you don't feel anything at all," I suggest.

"Maybe after you die your body hurts real bad so you just lay down and don't ever move again."

"Here's how I see it. Do you remember what it felt like before you were born?"

"No."

"That's what I think it feels like after you die."

Victor pauses for a few seconds and then says, "I think when you die, you go into another body, but you don't remember anything. It's a new life. You just start over."

"Kind of like dying on your math quiz, you get to do a total do-over."

Victor looks at me. "Not really, Mr. Tucker," he says. He picks up the empty pizza box, folds it in half, and puts it in the garbage.

■ ■ ■ ■ ■ ■ ■ ■ ■ ■ ■ ■ ■

Write About It

The students sit at their desks. They are unusually subdued today. A middle-aged social worker stands in front of them, speaking softly. The week before they all finished reading *Bridge To Terabithia*, a book in which a young girl dies. In the last part of the book, after the girl dies, her best friend feels guilty, angry, and confused. The majority of the students seem to have a visceral response to this boy's psychological struggles. I decide to bring in a guest speaker to talk to my homeroom class about death and mourning.

The speaker is a fragile-looking woman. She smiles only a little. "Losses can be all kinds of things," she says. "Death, divorce, grades, break-ups, switching schools, even moving. For example, what do you lose when you move?"

"Your house," Jairo shouts out before any kids have a chance to raise their hands.

"Your family," interjects Victor, only a second behind Jairo.

"Well, you don't necessarily lose your family," the woman says, not hearing Victor whisper "your fun" after realizing his first answer made no sense. I see him looking over at me.

"What about a divorce, what do you lose then?" the woman goes on.

"Your mom and dad separate," Victor shouts, as if by reflex, even before Jairo this time.

"Yes, a divorce is the death of a marriage," the woman smiles kindly. Victor doesn't understand her smile. He has a triumphant look on his face.

"What are some other kinds of losses?" the woman asks, looking out to the rest of the class. She waits for a moment as several children raise their hands.

"Pets," says Adrianna.

"Good, you need time to grieve when your pet dies. You might want to get another, but not too fast."

The woman calls on Nayeli. "Marriage," she says proudly.

"Okay, getting married could be a loss, like a loss of freedom." I wonder if this is what Nayeli means.

"Family," Jamal volunteers in a serious tone.

"Good. For example, when your grandparent dies, that can be hard, because you're sad and your parent is sad too."

Jamal raises his hand again, and the woman calls on him. "Your dad," he adds, and puts his head on his desk.

Freddy frowns as he wipes his eyes. His mother died three months ago.

"How many of you have lost a parent or close family member?" the social worker asks.

Almost every child raises his or her hand.

The social worker appears a bit surprised. "After a loss, people can go through a lot of different stages, all normal ways to express grief." She looks over at me, wipes her forehead, and looks around as if she's searching for something. "I'm going to need a volunteer to help me hold my grief poster," she says, picking up a green poster on the side of the room.

Victor raises his hand immediately, while a half dozen other students raise their hands also, but less assertively. The social worker does not choose Victor. As another boy walks up to the front of the classroom, Victor stands, picks up a ball of paper, and meanders over to the trashcan to throw it away.

The woman reads the stenciled words on her poster aloud, "Denial, shock, sadness, anger, fear, acceptance, guilt."

"For example," she says, "you might feel angry." She points to the word 'anger' on her green poster. "How could this person miss all my birthdays and graduations? You feel a big gaping hole, like someone put their hand into your chest and pulled out your heart."

Several students put their heads on their desks. Shamika gets up and comes to the back of the room where I'm sitting.

"Mr. Tucker, can I go sit outside? I really don't like to talk about this kind of stuff."

"Sure Mika. Go ahead."

The social worker continues. "Everybody's different. Some people need to cry with their friends. Other people want to keep their grief inside."

"Mr. Tucker," Victor gets up and approaches me, "Mr. Tucker," he repeats, but I ignore him and say nothing. I want him to see that I'm concentrating and that he's interrupting me and maybe other people as well. Out the corner of my eye I watch him return to his seat.

"After you lose someone, what are some ways a person might express sadness?" the social worker asks.

"Crying," "running," "looking at pictures."

"Good, very good," she responds, writing the children's ideas on the board.

A minute later, Victor gets up and quietly walks over to me again. He takes my glasses off the table without asking. "They help me see," he says.

"They help me to see, too," I say in a cold tone.

"Oh, sorry," he says earnestly, but returns to his desk still holding my glasses. I want to get back my glasses, but I don't want to interrupt the class. It doesn't even occur to me to wonder why exactly he doesn't have his own glasses or what exactly Victor wants to see.

"How else do people express their feelings?" the social worker asks.

"Talk about it with your Mom," says Jamal. He smiles when the social worker nods.

"Clean out the basement," Ashley says.

"A punching bag," Cameron adds in.

Freddy picks up his head briefly. "Your stomach starts to hurt," he says. "And you sweat a lot." He then drops his head back on its side as if it's too heavy to hold up.

I look over at Victor wearing my glasses and shake my head. He sees me.

"I'll be good," he mouths, so I can read his lips.

"You write about it," Victor says loudly and then looks over at me.

"Yes," says the social worker. "Some people eat, other people starve themselves. Some people cry a lot. Others can't stop talking. A few just like to write."

By the time the social worker finishes discussing the importance of talking and listening, of memories and impermanence, of not avoiding and not pretending, most of the students have their heads on their desks and appear exhausted.

As the social worker is closing her discussion, Victor raises his hand. I realize he is still wearing my glasses. "Excuse me, ma'am, can I ask a question?" he says. The social worker nods. "What if you get shot? When they bury you, do they keep all the holes in your clothes?"

■ ■ ■ ■ ■ ■ ■ ■ ■ ■ ■ ■ ■

Travels

A quart box of General Tsao's chicken, a box of rice, and five pairs of chop-sticks bring Victor, Miguel, Jairo, Jamal, and me around the Salvation Army coffee table in my classroom at about five-thirty this afternoon. We had been eating pizza, at Victor's request, but ever since I taught the boys how to use chopsticks, Chinese has been the afternoon food of choice.

We all wait while Victor distributes the chicken evenly. Once we start eating, we imagine what we'll do when the summer finally arrives. The boys and I decide to go to a city, and then the boys decide to go to a big city. "New York!" one person says. "Texas!" says another. "New Mexico!" shouts a third. And then all at once "Mexico!" and then "Las Vegas!" and then "California!" almost in rhythm. "What about San Diego?" I suggest.

With this idea, the kids get really excited. "We'll bone lots of girls there," says Jairo.

"Mr. Tucker can get us a big bag of condoms," says Victor.

"No, guys. No," I say, trying to steer them away from this world, "I don't want you guys doing that kind of stuff."

"Come on, Mr. Tucker, we was just joking," says Jamal.

"I ain't gonna get no girl pregnant or nothing," adds Jairo.

Victor speaks up. "Mr. Tucker, how long are you living in Phoenix?"

"I'll be here the rest of this year and one more. Then I've got to move to Boston."

"Could I stay with you when you leave?" he asks.

I put my chopsticks down and look at Victor. "I'll be in medical school, Victor, and I'll be living really far from here. How would you get there?"

"You could buy me a plane ticket." He stands up and looks straight at me.

"I'd love to," I say nervously. "That'd be really fun, but I'll be living in a dorm, so I think it'd be impossible."

"You'll be here till I finish eighth grade?" he asks hesitantly and then walks over to my desk to get a napkin.

"You're in sixth grade now, so I'll have to go when you're finishing seventh."

I've stopped eating. I can't look him in the eyes.

"Don't leave us here, Mr. T," he replies as he walks back to the table and sits down by his food. He sounds earnest.

"I don't know, V. We'll have to think about it."

Even though I say, "I don't know," the truth is I do. I'll only be in Phoenix one more year. I was granted a two year deferral from Harvard Medical School so that I could teach in Phoenix. I know I won't be able to extend that time even if I want to, and I'm not going to be able to bring Victor to Boston.

Jamal, Miguel, and Jairo sit silently beside Victor. They understand what I'm saying better than Victor seems to.

"Look, you guys, I'll be back here to visit," I say cheerfully.

"You gonna come to our graduation, Mr. T?" Jamal asks. Eighth-grade graduation means a lot to these children. It is the last graduation many of them ever have.

"Definitely," I answer. "Nothing will keep me from it. I'll come to all your graduations. Just send me an invitation so I'll know when it is."

"Hey, Mr. T, will you take us on a camping trip?" Victor asks. "That'd be tight."

"Maybe when the school year is over we could do something," I answer, not sure if I should be agreeing.

"But let's go out of Arizona. We could camp in New Mexico. At the mountains," Victor says, as if mountains mean something important.

"New Mexico mountains are far."

"They'd send me to Mexico, Tucker," Miguel says in a serious tone. It's one of the only things he's said all afternoon.

"Nah, there's no relation between Mexico and New Mexico," I answer, assuming that's what he's thinking.

"My green card's for Arizona," Miguel says. "I no cross to other state. We stay in Arizona."

"You've never been outside Arizona?" I ask, perhaps being a little naive.

"No," he says as his body folds a little.

"I don't think it'd be any problem," I say without really knowing. "As long as you stay with me, I don't think anyone would bother you. They probably wouldn't even ask you for a card."

Victor adds, "We're just little kids, and you're white, so we'd be fine."

We all agree.

before a canyon

Victor Villanueva
Sixth Period
Creative Writing Class

Take the Day

Take the day Jovino jumped out the bridge and landed in the
water they don't know why but they told him that he can't do
that no more but he said "if you tell me again I will jump it
all over again" he said "I don't care" but they told him "but
I do" and they had to go to jail because he was not good and
his mom did not care and he jump and a boat was going by
and he killed himself on a boat.

by Victor

Textbook

Today is my last day of school and my last day teaching at Hatfield. I'm switching to a different school next year, Garcia, where I'll be teaching a self-contained class. This means that for my one group of students, I can make social studies and science applications of reading, writing, and math. So we'll essentially be doing reading, writing, and arithmetic all day.

I probably won't see most of my students again. In some ways I'm happy I'll be leaving the school. I always felt under attack: I never held the textbooks in much esteem and I made the vice-principal uncomfortable by getting too close to my students. She didn't approve of children coming after school to my classroom to hang out and talk to me. She also didn't like the burgeoning friendship I had with Victor. Still, I'm sad to be leaving. A part of me would like to stay.

During the first part of the day, we play Seven-Up and several other games Victor and Miguel came up with the afternoon before. After a couple of hours, Victor takes my camera and becomes the class photographer. The children pose in different groups while he takes their pictures.

Meanwhile, the kids write in each other's notebooks. Then, before lunch, they ask to go outside to jump rope or play soccer. When lunch is over, I decide to leave my door open and let them trickle in and out whenever they want. Trains of children hoot and holler as they enter and exit my classroom. I stand in the doorway to make sure no one gets hurt. The radio is blasting in my room, and more kids than I can count are dancing and jumping around.

Mr. Tucker, why are there kids from all the other classes here? Mr. Tucker, what was my grade for reading? Mr. Tucker, will you sign my shirt? Mr. Tucker, can I come to your party too? Mr. Tucker, where are the—

Report cards! I have forgotten the report cards. I send one student out to retrieve Victor from the soccer field where he still has my camera and another to retrieve Nayeli who is gossiping at the back of the field beneath a tree. I then turn off the radio and stop the party. "We need silence, everyone. It's time for report cards!" Everyone gathers around.

"Adrianna Alfonso, promoted to the seventh grade," I say dramatically, and the kids cheer, some of them in my homeroom, some not. "Rubia Angeles, promoted to the seventh grade" and Rubia smirks because it was obvious she'd pass all her classes.

I go through the kids one by one, until suddenly it's nearly two o'clock, and we have only fifteen minutes left before school dismissal. I realize that post-party, my room is a complete mess.

"Victor, get to work. Jamal, what are you doing? Alma? Alma, get this garbage off the floor." I panic. "No one is going to leave this room until it is completely spotless."

At this point, a leg on one of the tables somehow breaks, and the cheese dip slides off the top and spills onto the carpet.

"That's disgusting" Alma cries out.

"It weren't me," says Victor.

"I don't care what you have to do, get that stuff off the ground," I shout. Jairo dips his whole hand into the cheese to pick it up, but I don't even smile, and I hear kids outside beginning to file out of their classrooms, and I realize the cubbies aren't cleaned out yet. "Clean out your cubby. Take everything," I pause. "Or else it's trash!" I don't really mean that, because I always save everything.

Another minute passes, and the kids begin to cluster around the door. "Please Mr. Tucker, the bus Mr. Tucker." This is not how I wanted to end things.

"Goodbye, everyone," I shout as I swing open my classroom door, "Remember, from now on you can call me Jeremy." I wave and shake hands, while a couple of students give me hugs and a few others promise to come by tomorrow, and before I know it, my room has cleared out. There is no one left.

At this moment, I realize I haven't seen Victor for a while. I don't even remember dismissing him, although I do find an empty camera case sitting on top of the teacher-desk. I wonder if he took a lot of pictures. I wonder if I'll ever see him again and why he left without saying goodbye. I wonder if I'll get my camera back.

I look outside, but there is no one waiting to see me. The sidewalk leading up to my classroom is empty. I wish I could say, "Wait for me,

I'll be right back," but there is no one there. My world has emptied out. I decide to look through my backpack. The camera is on top.

So much for proposing a summer swim party or regular gatherings at Burger King. So much for saying your stories are beautiful, and your lives are important. So much for a group hug goodbye. I hurry out of my classroom, hoping I'll see each of my students one last time, and that the ones I see I'll be able to tell one last important word. I imagine the great difference these few frantic moments could make.

Except I know that's a lie. The truth is that these last few minutes are for me, not for them. I want to see them. I want a kind word from them, a goodbye, an 'I'll miss you,' maybe even a hug.

I see Shamika first. I tell her goodbye and that I'll send her newest story back to her in the mail. She says, "See ya, Tucker," and I remember what she wrote to me earlier. Thanks for being my teacher, Mr. Tucker. You're the only one who understands my stories. I wish I could hear her say something like that out loud, but her expressive voice is locked inside her writing.

Next I see Jamal. I wave, continue to walk, and then I pause. I turn back, and he's still standing at the door, waiting, looking at me. "Goodbye Mr. Tucker," he says with the same smile he wore every time he got an answer right or put his hand on my shoulder or when he walked with me to the copy machine or sat beside me at the library. I wonder if I'll ever see him again. "Goodbye Jamal," I say sadly, watching as he disappears forever.

Then, I see Jairo by the swing set. "I've loved having you in our class," I tell him. "You made me laugh all the time," I add. "And your after-school craziness, too."

"Thanks, Mr. Tucker," he says smiling.

And then Anthony after him. "You are a fantastic kid, Anthony. You're going to go places." Anthony has been an incredible student, always trying hard, always easy-going, never showing off. I promise Jairo and Anthony that I'm going to keep up with them, follow their progress, and make sure they are doing well. It doesn't occur to me that this may not be possible or that they may not always be best friends.

I see Domingo. I walk over to shake his hand. "Remember how you used to say Lucia's the brain. Well, guess who's the brain now?" I ask.

"Anthony," he says.

"Well, Anthony is a brain, but you're the brain too, Domingo. You have become a fantastic student. You know, there can be more than one brain in a class."

Domingo asks me if he can take my picture. "Have a good summer," he says. "Goodbye, Mr. T. You were my favorite teacher."

"You too," I reply.

As I race to the other side of the school, Regina, Adrianna, and Nayeli come up to me in the hall. They give me a group hug. "You're a great teacher," Adrianna says.

"Can we come visit you tomorrow? We can help clean the class," Nayeli offers.

"That'd be great," I say because it would mean a lot to me to see the girls again. Nayeli and Regina were both smart and mischievous, both inconsistent students at first who did really well later in the year. And Adrianna, who looks at me with sad curious eyes, whose mother and teenage sister both had babies this past year, became an all-around terrific student, one of the best I had. Near the end of the year, she wrote me a note and put it in an envelope marked "private." You used to be my second favorite teacher, but you changed, and now you're my favorite. Students like Adrianna taught me never to give up on anyone.

I briefly see a few other teachers during my after-school frenzy. Standing on the sidewalks outside, they are watching the buses fill with students and then depart. With their whistles, sunglasses, and clipboards, they seem nonchalant.

I wonder if any of them feel as frenzied as I do.

I'm sure they did a better job of collecting textbooks.

When I return to my classroom, I feel a rush of happiness and relief to find Victor standing outside, his backpack over one shoulder and a paper in his other hand. He gives me the paper to read. I see the word "Bonus" at the top of the page.

"Mr. T, I'm coming tomorrow to help. I'm gonna help pack all your teacher things," he says. Then, without explanation, he gets on his bike and leaves.

I sit with his bonus paper on the concrete walkway to my classroom and watch the empty school. I sit without moving. I don't know how long I sit. Five minutes or thirty-five. The time seems to change fast. At sunset, South Mountain turns a dim, gray-blue like the sky. A sunset here is not filled with yellow and red like a sunset painting. It is blue and silver and carlight. It's strangely serene.

■ ■ ■ ■ ■ ■ ■ ■ ■ ■ ■ ■

Asshole

The next day, Victor, Adrianna, Miguel, Nayeli, and Jairo are helping me in my room. Victor asks if he still has to wear the uniform to school even though the year is over.

"Well, probably not," I say. "How come?"

"I wanna come in my baggies to school. I'll look bad like a gangster."

I'm furious at Victor for saying this, but I say nothing. Usually I listen to his comments and stories, and say very little. I've been planning all year to give him a full taste of my anger, to give him a lecture where I swear at him and tell him how I feel. Now that I'm not his official Hatfield teacher, I want to break all the rules of what a teacher should say because I know that the first time I swear at Victor, he will remember. It's why I've been waiting for the right time and why I want the lecture to be about something important. I want to be in full control of the moment when Victor thinks I'm so angry at him that I've lost all control. Finally, the time has come.

After taking a few minutes to gather my thoughts, I tell Victor I need to speak to him in private. While the other four students continue to work and chat in my room, he and I walk through the fire door (rather than through the front doors) into Mrs. Pass's room and shut the door. No one is there; we turn on the lights. Victor leans up against Mrs. Pass's desk at the back corner of the room. He has no idea what I've got in store for him.

I comb my hands through my hair, tense up my body, and remind myself of exactly how I've been planning to start this speech. Just as my dad did when I showed him terrible disrespect and called him "cheap." He called me a "fucking asshole." I remember the strong impact his words had on me. I recall that afterward I repeated his words over and over to myself. Even ten years later as I stand in a classroom where I am a teacher and an adult, I still can hear my father's unusually angry voice responding to my ingratitude.

I felt both astonished and horrified that he swore at me; it was the only time he had ever used that kind of language with me. I had heard him swear "asshole" into our window at drivers on the freeway and "fucking idiot" at referees on TV who made bad calls against the Oilers or the Rockets. But until that day, I never had heard him swear at some-one who could hear him, and certainly never at me. I didn't know he was capable of talking that way face to face to me or any other human being. It was the most frightened I had ever felt.

With my father's words resonating in my ears, I look Victor in the eye.

"Victor," I say slowly, "You're acting like a fucking asshole." I pause. Victor freezes. "Boy, you better know by now that I'm not dumb. You and your talk about the gangster clothes, being all baggy and shit. You think it's so cool to look like a gangster. Well, it's not. You're dressing like you're ready to get your ass blown away and into the grave. You ever seen a kid in a bright blue body bag? It's ugly, and that's what you're asking for. Those gangs are just stupid. They're for little assholes like you who are so damn weak that they need to be surrounded by a bunch of other little assholes to make them feel strong. They call themselves G's, dress all baggy, and then screw up their lives or get themselves killed.

"But you don't care, do you Victor? You don't give a fuck. You know, I finally understand you. Everything that happens to you, you think to yourself, 'So what? So what if I get a detention? So what if I get suspended? So what if I get expelled? So what if I get killed?' You figure, 'Why not be a fuckup 'cause my life ain't gonna amount to shit, anyway.' To you it's not a risk, 'cause you think you've got nothing to lose. You figure death is no worse than life anyhow.

"Well, you know what, I know it's been tough this year, since your dad died and all, and I'm not saying that it's ever gonna be easy. It's not. But don't think that just because he died, it means that you have to die too.

"I mean, here you are, practically my favorite kid at the whole damn school, and you do nothing but treat me like I'm stupid and then you have the nerve to tell me about how cool gangs are. And you know what, I'll cry like hell if you get yourself killed. I'll be so damn angry at you for wasting yourself like that. You've got so damn much you don't even know it, and I'm working like hell to show you how much you've got and you don't do crap but act like a fucking asshole ready to throw it all away. And here I think you're such a great kid that I want to kill you sometimes when you don't think that yourself. You make me so damn mad I can't say what I've gotta say right now without cussing. You piss me off when you act like your life is worth shit."

Victor looks at me with tears in his eyes. He laughed at first because I was swearing, but then he stopped. He looked serious and said nothing. When I finish, he asks to go back through the fire door into my room. He doesn't want to talk at all. But he has heard what I said: after that day when he's talking to me and no one else can hear, he calls himself my 'special student.' He also tells me a week or two later that he doesn't wear baggy clothes anymore. He says he doesn't want to look like a gangster.

■ ■ ■ ■ ■ ■ ■ ■ ■ ■ ■ ■ ■

Dad

It's a Friday in the middle of July. I'm finishing in my Hatfield classroom and then taking Victor and his younger brother, Tommy, to the movies and bowling. It's the first time I've ever offered to drive Victor in my car. I know there are school rules about not driving students, but I figure, since the school year is now over, I'm not breaking any school rules. Still, I feel nervous. I don't want anyone to see the kids get into my car.

I've already talked to their mother to get her permission. She said "Yes" before I even told her where we were going.

Victor's brother is an agreeable seven year old, does whatever he's told, and seems to listen more than he talks. He's wearing the same purple shorts today that I've seen him wear when he has come with Victor to my classroom. When Victor asks to bring him along on our outing today, I agree. I wonder if my friendship with Victor will become a friendship with his family.

Victor, Tommy, and I make a plan. They run across the field to the street behind the schoolyard, which no one in the building can see. I leave the classroom and walk to my car. I drive it around the block to a street we have agreed on, and find the two boys waiting on the side of the road. A part of me is surprised they are there. I worried that maybe they weren't going to follow through on our plan and that today would be the last time I'd see them. Relieved, I stop the car. The boys quickly get inside, and we head off. Victor tells Tommy to duck until we get to a main road.

On the way to the movie, Tommy asks me a question: "What would you do if Victor was your kid and he acted bad in school?"

"You mean if I were his dad?" I ask.

Victor answers before I have a chance. "If you was my dad, I would be good in school. I wouldn't be bad." I'm surprised to hear him say this. I'm not sure it's entirely true, though I'd like it to be. I tell Victor that I believe him.

I then tell Tommy that if my son were to act the way Victor did at school, I would take away everything from him until he improved one hundred percent. He'd lose his television privileges, his phone, his stylish clothes, and he'd eat nothing but vegetables, tofu, and rice. At the same time, I'd spend as much time with him as it took to help him get back on track at school.

"Toe who?" Tommy asks.

"Tofu. It's this healthy, hardish, softish white stuff."

"That's nasty, Mr. T," Tommy says.

Victor tells me that his mom went to a fortune teller who told her that he was going to become a lawyer or a teacher.

"She thinks I'm going to get a good career," he says happily, as if her simply saying it guarantees success. I think of a few of the stories he wrote during the year about boys and their mothers. Perhaps what his mother said is the kind of affirmation he has been looking for.

I bring Victor and Tommy to a movie called "I Got The Hook Up."

Victor has told me that it looks like a good movie. I don't know what the movie's rated, who's in it, or what it's about. We arrive early enough for me to find out, but I don't. I'm distracted. I'm happy we've made it this far without problems. Victor chooses the back row of the theater, which turns out to be a good thing because Tommy doesn't want to sit during the movie. He's either standing or kneeling on the floor in front of his chair. That's probably because the movie is about two guys using sex to create a cell phone business, and every other word in the movie is "motherfucker." I happen to love movies like this, and it doesn't occur to me to leave. When it's over, I realize that we should have left, but luckily Tommy says his favorite part of the movie was when the man inside the port-o-potty got turned upside down. He also says that all the swearing sounded stupid.

After the movie, we go bowling and then for burgers. By the time I take the boys home, it's already dusk. Tommy goes to his room to get ready for bed without any argument, while Victor and I sit outside and talk. His mom is home and passes by us a few times to go to her car, but she can't understand what we're saying. I feel selfishly glad that she doesn't speak English. It keeps the conversation between Victor and me.

■ ■ ■ ■ ■ ■ ■ ■ ■ ■ ■ ■ ■

Saved

Sitting on the back patio in rubber lawn chairs, Victor and I look at the South Phoenix sky. The sun has already set and it's now eleven o'clock at night, later than usual for us to be talking.

"My mom said something weird, Mr. Tucker," Victor says. "She said maybe you can save me."

I fidget. I shift my legs and sit up straight. These are the words I have wanted Victor to say all year. You can save me. You have saved me. But for some reason they don't sound right.

"Help me get a good career, I guess."

'A good career?' Was it all for that? I wanted to hear Victor say 'save me,' but without a 'maybe' or 'something weird' or 'my mom said' to preface the saving. That's what I wanted. But now I'm not sure what it means. Save.

"Victor, I don't know."

"She said maybe you can adopt me, you know, fill out some papers or something, bring me with you to Boston."

"Adopt you?" Jesus.

He's already asked to come with me to Boston. My mind drowns in a flood of advice from friends and family: "It's not your job to save him" and "You've got to think of yourself" and "You can never be his father." But still I can see a shared apartment and a Doing Something Important sign hanging from my front door.

I think of my mother and what she would say at this moment. I look Victor in the eyes.

"What about your mom? With you in Boston and your mom in Phoenix, you'd almost never see her."

I forget that Victor hates his mother.

"That don't matter. I'd see her sometimes. I'd be good, Mr. Tucker. I'd be good with you."

I believe Victor, and I'm flattered. I feel stupid for feeling flattered. I should be rejecting the idea quickly, telling Victor it's impossible and unwise and wrong. Instead, I find myself almost enthusiastic. I like the idea of being a dad.

"This isn't a good idea, Victor. I can't be your dad. I'm only twenty-three."

"I know. That's weird."

I think of the advice Dr. Marans gave me about kids like Victor.

"The worst thing your kids can think is that if they do something wrong, you're going to give up on them. And the worst thing you can think is that if you don't give up on them, you're going to save them."

"I wish I could bring you with me," Looking right at Victor, I try to speak gently.

"You know I really care about you and enjoy your company. But when I think of you living with me in Boston, Victor, of me adopting you, for some reason, well, it just doesn't seem right, and I think to myself, 'How could I?' you know, 'Why would I?'" I pause.

I've forgotten what I want to say. "I mean, for one thing, why you? Of all kids, why would I work so hard to help you?"

"'Cause of my grades. I don't know."

"You weren't the only one with bad grades. But you were one of the few who stole from me." I still haven't realized that Victor stole from me then for the same reason we are talking on his patio now.

"I didn't steal from you," Victor responds. "I was passing stuff out to all the kids." That's not true. Victor was showing off. But I am missing the larger point.

"You stole from me and disrespected me. And you know it's true."

He giggles. I shake my head. "So why should I try to help you?"

■ ■ ■ ■ ■ ■ ■ ■ ■ ■ ■ ■

A Glass Angel

After talking a while longer outside, Victor and I decide to go inside. The front door is partially open, so we don't have to knock. His mom is sitting at the kitchen table. There is no one else around.

"Mr. Tucker," Victor says, "this woman was looking at my hand and told me my life was going to be real long." His palm is not much smaller than mine, but his knuckles are much colder. "Look at this line here," he says almost secretively. "This is my life line. See how it goes all the way from here to here. That's a long way. When I'm old, I'm gonna get sick and die. That's what this woman said, Mr. Tucker."

"She's right, Victor. I think she's right." At this moment, as we sit quietly in his living room, I believe this fortune will come true.

"Let me see yours." Now he holds my hand in his.

"Look," he says enthusiastically. "Your life line's even longer than mine. You're going to live a long time." I look at the wrinkle crossing my palm. It's yellow in a sea of pink.

"Will I ever have a wife and kids?" I ask, hoping to hear a "yes."

"Look, these lines here, on the side, they mean you're going to get married. See, you'll get married once, and you'll have…" Victor pauses, "six kids."

"Six kids? That'd be great. But what about my wife? That's a lot of babies to have." I forget that Victor's mother had seven.

He returns to his own palm. "I'm going to have two wives and three kids," he says pointing to another wrinkle on his palm.

"You mean you're going to get divorced?"

"I guess. I'll have two wives."

"I don't know. Do you really think the lines on your hand are going to control your life?"

"I know. I think I'm going to live to be a hundred."

When Victor says this, predictions and odds and reasons mean nothing.

Teachers and principals know nothing. I feel a cold tingle through the side of my face. Victor has just said what I've been waiting to hear. It feels better than "saved," a word that's impossible to define anyway. "Live to be a hundred." This is an affirmation of my hope that the rest of the world is wrong and that Victor's life truly is his own.

I take a while to respond. "Personally, if I made it to eighty, I'd be happy. But a hundred, that'd be really good." I am smiling.

"Mr. Tucker, I wonder if I'll know you when I'm older. What if we're still friends?" he asks.

"I'll always know you, Victor," I answer. As I look at him, I notice that his dark hair isn't pulled back with gel today. It appears more free than usual, floating almost sideways. I wonder how Victor's hair will look when he gets older, and if his face will be smooth or if his pimples will leave scars. Sometimes, I imagine that twenty years from now, when Victor and I are both fathers, that he and his family will be living next door to me and mine. I imagine we'll have barbecues together in our backyards and that our backyards will have no fences so that our children can play touch football, and we'll sit back with our wives, all four of us chatting, laughing loudly, and enjoying cold beers.

"Maybe when you're in Boston, I could live with you," Victor says.

My mind returns to the present moment. We discussed this a couple of times before, but I guess Victor needs to hear it from me again, just like I needed to hear him again and again after he told me about his dad.

As I speak, I'm afraid of sounding as though I don't care.

"The thing is, I'm going to be living in a little dorm room, and it'd be too much for me to take care of you."

"I'll be in eighth grade," Victor pleads. "I'll be good." He is still sitting upright on the couch beside me, but his eyes look damp, and his body is turned to face me. I have never seen him sitting like this before.

"I'll never be home," I say. "I wish you could come with me. I wish I could do it." I lean back and look at the glass angel beside the front door. Located there, it could easily break. "We'll stay in touch. During the summer, or when I have spring break, or something like that."

■■■■■■■■■■■■■

Baseline

The last time I saw Victor before I left Phoenix for the summer, he decided to cancel his plans and called me at the last minute about lunch.

I pick up Victor early in the afternoon. My stomach has been hurting all day, but I still want us to spend time together. What if today is the last time we'll ever talk? I still don't trust my relationship with him.

"I've got to stop by the new school to sign my contract," I tell him. "If you want, you can go in with me to meet some of the teachers."

Victor has been talking about switching from Hatfield to my new school next year.

I've been transferred there by Teach For America, a school change that is very unusual. I'm happy to have an entire class of students for all the subjects, and those kinds of self-contained classrooms are at Garcia Prep Academy. It's about the same size as Hatfield, but it has students from kindergarten through twelfth grade. Victor and I park and find our way to the front door.

"I want you to switch schools," I tell him as we walk, "But if you do, you're not going to be able to get away with whatever you want, just because I'm there."

"So, if I'm bad in a teacher's class, they could just send me to you."

I can only imagine the problems this would cause. I'm not sure if I want to be made responsible for Victor's behavior.

"I'll tell the other teachers that they should not send you to my room no matter what. I can't be a teacher to you anymore." That isn't what I mean to say.

We walk through the computer room and find the main office. Bright yellow paint dominates the cement ground by the front windows and is on all the classroom handrails around the school. I chat briefly with my new principal and introduce her to Victor. He shakes her hand and acts decently. He doesn't embarrass me at all. After we leave the school, I ask him where he'd like to go for lunch.

"I'm not very hungry, so why don't you choose where we go for lunch."

"You don't really want to have lunch with me, do you?" he says as we pull out of the parking lot.

"It's not that, Victor. I just don't feel well. I really do want to go with you for lunch. Anywhere you want. Tell me where to go."

I am heading toward Tempe. I expect Victor will choose a nice restaurant, a place where the items on the menu cost more than burgers and fries. This is the celebratory lunch we've been talking about for a while.

"It's up to you. What do you want?" he says. He seems uncomfortable, strangely insecure.

"I'd rather let you decide. I'm not going to eat that much."

"You don't want to be here," he says.

I glance over at him. He is facing straight ahead, not looking at me at all. "I do want to be here. It's just my stomach feels really bad."

"You wish you didn't come."

"That's not it. I want to be here, I just don't feel good," I respond. We stop at a set of lights. I'm not sure what's the best way to explain how I feel.

"Suppose you drove with your family all the way to California, but then you got sick," I say. "If everyone were going to Disneyland, wouldn't you want to go too, even though you felt lousy?"

"Yes."

"Well, that's how I feel. I want to be here, I just wish I didn't feel like this, but I can't help how my stomach feels. So let's figure out where to go eat," I finish.

As we approach 48th Street, we see the Pizza Hut where we usually go. Victor suggests that we should eat there. He seems nervous about the idea of going to a restaurant in Tempe.

Once inside, we order a large pepperoni and jalapeño pizza. Victor has shown me that jalapeños make pizza taste much better. The waitress brings two cups of water.

"I wish I were more hungry," I say.

"Do you feel sorry for me?" he asks.

"Feel sorry for you? Why do you say that?" I don't understand what brought on the question. I also don't want to say "yes," because I don't think I do feel sorry for him, and I know it's the wrong answer.

"Sometimes you do things just 'cause people want you to," he explains.

"I do what I want to do," I say. "And I don't feel sorry for you. You're smart and you're gonna do great things with your life. There are a lot of people I do feel sorry for, but you're not one of them."

"Like who do you feel sorry for?"

I pause. Victor is not making this easy. He's testing our friendship, trying to define it. It's hard for me to figure out what to say.

"I feel sorry for old people who have to live in old age homes. I worked at one for several months when I was in college, but after a while, I just couldn't take it." I'm good. Off the top of my head, I thought of a straightforward and true example.

Eventually our pizza comes. I try to eat it enthusiastically. I don't want Victor to think I'm doing him a favor. While we eat, we talk seriously about next year. I tell Victor that I am proud of him for changing his attitude about life, but that he still has one thing left to do: hard work.

"The time has come for you to put your money where your mouth is," I say. He laughs as red sauce dribbles out of his mouth.

"I'll bet you a hundred dollars that I'll make straight A's by the end of next year," he says once he finishes chewing.

I say "yes" to the bet, even though I wish he had said A's and B's. I don't think he's got a chance at straight A's, and I want to see him win.

On our way out, after I pay at the cashier, Victor gets a hold of my bank card. I tell him it isn't funny and that I need the card back, but it's no use. We go to our respective sides of the car as I unlock the doors.

"I'm not giving you your card unless we go bowling," he says as he gets inside. I think he's kidding. I shouldn't have allowed him in the car until he had returned the bank card to me.

"Boy, if something happens to that card, you're gonna get it bad."

Victor continues to beg. "I want to go bowling. I want to go bowling." His tone of voice alternates between desperate and threatening. He sounds like Miss Piggy at both extremes.

"I know you want to go bowling, Victor. But today I have to say 'no.' I've got other plans." We pull out of the parking lot.

"So, call your friends and tell them you can't go."

"I know I usually say 'yes' to you, but today I can't. I've got a million things to do before I leave town tomorrow. You have to understand, Victor, I can't always give you what you want." We are driving back to Victor's house on Baseline. It is a straight shot, from 48th back to Central.

"I want to go bowling. Come on, Mr. Tucker," he begs.

"Victor, give me my bank card. It's not funny." We are going about sixty miles an hour. As I argue with Victor about the bank card, I am also turning down the radio every few seconds after he turns it up.

"I'm going to break your card," he says unconvincingly. I know he won't do that.

"Victor, give it to me. I don't have a credit card right now. I really need that bank card. If something happens to it, your mother's going to be very unhappy, because I'm going to need her to give me money so I can afford to drive home to Houston." We stop at a large set of streetlights.

"She's not gonna give you shit."

"She's gonna be giving you a lot of shit if something happens to that card. Victor, I need that. That's how I get money, and I need to be able to get money. I'm going home tomorrow." Victor rolls down his window when the car accelerates as the light turns green. "Don't you go putting that window down," I say. "Boy, if you drop that card..." We return to driving sixty miles an hour on Baseline, except now my bankcard is on the other side of the windshield.

"What? What you gonna do, nigga? Ew, I dropped it. Mr. Tucker. Ew. Look, it's not here." I look over. Victor has put his hand underneath the window where I can't see it.

"Get your hand in the car, boy! I don't have time for all your games right now. And I'm not going to go grab at you while I'm driving." I glance over at Victor again. "And wipe that silly smile off your face," I add.

"You gonna bring me bowling? Huh? huh? huh?" Victor says in his trash talk tone of voice. I feel as though he's trying to punk me.

"We're going to your house. You think I'd bring you bowling with you acting like this?" I'm not angry at Victor, but he is getting on my nerves.

"I'm gonna drop your bankcard out the window, and then you'll lose all your money," he says. He rolls down the window a bit more and waves my card around in the wind as I drive. Now I can see it through the front windshield.

"Boy, it'll be your ass if you let go of that card." I am trying to drive safely while we bicker, but having the window down is a bit distracting.

"Watchu gonna do? I'll fuck you up if you try to mess wit' me, nigga!"

"Look here, you little fucker. If you drop that card, you're gonna have to walk your dumbass up and down the street till you find it," I shout over the wind rushing into the car. "And that won't be pretty. These cars on Baseline are going sixty miles an hour, and it'd hurt you real fucking bad if you got hit." I don't realize this conversation is different from our normal banter when we play basketball or bowl or bicker over the radio volume. I figure that Victor isn't clumsy enough to drop the card by accident and that he likes me enough not to ruin it on purpose. Once we get to his house, I'll straighten things out.

Except we never make it that far. Here we are, going sixty down Baseline with the windows down and Power 92 blasting when Victor starts to yell in terror. "Oh my God, oh my God, I dropped it. Mr. Tucker, for real, I dropped it. Oh my God. Mr. Tucker, pull over, really, I dropped it. Come on, I did."

"Don't play with me, Victor," I say unemotionally. I don't slow down.

"No, really, Mr. T, I'm not playing, really, JT, I dropped it."

I look over at the passenger seat. At a quick glance, I don't see the card in Victor's hands.

"All right, fine, I'm pulling over. Give me a minute." I still think Victor is making this up, but I decide the best thing now is for me to wrestle the card out of the boy's hands.

"I can't believe I did that. JT, we've got to stop!" He sounds more desperate than he did before.

I switch to the left lane, and when oncoming traffic clears, I make a quick u-turn.

"I hear you, but I don't want to get us killed." I'm not going to stop the car suddenly and swivel turn as if we're the Dukes of Hazard. I'm still not sure if I believe him, but I realize that we're going to have to stop. Victor isn't ready to go home.

As we drive back on Baseline, Victor looks at the different trees and streets to try to figure out exactly where he dropped the bank card. I now do believe my bankcard is gone, getting run over by speeding cars somewhere on Baseline. We drive back for less than a minute when he says he thinks we're close. I nervously drive into the middle lane to turn left across Baseline traffic. I wait between two yellow lines that come together and form a 'V' as they narrow into nothing. Inside the "V" I feel trapped by the cars zooming past us on both sides.

This isn't a safe place to be, here, with Victor, with my bank card in the middle of the street. Finally, when there's a break in the traffic, I drive across Baseline and pull into an empty church parking lot that's on the side of the street where Victor says he dropped the card.

"I can't believe I did that," Victor says as we get out of my car.

"Me neither," I say flatly. "I hope we can find it. We might walk some on Baseline."

"God I'm stupid. Are you really mad, Mr. Tucker?"

"Just frustrated. I never should have let you in my car."

"Why did I do that?"

"Because you're twelve," I say. We walk along the road behind a row of palm trees. The ground is dry dirt, and my feet are stinging as if I'm stepping on ants.

Victor looks around. "Let's go all the way to the last tree. I think it was around there." He points at the last major intersection we crossed.

"It might be, but when cars hit it, it'll get thrown around. It could be anywhere at this point, knocked off the road, even on the other side."

We walk toward the cross street, both of us concentrating on the road. "I don't see it. Let's go all the way to there."

As we walk, we keep our eyes on Baseline.

Suddenly, I see a small shiny card flip up into the air after a truck drives over it.

"Victor, I think that's it," I say, amazed that we may have found it. "Look, it's there in the middle."

And then, before I've even thought about how we can try to get it back, Victor darts toward Baseline and runs into the road.

"Victor, hold on, don't go, Victor!" I yell out. "The cars are coming. Wait, don't go, Victor, stop, don't—" but I am several steps behind him and can't catch him.

We're driving down Baseline, sixty miles an hour through the heart of South Phoenix. We're coming from Pizza Hut and he wants to go bowling. I say I can't and he says I'd better. I say this August and he says right now. And then my window goes down and my bank card goes out and that's when the yelling begins. He calls himself clumsy and says that he's stupid. He asks why he did it. I say 'cause he's twelve. And so we walk down and stare at the street. And that's when we see it, by miracle we see it.

And then, even with cars coming and my shouting, even with my "don't go" and "don't go," he still doesn't wait. I want him to wait, I want him to stop, but I'm too far behind and I can't hold him back and I can't stop a car, a silver bullet racing at him. He thinks he's got time and I pray he won't trip. I stand without moving, my body is frozen, and I pray. It's the only thing I still can do. He jumps into the street and I can't catch him.

Until this moment, as I watch Victor run onto Baseline, I've always assumed that in the end, he will be fine. But now it really hits me, the truth, it really hits me, how often Victor runs across streets without looking, how close to life's edge he must live.

"Jesus, Victor, I can't believe you did that. Here, let me have it," I shout out as I grab him.

"Can I hold it?"

"No. No more." I hold him to the side of me away from the street. We stroll back to my car.

"Okay" he says without arguing.

"Victor, if that car had hit you, you'd be dead. Why'd you have to do that?"

"I don't know. I had enough time."

"You did. But still, what if? You never know."

"So? I'd probably just hurt my leg or something."

"If you were lucky and the car hit only your legs, you'd be in a wheelchair for the rest of your life. That'd mean no more soccer, no more running, no more gym. You couldn't even drive. And that's if you were lucky. What if that car had run over your head, and your brains were all splattered, and then, well, how could I— what would I tell your mother? With all your potential, if you got yourself killed—"

"A car would kill me if it hit me, huh."

"It's just not worth it. If it's a choice between my stupid bank card and you, I'd forget the card. Your life is more important than all the money I've got. If something happened to you, I couldn't forgive myself. After all the time we've spent together, to lose you, over a plastic bank card, I think I'd be, I'd feel—I don't know. I'd rather go out there myself."

"What if the car hit you?"

"That'd be better than having it hit you. At least I wouldn't have to live through seeing you die. At least I wouldn't feel anything." I pause. "What would you do if I got killed right there?"

"I don't know. I'd probably take your bank card and go get your money."

I stop. These are not exactly the words I was hoping to hear. "You'd get my bank card and money?" I ask incredulously. "Here I tell you how much I care about you, that I'd never forgive myself if something happened to you, and all you say is you'd take my bank card and money!"

Victor is laughing.

"Take my bank card and money. Figures. What a punk!" I knock him on his shoulder lightly. I'm laughing too.

We're walking side by side, along Baseline, and Victor hugs me with his left arm.

"I love you, Mr. Tucker," he says.

I smile.

"I love you, too, Victor."

It seems like it should, but time doesn't stop.

"Do you think your card is still working?"

"I don't know. How many cars do you think ran over it?"

"Maybe ten."

"No way. It was there five minutes, and cars were coming really fast, probably ten each minute."

"Fifty cars. I don't know."

Victor is right, but I'm tired of playing teacher. I change the subject as we get back to the empty church parking lot.

"Hey, Victor, there's something I've been wanting to ask you about. How are you feeling about your dad these days?"

"I'm okay. I used to cry all the time when I saw his picture, but now I'm okay. At first I didn't believe he was really dead, and seeing his picture made me cry a lot. But now it doesn't usually bother me," he says. We stop in front of my car.

"I'm glad you look at his picture. And if you cry sometimes, that's okay," I say. I lightly touch his back as we stand in an asphalt parking lot in front of what appears to be an abandoned church.

"I've got his picture on my necklace. Look— that's him," Victor says. He takes his necklace out from under his shirt. It has tiny silver objects dangling at the bottom. He holds the round pendant in his hands and opens it slowly. Inside is an old picture of a man who appears about thirty and has sideburns and dark skin. The photograph isn't more than a half inch in size. This is the first time I've seen Victor's father.

"When did you start wearing that?" I ask.

"Just in the last few weeks."

"I'm proud of you, Victor."

We get back inside my car and finally head to his house.

"Hey, Mr. Tucker, can I borrow ten dollars?" Victor asks as I pull back onto Baseline.

"I swear I just heard somebody ask me for money. Did you hear that, Victor? Crazy, huh, since I may not even have a working bank card anymore."

"No, really, we're going bowling tomorrow at the rec center, and I need some money," Victor says without chuckling or cracking his voice. I wonder if he's serious.

"You're going bowling tomorrow? Bowling? After all that begging? I can't believe you're telling me that, and then asking me for ten dollars on top of it. I don't even know if I'm going to be able to get enough money for me," I say.

We pull up in front of his house. Victor looks at me as he opens up the car door.

"How 'bout just five?"

before a canyon

PART II
victor and the quiet

Reading

Chronologically Victor's youngest brother, Jackson, is six years old, but to me he's anything but six. On the street, he tries to act thirteen, when asked directly, he claims to be ten, and inside his house when it's late at night, he seems about three. I've noticed that in general his only well-developed ways of communicating are swearing, fighting, crying, and lying. That said, I always enjoy bringing him out because no matter what we do, he loves it. The biggest problem I have with Jackson is that any time he thinks of it, he asks me to buy him a burger.

Lately Jackson has been really excited about what I've been teaching every morning at my new school, writing fictional stories, so he and Tommy have both been testing out the lesson plans. It's the fall of my second year in the Teach For America program. In my new school, Garcia, I have a self-contained class of fourth and fifth graders, so I can include quite a bit of writing.

Meanwhile, I've been stopping by Victor's house once or twice a week to see him and the rest of his family. He didn't switch schools; his mother didn't take the time to make that happen. He and his younger siblings love to hear about my lesson plans at this other school. To them, it's as though I'm sharing the tricks of my teacher magic.

"JT, JT, we finished our stories," Jackson runs over to me as I walk through the door. He bolts through his house to grab the spiral notebook I bought him a week ago and hurries back to jump on my lap. His story is called "The Fat Cat."

Third-grade Tommy transcribed the title and the first few sentences for him in brown crayon. The rest, which Jackson wrote, is a conglomeration of partially legible letters in various crayon colors strung together with breaks only at the end of each line on the page. Jackson pretends to read his story as he speaks aloud. He says the title correctly but then makes up the rest. Tommy and I listen. I'm amazed at Tommy's patience as he giggles, even though Jackson's story goes on and on.

Because Jackson seems to be composing a story for us that has no end, eventually I ask him to give Tommy a turn. He passes the spiral to Tommy, who flips through a few pages of scribble until he finds a page with writing. Jackson sees it and shouts, even before Tommy says a word,

"That one, Tommy, that one. Read JT that one!" Victor, who's now in seventh grade, walks in just as Tommy is about to read aloud the story that he and Jackson composed together. Tommy reads slowly:

Once upon a time there was a bear that resels. He was reseling with a lion. The lion accendently scrached the bear. The bear got mad. The bear headslammed the lion. The lion was still on the flore. Then he got up and the lion bodyslammed the bear.

The boys laugh and laugh. "Do another one, Tommy, do another!" Jackson exclaims.

Victor laughs out loud when the lion in the story body-slams the bear. "That's real good, Tommy. He's smart, huh JT?" Victor's voice doesn't crack. It's now mostly changed.

"I know, Tommy's awesome," I say. When it comes to Tommy, this has become my refrain.

"JT, let's do another story," Tommy says.

The last time I was here, I wrote the words while Tommy and Jackson spoke out loud. "You know what?" I say. "My hand is tired because I've been working at school all day. Victor, could you do it?"

"Okay, I'll help them. Then we'll read it to you when it's done."

Tommy and Jackson banter back and forth as they create their newest story.

"Once upon a time there was a lion who lived on a giant volcano. His father was really mad…" The kids talk quickly, with a 'no, like-this, like-this' every few seconds.

"Slow down, putos," Victor squeals, and the kids both laugh. He writes almost as quickly as an adult. "I'm fast, dude. I write real fast," he says to me.

"Too bad no one else can read it," I say with a smile because my handwriting is terrible as well.

"I do it that way on purpose. This is Mexican English," he says with an added emphasis on the word "Mexican."

I stand up and tell the kids I have to run to the store. "Finish the story while I'm gone so you can read it to me when I get back."

"Huh homies, we're gonna make it funny," Victor says. "He'll wish he had wrote it."

"Let's have a monkey named Jermy," Tommy suggests. They write Jermy for Jeremy, and say Germy. Jackson grins big, showing the giant gap in his front teeth.

When I get back from the grocery store, the kids are kicking a soccer ball around on the driveway. It's about nine o'clock at night. They tell me they've finished their story and brag about how funny it is. Apparently Jermy, the monkey, turns out to be a big dope.

Victor, now thirteen, Tommy, now eight, Elizabeth, Victor's seven-year-old sister, Jackson, chronologically six, Clarissa, Celia's two-year-old daughter, and I sit in a circle on the driveway to listen. Victor reads out loud. The story is one-and-a-half pages long and everyone laughs, especially at the parts about the monkey named and spelled Jermy. When Victor finishes, I tell the boys they could publish it and become famous. I mention that I have another story in my car that I think they might enjoy called "The Adventures of Captain Underpants," which my fourth and fifth grade students have been reading. I ask them if they'd like to hear it sometime.

"The adventures of what?" Tommy asks, sitting straight up. "Underpants?"

"Captain Underpants," I answer. "He's a super hero."

"Underpants!" Tommy repeats.

"We could read it now," says Victor.

I agree. I go to my car to get a copy out of my trunk. My car is on the street beside the front curb. Tommy and Jackson jump up to follow me to the car, both peering in the trunk when I open it. I keep my eyes on the street to be sure we're safe.

"Why do you got so many books?" Tommy asks.

As I explain about library books and lesson plans to Tommy, Jackson bends over my trunk and falls in. He then jumps out of the trunk and grabs Captain Underpants out of my hand. He runs back to show Victor. He doesn't wait for Tommy or me.

"I wanna read it, I wanna read," screeches Jackson. Waving the book around in the air, he points at the picture of the large man wearing white briefs and a red cape on the cover.

Victor sits on the driveway with his back against the house. It's pitch dark outside, and the only light for reading is a small lamp built into the garage. Jackson stands on Victor's leg. Clarissa sits in my lap across from Victor, bouncing joyfully. And Tommy and Elizabeth stand on both sides of Victor. He manages to read the book out loud and to show us pictures at the same time. He inflects his voice, making goofy sounds for the book's protagonist, Captain Underpants. After reading the first chapter, which takes him only five minutes, he passes the book to me. Now I read, trying to maintain Victor's energy. The kids shift their positions so that they remain close to the book, but they start to let gravity pull them down a bit. Tommy begins to kneel. Elizabeth and Jackson lean against my shoulders. I read chapter two, and then pass the book back to Victor. By chapter four, everyone's sitting. Clarissa has gone inside.

We pass the book back and forth for half an hour or so. By the time Victor and I finish reading it, all of us are lying on our stomachs, still giggling at the silly cartoons, but more softly. It's now almost eleven. Everyone goes inside to sleep except for Victor and me. His two older sisters, Celia and Vanessa, come outside to join us. They sit on plastic beach chairs while Victor and I lie still on the ground. Lounging on the driveway, we spend another hour together in the quiet darkness.

■ ■ ■ ■ ■ ■ ■ ■ ■ ■ ■ ■

Schooled

"Hey V, thanks for coming with me," I say. Victor has helped me every weekend in my classroom with cleaning and grading since the school year began three weeks ago.

We are sitting at one of the tables in my classroom and working quietly. I notice that Victor works quickly and never moves his eyes off the paper.

"It's fun, Jermy. I'm like a teacher. I already know how to be a teacher."

Victor's names for me have gone from Mr. Tucker to Mr. T to JT to Jermy.

"You're definitely learning," I say. "You'd be a good teacher if you wanted to be one. You'd know how to handle all the bad kids."

"I'd be like, 'Hey, homie, I know all your tricks, so don't try them on me, 'cause I already did them to my teacher.' "

"I know that's true." I look over. "Hey, V, don't forget to put the scores on the tests." Victor is grading vocabulary tests, using an answer key I made.

"You're a good teacher this year," he says while we work. "You got couches and tables. You got all your folders and everything neat. And you do an auction every Friday. Your students really like you, huh?"

"I don't know. I think so. Sometimes I'm kind of mean, though."

"They get detention when they're bad? Not like me. I got away with murder."

"Exactly. I'm not letting anyone act the way you did. They're good, though. They're an easy class."

"I wish you could be my teacher this year."

"You're a spirited person. Honest and fun. Nothing's a secret with you. I've loved getting to know you as a person," I say. "But as a student.... I don't think I could be your teacher," Victor laughs.

"I'd be good. I'd be cool with you. I'd help you do everything, and I'd make good grades, too."

"You'd try to, but I don't know—I make my students do homework every night."

"Even weekends?"

"Every day the kids see me, including Fridays, I give them work to be done at home." That's just the way it is."

"Damn."

"They do it too."

"I probably would," Victor says. Now that I'm thinking about it, he probably would do it. He flips through several papers, marking in blue pen answers that are different from my answer key. "Hey Jermy, this kid got them all right. She's smart."

"Who is it?" I glance over at the paper. "Oh, Karina, yeah, she always does well. She's great at spelling and vocabulary."

"I bet she studies a lot. She probably does all her work."

"She does, and it's hard doing all your work every day. She's an amazing student."

"Hey, Jermy, look at this one. Do I have to count it wrong?" The student chose the right vocabulary word for the blank and he spelled the word correctly, all except for one vowel.

"Yeah, go ahead and fix the spelling and mark it wrong."

"You're hard," he says as he does it.

"I know, but these kids are really smart, and it's good for them to learn to be careful. Even if he gets that one wrong, he'll still get an 'A' on the test. So it's not such a big deal."

"My teachers don't even fix our work. They just collect it and put checks on it. That's probably why we don't learn that much." Victor is still at Hatfield.

He works with me in the classroom for a couple of hours. After he's finished grading three weeks of vocabulary tests, he helps me enter the grades onto my computer spread sheet. Meanwhile, I'm figuring out lesson plans for the next week and reading through the green folders, in which my students write their fiction stories every morning.

When we leave, we go to Pete's Fish and Chips for burgers, and then we head back to Victor's house to pick up Jackson. I promised him this morning that he could come with us to the river in the afternoon.

■ ■ ■ ■ ■ ■ ■ ■ ■ ■ ■

before a canyon

Leaving Mexico, Part 1
By Celia

One night my mom decided to leave Mexico. She didn't even think about it. My mom and dad started fighting, and we just went. He treated her very bad.

It started when my dad came home drunk, and he had a big dog, a wolf dog, and they tied the dog to a small tree, but the dog messed up the tree and attacked my dad. My mom didn't take care of my dad. She didn't feed him or think of him. She didn't put anything on his face after he got bit. She didn't even take him to a hospital or nothing. My dad got all mad and left. He was bloody, but she didn't think of him at all.

When he came back, my mom started fighting with him. The only thing I remember is that she got a chair and threw it at his head and broke it on his side. We only had a couple chairs, and we didn't have beds or anything. Everybody had to sleep on the ground like children, so it was bad she broke that chair.

The River

"Come on, JT, don't bring Jackson. I hate Jackson. He asks for too much."

"We don't have to bring him if you don't want to," I say hesitantly.

"No, fine. I feel bad," Victor gives in, so we return to his house. Jackson is waiting outside, playing in the driveway. He runs up to the car before I've even parked.

"Where was you guys?" Jackson asks as Victor reaches around to open the back door for him. "You got burgers? Hey, gimme the front, mother-fucker!" he says to Victor.

"Fuck you, stupid," Victor responds. Jackson hops in the backseat without another word. "See JT, Jackson always getting on my nerves. You lucky we brought you," Victor says in a deep voice.

On our way to the river, after going to Wendy's to get a burger for Jackson, we stop at a beef jerky stand. I've never been a fan of jerky, but Victor says he's been to this stand before, and tells us there's one type of jerky that's particularly good, so we buy it. He's right. It's spicy and sweet, and all three of us keep ripping off little pieces for ourselves until all ten dollars worth of jerky is gone. The whole thing lasts for only five minutes.

The river we go to is called Rio de Salado. Climbing over haphazard tree roots, we walk downhill across lots of rocks to get to the water. There are hundreds of people already there when we arrive, mostly families, barbecuing, sitting on blankets, and carrying fishing poles. Most of the people are speaking Spanish, so I feel somewhat dependent on Victor and Jackson.

As we make our way to the water, the kids race across the rocks while I walk slowly and watch each one of my steps. I'm not taking any chance of twisting an ankle and depending on Victor even more than I already am. By the time I get to the riverbank, the kids have taken off their shoes and are running into the water. At my request, Jackson has put on his bright-orange flotation devices.

"JT, JT, watch me, watch, JT!" Jackson jumps into the water and paddles around, splashing Victor and the other kids around him.

"I'm gonna mess you up," Victor says jokingly as he dives into the water and swims at Jackson. The boys laugh and run through the water.

As they swim, Jackson sees a girl who looks about twenty in a pink one-piece bathing suit standing beside the water. He stares at her. "Dammmmn, you look good," he shouts out.

The girl doesn't move or say a thing. I think she's a lifeguard. Jackson looks tiny in the water even though his voice is big.

Victor laughs. "That's my brother," he says to the girl. "Don't be mad. He's stupid."

"I'm not mad," the girl says.

Victor continues. He points up at me. "My homie up there says 'What up?' He's like twenty-four." I'm embarrassed. I don't know what to say. Luckily, the girl doesn't say anything either.

"So what up? Why are you shy?" Victor continues.

"I'm not shy."

"So can I get at you? Can I get your number?"

I'm not sure if Victor thinks he's being ridiculous, but to me a thirteen-year-old kid hitting on a twenty-something-year-old woman looks funny. Jackson doesn't know the difference. "Hey, hey, girl, shit!" Jackson shouts out, "Are you white or Mexican or Italian or Chinese?"

"I'm Mexican," the girl replies, and she starts to walk off. I'm surprised she answered a small child with a big voice and orange arms.

"Don't you get burned up there?" Victor says up at her, but she doesn't answer. Her back is now turned, as she is talking to another girl. Victor turns around and quickly dunks Jackson.

"Mother fucker bitch mother!" Jackson shouts at Victor as he re-emerges from the water. Victor laughs and shoves him again. The boys joust, trying to dunk each other's heads, having lost interest in the girl. After a while, they decide to look for a part of the river that's deeper. They see that upstream there's a rope spanning across a section of the river where the water rushes fast between a cluster of large rocks. "Come on, Jackson, let's go up there. That's bad!" Victor shouts as he gets out of the water.

"That's bad, JT," Jackson shouts up to me in the same tone of voice as Victor's. He follows Victor and runs over to the part of the river that is slightly upstream of the rope. Two men hold a several inch thick rope across the river to make a game of the tides. Kids float downstream, grab the rope, and hold themselves against the current of the river, trying to pull themselves up and partly out of the water. Eventually when they can no longer hold on, they let the current take them through the rocks to a less turbulent area below where they can get out and do it again.

Victor runs to the river to join in the game. Jackson helps me find a high rock that stands above the river where we can put our shoes and shirts. I like the location, because I can sit here and see most everything. Jackson stays with me—he watches Victor, longing to join in the game, but somewhat fearful of it, as well. He would never admit it, but Jackson knows he can't really swim. After Victor takes two turns riding the river, he comes to find us on our rock, carrying his soaking shoes. He sits down to take a break. As I listen to Victor recount the details of his encounter with the river, I decide this is definitely not for Jackson. But before I say something to Jackson about not doing it, he has slipped off. A few minutes later, Victor and I see him floating down the river. He's shouting and laughing with his typical intermittent Jackson-look of terror.

"Jesus, is Jackson okay doing this? He can't really swim," I say.

"I know, Jackson's crazy. Look at him," Victor is laughing. "He's stupid. I think he likes to be scared."

These are not words I want to hear as I watch Jackson get swept down the river and reach out with his arms to grab the rope. Only one of his hands holds on, but Jackson laughs maniacally even as the water tugs his body down. His laugh appears as an upside down grin, and his shrieks of pride are indistinguishable from shrieks of fear. Suddenly his hand lets go of the rope and that's when his head disappears and he becomes silent. The river may be too strong for his orange floaties.

Victor stops laughing and jumps to his feet, his shoes already on the ground as he pulls off his shirt. He runs to the edge of the rock and is ready to jump. I stand beside him.

"Wait, stop, Victor. Don't jump!" I shout, my hand on his shoulder. He looks like he's thinking about jumping ten feet down onto a rocky river. That's when we hear Jackson's muffled cries.

"Ahhhhh" he yells out, and then we hear nothing again.

"You can't jump here!" I press on Victor's shoulders, praying he won't pull away, not knowing what to do about Jackson.

"That's my brother!" he says. He doesn't move. We can't see Jackson anywhere. We don't know if he's drowning underwater or hidden behind a rock.

"I know, but you'll end up getting yourself killed if you try!"

"That's my brother. I wouldn't even feel pain if I landed on a rock."

My heart beats oh God oh God oh God and I'm frozen and my hand is still pressing on Victor's shoulder. "Where's Jackson? Where's Jackson?" I keep saying.

"That's where he'll be," Victor says, pointing slightly downstream of where I'm looking. All I can think to do is wait. Then Victor adds, "If he's not there in the next thirty seconds, I'm going in." We wait for Jackson to reappear. I've stopped breathing.

Suddenly, from behind a rock, we see his orange arms and head emerge, bobbing only a few inches above the surface of the water.

"Look it, look it!" Victor shouts out.

"He's okay," I say, breathing hard. Jackson seems to be all right. From what I can see of his face, I can't tell if he's laughing or crying, but either way, he's clearly conscious.

"You would risk your life for Jackson?" I ask Victor.

"I'd do anything for my brother."

"But you said you hate him, and you're always cussing at him."

"I'd never let anyone hurt my brother," Victor says quickly.

He stands at the edge of the rock, holding his shoes and shirt in his hands. He doesn't move as I sit down again. Neither of us speaks a word.

We continue to watch Jackson, kicking and squirming to keep his mouth and nose barely above the level of the water, only the bright orange balloons on his arms floating easily. Victor concentrates all of his energy into his legs. He stands quietly.

When I look up at his face, still, his eyes are on the river.

■ ■ ■ ■ ■ ■ ■ ■ ■ ■ ■ ■ ■

Belting

Victor's mom is home tonight. We're all sitting in the living room, watching TV, me on the couch, Victor beside me, Jackson in my lap, and their mom on the other couch. Victor and his mom get into a fight after some of his friends come over and want him to go out with them. He starts to leave, but then she tells him he isn't allowed. It seems strange to me (and probably to him) to have someone say "No." Usually he goes out whenever he wants, since there is no one there to ask.

Victor comes back inside and sulks on the couch. His mom lies on the other couch. After a few minutes, he says something in Spanish that I don't understand, and then she orders him to go to his room. After he goes, she follows him with her belt in her hand. A few minutes later, he is back out of his room, doing the dishes, with his mom standing next to him and watching. He seems angry. Meanwhile, Jackson and I face the TV. Victor joins us after a few minutes.

Before I have a chance to find out from Victor what happened, Jackson turns to me. "JT, can we go get burgers?" he asks.

"Jackson, I don't know. It's already late." It doesn't feel like this a good time.

"Please," he begs.

"Let's see what your mom says." I'm nervous.

Jackson walks over to his mom and asks her in broken Spanish. She is lying down, resting. She answers decisively, "No."

I don't mind. I'm just as happy not to go. It's been a long day, and I want to get home soon, anyway. But Jackson seems utterly dejected. He whimpers softly.

His mom starts to laugh. She looks at me, smiles, and says, "Ay, Jackson." Then she stands up, takes out her belt, and smacks him hard on the back. Jackson howls. Mom laughs. Victor laughs. She hits him again, still laughing. Jackson runs out of the room. Victor shouts in Spanish as Jackson runs. Their mom returns to her couch. She looks at me again and laughs.

I smile back. I'm shocked, but I say nothing.

A minute later, Jackson returns to the room. He sits on the floor in the corner and pulls his knees to his chest, making him appear even smaller than he already does. He's wearing no shirt and his chest is as red as his face. He mutters something to Victor and Victor tells him to shut up. Responding with his mouth open upside down, looking toward Victor but not at him, Jackson screams out, "You shut up, you stupid motherfucker."

Mom laughs. She looks around for a minute and then she looks at Jackson.

"Poor Jackson" is all I can muster.

"Jackson's stupid," Victor says without looking.

She says nothing. She walks over to Jackson, and he pulls away from her, his mouth open, but no breath coming out. She laughs again, and he sinks deeper, and she swings her belt back, and she laughs, and his red body falls deeper into the corner still, silent, and her body looms over his.

And then in one sudden motion she smashes him on the legs, her belt hugging his legs. He shrieks, but nothing comes out except tears.

She smiles, "Jackson," and shakes her head. Victor and I sit quietly.

■ ■ ■ ■ ■ ■ ■ ■ ■ ■ ■

Leaving Mexico, Part 2
By Celia

In the middle of the night that same day, she got us and took us. Victor was one, Vanessa was three, I was four, and José was five.

We were walking barefoot through a desert with cactus and prickles on the ground. We didn't have no shoes, and it was the middle of the night, and there were wolves and everything.

When we got to the street, we borrowed some money from our friends. We took a bus to Nogales, and from there we took a truck with a lot of people, like five or six families. We were sitting in the back of an old pick-up truck.

Chaos

"We're gonna go on every ride," Victor announces as I pay for the two of us and Jackson to enter the annual Arizona State Fair. Elizabeth's out with her mom and we can't find Tommy—he's out on his bike somewhere—plus Vanessa won't ever come with us—she's too mature. Celia's always too busy cooking to leave home. But Jackson seems to be at home a lot, so he can always join us if Victor will let him.

"Look, Jermy, look, look!" Jackson shouts out, pointing at a giant slide.

"There's a lot of people here," Victor says.

Jackson hears his brother. "Hell yeah. Look at that bitch," he says.

"Man, don't talk like that, Jackson," I say, putting my hand on Jackson's head, which is barely as high as my waist.

"She's fine," he continues. "She got a big booty."

"That's my little brother. You be embarrassed." Victor says to me with a smile.

"I mean, he's hooting at girls we don't even know," I say back. Jackson lets out a squeal of pride.

"That's why I got me a lot of bitches. I got me a grip," Jackson says. I hate hearing this from a six year old, but I say nothing.

"There's a lot of booty here, huh Jermy," Victor says in a nonchalant tone.

I nod.

"I didn't dress nice," he says. "Damn JT, my shirt's all dirty." He is wearing the white soccer shorts and purple soccer shirt I bought him last summer. I think he looks fine.

"I can't really tell," I answer honestly.

"I'm wearing a dirty-ass shirt. I didn't even notice. I'm going to the fair in a dirty-ass shirt." I look, but I can't see what he means. He scrubs his shirt with his hand, twists it, even applies some saliva to it.

After a few licks, he says, "It don't matter. I don't have to impress no females. I just came to ride the rides."

Jackson is now facing backwards, still eyeing the giant slide. It's yellow, plastic, and arched in multiple places. Kids are given blue plastic boards at the top and then ride them to the bottom.

"Come on, Jackson," Victor says, "That ride is for babies. Don't be so gay."

Jackson turns around. We continue walking, and then we enter the area that's cluttered with expensive games and large stuffed animals. As we discuss various games and strategies for winning, I remember that when I was in middle school, I used to be fascinated by the amusement park games in the same way Victor and Jackson are now. I had to limit myself. I recall that one time I won a giant stuffed dog named Spuds McKenzie, who used to appear in Bud Light ads wearing sunglasses and a bandana. Winning that dog was one of the highlights of my adolescent years.

Thinking about Spuds, I decide to give Victor and Jackson five bucks each to spend on games. Victor decides to play a dart game. With five darts he pops four balloons, but he needs five popped balloons to win the prize. Jackson then decides to spend his five dollars on five more darts. He misses with each of his first four, so he gives the last dart to Victor. I feel nervous because I know a prize is at stake. Victor quickly picks up the dart, throws it, and pops the fifth balloon. The prize is a framed picture, and there are about fifty of them. He and Jackson choose a gray drawing of smiling and frowning masks with a zoot suit man above them and the words "Sick Life."

Jackson begs to carry the picture. He brags about how well he had thrown his darts, telling Victor and me the story over and over, as if we hadn't been there, as if we hadn't seen his darts.

As we continue to walk, the horizon fills with the rides Evolution and Kinetics, outlined by fluorescent lights and enhanced by hard rock and rap. All of the rides seem to cost several dollars, and the riders sit in small metallic cages that revolve around non-sedentary central axes and turn upside down for a good quarter of the time they're in the air. I find these rides fun.

I study the rides. Victor seems to study them too. He turns his head toward me, "What kind's not crackable, you know, where you can't steal them or nothing?"

Unsure what he means, I say, "Personally I don't want a bolt to fall out and the whole ride to come apart."

"That one, look! Dammmmn." Victor points up at a ride called Gravity. It is different from the others in its simplicity: it lifts you higher than any other ride in the park, and then it lets you drop straight down.

"That looks nice," I say.

"You'd do it?"

"Hell yeah. I'll do it if you'll do it," I say, feeling only slightly queasy as I think about the ride.

Victor says nothing. He points and grins. We watch a doughnut-shaped chairlift slowly pull up a group of shrieking people. Once they reach the top, they sit suspended in the air, their seats hanging. Then, suddenly, the donut magnet releases their chairs and they seem to free fall. Victor laughs as they shriek. He then looks over at me.

"Hell no," he says, "I'm not doing that."

"What about you, Jackson?" I say, laughing.

"I don't like the big ass rides, JT," Jackson says with his arm around my knee.

"I like roller coasters better. Come on, JT, let's do that first," Victor suggests.

"That's cool with me," I reply.

Victor leads us off to a more standard looking, cart-follows-hilly-path rollercoaster. It appears to be the only one of its kind at the fair.

Jackson whimpers as he drags behind, "I don't like this one. It's a big ass ride. Can I do the slide, JT?"

"Let's do the roller coasters, Jackson," Victor says. "It'll be better."

"I don't like big rides," Jackson says again, unwilling to concede. "I'll do the slide."

"That's stupid, Jackson. That ride's for babies."

"Fuck you, mother fucker," Jackson says. "Can I have three tickets, JT?"

We alternate for the rest of the evening between rides Victor wants and rides Jackson wants. For each one, we stay together, one of us watching from below and holding "Sick Life," the other two going on the ride. My favorite is a wobbly ride called the Zipper. Victor and I jump into a seat whose position depends on our body weight while Jackson stands below and waves, thankful that he doesn't have to go. The seats on the ride are attached to a chain that carries them from one end of the ride to the other. Meanwhile, the stick-like apparatus, holding the seats, revolves around the center of the ride, and the seats revolve around their own ax-les. It is a lesson in torque, and for me and Victor, it is also a lesson in who can shout obscenities the loudest. 'Jackson's a fucking midget! JT's a fucking whore! Victor's a fucking bitch!' We can't believe how fast the ride twirls our bodies upside down. We are laughing and screaming like we never have before.

As we leave the fair, I see one more ride I still want to do. It is called the Tilt-A-Whirl. The main character in Sandra Cisneros's "The House on Mango Street" says her life is like a Tilt-A-Whirl. I imagine she means dizzying, but I want to experience it myself.

"I think we should leave, JT," Victor says. "It's already late."

"Really?" I'm disappointed. "You don't want to stay a little longer?"

"I want to go to sleep," Jackson says in the same tone he uses when he's bragging. He seems proud to agree with Victor.

I concede. We make our way back through the park toward the en-trance. As we walk, I am still thinking about what it would feel like to be on the Tilt-A-Whirl. I figure it isn't a good life metaphor for any of us, anyway.

"I got a question for you, Victor," I say. "Of all the rides at the fair, which one do you think is the most like your life?"

At first, I wonder if Victor is annoyed. He says nothing and doesn't smile. I realize that eight-thirty on a Sunday night as we're walking down 19th Avenue in west Phoenix in search of my car is probably not the best time for me to ask an abstract question.

But before I have a chance to retract it, Victor speaks up. He doesn't sound annoyed by the question at all.

"That last one we did, Chaos," he says. "Because I make a lot of chaos all the time. I'm always making chaos for everybody." He has misunder-stood my question. He tells me not how life does something to him, but rather how he does something to life.

■ ■ ■ ■ ■ ■ ■ ■ ■ ■ ■ ■ ■

Leaving Mexico, Part 3
By Celia

I had a little cup of glue that my mom bought for me. I didn't have no pens, no toys, no nothing. Just the clothes I had on and my glue.

It was just regular glue in a little bottle. I always had it with me until the other kids took it away from me. Another girl wanted it to fix her tennies. She wanted to glue them because her tennies broke. She took the glue away from me.

I was fighting over it. It was the only thing I had. I got too excited about it.

Phone Fight

Jackson opens the door to my car and begins to climb over me before I've even parked. He reaches for my Dr. Pepper. "Hey, that's my pop!" he shouts.

"Hold on," I say, "I've got to turn off the car." As the car comes to a full stop, I try to hurl Jackson's wiggling body off my lap, but when I stand up, he ducks under me. I have to yank him from behind and hold him in a body-lock. Jackson keeps trying to squeeze between my arms, but I block him with my leg. I kick him back and slam the door shut.

Forgetting the Dr. Pepper, Jackson jumps into my arms. "Where you gonna bring us today, JT?" he asks.

"Hey V, ready to go?" I say. I talked to Victor yesterday about taking a trip to the library today. He has a science project to do, and I offered to help him find books. Jackson and Elizabeth said they wanted to go too. Tommy, as he had before, preferred the independence of a bike.

As Victor and I walk down the driveway to my car, Jackson bursts out of the house and runs past us. He opens the passenger side and jumps into the car.

Elizabeth, who's in second grade, stands beside the front door of the house.

"I don't want to go no how," she says, sulking, and then steps back inside. She has to go to a Saturday detention at school, so she can't go with us.

"Victor, you're letting him take shotgun?" I ask, amazed.

"I'm a gangster," Jackson answers.

"I don't even let my homies get the front."

"I know," I say, as we pull away from the house.

"It's 'cause I'm a G," says Jackson immodestly.

"He's my brother," Victor replies.

"It's on Roosevelt, right, Victor?" I've driven to the downtown library before, but can't remember the name of the street.

"It's on Roosevelt," Jackson answers my question instead of Victor. "I know where it's at."

"We went to it before, right Victor?" I ask.

"Yeah," Jackson replies again.

"Let me answer, Mr. Tucker!" Victor gripes. "Oh yeah, I forgot to call you Jermy."

"What if I called you Mr. Villanueva?" I say to Victor.

"That'd be better than Victor," he says. "My friends call me Chivo, Chivito, Toshi, Toe, all kinds of names."

"Toshi?" I ask, confused.

"It's Victor and Chivo put together," he replies.

"What'd you tell me they call José?" I ask. I remember that Victor told me his older brother, José, has a funny nickname, too.

"Cactus. I don't know why they call him that." José is a large guy, the oldest of the siblings, thick around the middle, and when he speaks, he's very hard to understand. Still, I enjoy talking to him when he's around, but for most of the time I've known Victor, José's been in jail. He's usually drunk and doesn't seem to mind breaking the law.

As we drive up Central, Victor says, "I want to get me a little Euro, dude." I've never heard of a Euro as a type of car.

"Hell yeah, a Euro is bad," Jackson chimes in. "In my whole neighborhood, I drive around seeing Euros. My whole neighborhood."

Victor continues, "I want to get me one all black with tinted windows and white rims. And a fast diesel. That's what I want. I'm gonna get me one, JT, watch. I'm gonna get me one someday."

Jackson looks out my window. "That's a sorry car, JT," he says about the blue Chevy beside us.

"I'm probably gonna get a Honda," Victor says. "Or a four door. What I want is a four door. I want me a tight ass car," he says. "Like this car, a Honda," he says. "That's what I want. With NOS. I want to be able to haul ass."

When we get back from the library, we sit at the kitchen table for a while. Victor, Jackson, and I are the only people at home. Victor tells me about getting an "F" in social studies. I'm not happy to hear this, so I try to brainstorm ways for him to improve. Flashcards? Tutoring? Practice tests? I don't really understand the root of the problem, so it's hard for me to come up with solutions. I think first we need to find out the cause of the "F." He seems embarrassed about flunking, which tells me he's motivated to improve. His mom's feelings about this? She doesn't care, he says, as long as it doesn't interfere with her life.

While we are talking, he's holding the phone. Apparently, his girlfriend is supposed to be calling him this afternoon. Meanwhile, Jackson is sitting on my lap, with a plastic toy truck in one hand and a burger in the other.

Elizabeth comes bursting in through the front door. I wonder if she's been at Saturday detention since the morning.

"You've been gone all this time?" I ask.

"Stupid detention," she says. "I hate my teacher." She walks to the back part of the house without stopping.

"Elizabeth's a bitch," Victor says. "She didn't even say 'hi' or nothing. She's got spoiled, JT."

She comes back into the kitchen. "Victor, gimme the damn phone," she demands in an alto voice, speaking slowly, slurring and cracking.

"Hells no," he says to her. "And quit acting all hard." Elizabeth stands at the table where Victor is eating Ramen noodle soup.

"Don't be talking shit to me," she says. "Gimme the fucking phone." I am surprised at Elizabeth's language. She doesn't usually swear. She is unusually angry.

"Then come get it, bitch," he says.

"I'm gonna too. Then I'm gonna call my mom. You better give me the phone, Victor." He holds it over his soup and laughs. He refuses to hand it to Elizabeth. She lunges over the table to get it. Unfortunately, she knocks over the soup bowl.

Broth and noodles spill out. Victor jumps up and quickly finds a napkin. "Bitch," he says. Elizabeth then grabs the phone.

"Fucker," she says.

She walks back to their mother's room and Victor follows. I throw away the three wet napkins that Victor used to soak up the soup.

Meanwhile, Elizabeth sits down on the bed with the phone, but before she dials, Victor races in the room and snatches the phone back from her.

"Victor!" Elizabeth shouts out.

"Shut up, bitch," he says. I stand outside the bedroom and watch. I do not know what to do. I already feel awkward about being in the hall and would feel really awkward about entering the mother's bedroom.

"Give me the motherfucking phone," Elizabeth shouts. She stands up and goes after him in the doorway as he tries to leave the room. When Jackson makes her mad, Elizabeth will usually make one comment to him, ignore him, mope for five or ten minutes, and then forget the whole thing. For whatever reason, today Victor has brought out a different side of her.

"I'm gonna whup your ass if you don't shut up," he shouts at her.

"Shit, fat bastard, I'm not shutting up. Give me the phone."

Victor then snaps. He drops the phone and pushes Elizabeth. He swings his entire right arm backwards and slings the whole weight of it at her. His hand hits the right side of her face. I have never seen Victor slap anyone in his family. I am frozen in terror.

Elizabeth then starts swinging her arms. She hits back and forth, with both of her arms, against his shoulders. She has no control and he laughs. "What the fuck!" she shouts at him. "You shouldn't be hitting me." As she boxes at him, he pushes her back with his right arm. He holds himself stiff, trying to keep her away. But she doesn't stop, and she slips past his arm.

"I'm gonna kill this bitch," he says.

I look over and realize that Jackson is standing beside me, in the hall, partially behind my leg. "Calm down, Victor," Jackson shouts around me. "Calm down."

"Go get my gun," Victor yells out. But Jackson doesn't move.

"Calm the fuck down!" he shouts again. I press down on Jackson's shoulders to make sure he doesn't go anywhere. I think about going in the room to stop the fight, but I'm not sure I should intervene. It's not my place: I'm an uninvited guest, I reason to myself. Victor reaches with his left arm and grabs Elizabeth above her shoulders. He's holding her out with his one hand wrapped around her neck, almost like he's choking her. He pushes her on the bed and she falls.

She starts to cry.

"I'm gonna tell my mom and she gonna kick you out. She gonna kick you the fuck out for hitting me."

"Yeah right," he says. "Go ahead." He sees the phone on the floor, picks it up, and walks out, pushing past Jackson and me without a word. Within seconds, I hear the front door slam. Back in the kitchen, the phone sits in the middle of some noodles on the kitchen table.

About twenty minutes later, I look back in the room where I left

Elizabeth. I want to tell her to use the phone to call her mom. But she is asleep. So I decide to stay at the house and wait with Jackson. We watch TV until about six o'clock, when Elizabeth's mother gets home. I tell Mrs. Villanueva what's happened. She goes into her room and closes the door. I hear her talking to Elizabeth. I decide to leave.

A few days later, when Elizabeth and I talk in private, I ask her what happened. "I came home all mad. I had a bad attitude. It's 'cause of my stupid teacher," she explains. "And Victor was mean. But you know what, JT? When he came home later that night, he came home all nice. He started hugging me. He started asking me, 'Do you want something? I'm sorry, Liz,' he said.

"He was even being nice to Jackson. 'Hey bro,' he told to him. 'You want some food? We'll go get you a burrito or something, bro.' My mom never even talked to Victor. Then he brought me out for food with one of his homies. We went to Mariscos and we brought back some food to the house. He said he felt bad that he been hitting me and stuff. Victor's got a bad temper, but sometimes he be nice."

Leaving Mexico, Part 4
By Celia

On the way over here we had an accident. We were almost killed. I think we could have died. The tires broke down, and we crashed into a tree. We had no food, no nothing, just a cup of water, and then a police officer saw us.

Usually in Mexico the police are mean and always take your money, but this one was nice. He had candy and food. He fixed the tires on the car.

But then in another place, we ran out of gasoline. We didn't have no money for it. And we had no food left from the police officer, only a cup of water and some seeds. But somebody else helped us there, too.

Finally, we came to the border, and then in only ten hours more we got to the ranch, and that's where my mom's brother got us. He brought us to live with him in Guadalupe, right by Phoenix. My mom then got some jobs cleaning in a bunch of motels.

Sandra

I have to give Victor a bit of credit for helping me meet Sandra Cisneros, a great author and a rock star of a woman. She's almost fifty, beautiful and strong. I saw her outside the Phoenix Center as I was walking out of my art class one Saturday afternoon. I strolled over to the outdoor gathering where she was reading from her newest book of poetry. She was stunning, like an Indian goddess. Her voice was smooth.

While waiting in line to meet her after the reading, I wrote her a letter. I wrote about Victor and his family, about the neighborhood where they lived, and I begged her to visit my class. I told her what a huge difference it would make to him and his siblings and to all the children like them. I didn't mention that my girlfriend in college used to read her poetry to me on cold rainy nights while we lay in bed together.

The letter I wrote apparently worked because a month later I received a box in the mail from her. She sent me a few signed copies of her books to give to my students, several photos, and a handwritten letter. She thanked me for my words and told me to call her agent in New York to set up a time for her to visit us in Phoenix.

And now, after a year of phone calls and long silences, after months of creating lesson plans and assigning *The House on Mango Street* homework, the day of her visit has finally come. It turns out that the date she chose is a school holiday, but the plan doesn't change:

1— we will go to the Villanueva house

2— we will bring two Villanueva children and two former students with us to my school

3— we will spend time just with my class

4— we will go to the auditorium to spend time with all the students at the school

5— we will celebrate the school day just with my class

6— we will leave the school with the four children who came with us, and then go to a nice local restaurant where we can eat something before Sandra returns to the airport

I'm looking forward to seeing how she talks with children, and I'm excited to see her up close. I wonder how her face will look, if she's as powerful in person as she is on the page and in front of a crowd. I'm planning to say something to her about my crazy feelings, or at least to find a way to get her number. This is no date, but meeting her under these circumstances is certainly a fantasy, and Victor is, in large part, responsible for helping to make the fantasy real.

When I wake up in the morning, I pick out clean pants and a well-starched, blue shirt. I don't want my clothes to be wrinkled. When her plane arrives, I nervously watch people march single file off the exit ramp. A large group of people dressed in pink- and purple-floral patterns dance their way off the plane, and Sandra walks behind the dancing group. She is smiling as she watches. When I see her, I approach nervously.

"Hi, I'm Jeremy," I say. "It's great to have you here."

She looks me up and down and then gives me a distant hug hello. "I love that dog," she says, pointing at a toy poodle dressed in blue and strutting with the dancers. "You know, I love animals."

We leave the airport in my Honda. Sandra sits in the passenger seat where Victor has sat many times, where I used to sit years ago when my mother drove this car. She is wearing an Indian sort of dress, with a papaya colored scarf wrapped over her shoulders. She looks beautiful. My stomach feels weird.

Our first stop is at the Villanueva house. Victor, Vanessa, and their mother are waiting. "It's a pink house," I say with a smile as we pull into the driveway, "like the old Mexican ones you write about."

"Very pretty," Sandra responds.

When Mrs. Villanueva opens the door, Sandra smiles and greets her with a big hug. She then hugs Vanessa, who stands behind her mother and bends forward to hug Sandra as well. Victor waits behind his sister and mother. He reaches out his hand limply as Sandra walks inside.

Sandra touches Vanessa's shoulder. "Your home is beautiful," she says directly to Vanessa, who smiles quietly. "So clean." Sandra seems to know more about this house than I ever told her.

"Mr. Tucker showed us your book about Mango Street," Vanessa says. "It sounded like our family." We sit at the kitchen table and eat freshly made tamales. Vanessa tells Sandra about my first time eating tamales, and how I didn't take the paper off before I ate. She and Sandra giggle.

Sandra then speaks to Mrs. Villanueva for a few minutes in Spanish, speaking too quickly for me to follow.

Meanwhile, I'm looking at Victor. I mouth to him that he should talk some too, but he doesn't. "Be friendly," I whisper.

"I am," he frowns.

After half an hour, I tell everyone that we had better go. "My class is waiting," I say. "I think we're a little late."

We pile inside my car, Sandra and I in front, the two kids in back. We make two stops on our way. We pick up Adrianna first and Nayeli second, two of my former students, and all four kids squeeze into the back of the car. I got in touch with these two girls because I remembered how much they had loved Sandra's poetry.

"I didn't know you can say that," Adrianna told me from her desk the day I read Sandra's poem "You Bring Out The Mexican In Me." She wanted to see it again on her way out. Standing in the classroom doorway, Adrianna stared with giant eyes at the words on the page. "I wish I wrote that. She's bad, Mr. Tucker."

When we arrive at the school, Mrs. Rodriguez, the principal, comes bouncing out to greet us. She is a small woman, ill-appearing, and normally slow-moving, who speaks articulately in what to me sounds like a Canadian accent. Chatting with Sandra about the improvements they've made and the school's five-part philosophy, she leads us through the school. She points out the classroom-converted cafeteria and brags about the new swing set. Sandra says very little. Victor and I lag behind, while Vanessa keeps up with the two women.

Because it's coincidentally a school holiday today, the students who come are here by choice. When we arrive at my classroom, I'm amazed. All of the children are there, and they are dressed beautifully. They're not wearing their usual uniforms; they wear jeans and tucked in shirts, primary colors like red and yellow, stripes and a few flowers, and nothing bold or overdone. My twenty-eight students sit in their assigned seats at tables in the room. They become silent the moment we enter. I never have to ask for their attention. They appear star-struck.

Around the students, adults have filled the classroom perimeter. I recognize a number of parents and teachers from the school, along with several of my Teach For America friends. There are also four giant news cameras.

The twenty-eight children behave perfectly. They sit silently while Sandra talks and clap loudly after they hear her read. Sandra tells them about one of her goals as a writer, to be a translator, a cultural bridge. She teaches a succinct and brilliant lesson about writing with metaphors and helps my students come up with their own.

The children then show her a few projects they've completed for her book: a memorial to "The Four Trees," a mural about Latina strength and love; a three dimensional "House of My Own," titled by the book's chapter; and stories inspired by her style meant as additions to the book. Four children read their stories aloud. Me and Rachel cry soft like a pillow, not loud like thunder begins Eduardo, who's very bright, but often a clown. Meanwhile, Victor and Vanessa sit at the back of the classroom, Victor's chin rests in his hands. He smiles as the students share their projects, but he doesn't speak at all.

Next comes our question-and-answer session. The children completed Sandra's book the week before, and I asked them when we finished reading the book to write down difficult questions for Cisneros, questions about the book as well as questions about her life, things they want to know that we couldn't figure out on our own.

The children raise their hands and wait to be called upon before asking a question. My student Maritza starts. "Do you think it's better to be different or the same as other people?" she asks earnestly.

"You know, when I was young, I didn't want to be different," Sandra begins. "I wanted to be like everybody else. But now that I'm an author, I've found that the things that make me different are the things I write about, things that no one else can write about. And it's a funny thing, when you write about the things that make you different, for some reason, some magic happens, and people read it and say, 'It happened to me that way, too.'"

Now Eduardo raises his hand.

"What was the girl in your book going to do with the two bricks and a stick in the chapter 'Monkey Garden,' since there were five guys she had to fight, and she was only one girl?" This is a tough question. I'm not sure what Sandra will say.

Sandra breathes deeply and shakes her head. "Would it have made a difference if the girl had five bricks?" Sandra stops briefly. "Or fifty? Or a hundred?" She pauses again. "It didn't matter how many bricks she had. She wanted to do something with her anger, but if you conk someone on the side of the head, the change only lasts as long as the bruise."

She goes on to talk about the power of art and writing. While she speaks, I look over at Victor to see if he's listening. I wonder if he understands what she's saying. Maybe he's shy around a very strong woman.

Karina, one of my smallest, hardest-working girls, asks a question.

"Did you always want to write a book to be famous? Did you ever think you couldn't do it?"

"What's your name?" Sandra asks.

"Karina," the child answers in a small voice as she slouches in her chair.

"Karina, how old are you?"

"I'm ten."

"Karina, I want you to imagine the quietest person in your classroom," Sandra whispers, staring at her. Karina bites her lip. "I want you to imagine the shyest person, so shy that when you talk to her she can't even look you in the eye, so shy that she sometimes wishes she would disappear. Imagine the person that's not very pretty, the person who thinks she's not very smart, the person with no friends. Imagine that person, because when I was ten, that person was me."

Sandra looks directly into Karina's eyes.

"When I go to classrooms, I know that sometimes the person who's not the prettiest and not the most popular, sometimes she's tiny and she's watching things happen around her and she says, 'I wish I were popular,' but she's not popular. 'I wish I were pretty,' but she's not pretty. 'I wish the boys liked me,' but the boys don't like her. And she thinks to herself, why is all this sadness happening to me? But there is a reason."

Sandra pauses. No one in the room moves. I see Victor stare at Karina. It looks like he's not breathing. Vanessa leans forward, holding her face, also staring at Karina.

"Karina, do you know what the reason for sadness is?" Sandra asks.

The little girl shakes her head. "It's to help you. It's because if you're popular, you can't see other people in pain. But if you've suffered, you can. Maybe the president of the United States can't see it, maybe the principal of your school can't see it, but you can. That's a very special gift you have. And that gift is your life work."

Karina sits straight up. She looks up at Sandra in awe. I think we all do. I didn't think it would be possible after I met her, but Sandra sounds even more beautiful than she looks. The television stations interview her, the newspaper reporters photograph her, and the children swarm around her to talk to her about their lives.

After a couple of hours in the classroom, we decide to go outside to play. Sandra throws a basketball around with a bunch of the girls while the boys play tag. Victor and Vanessa stay behind with me. Sandra then speaks in the auditorium to all of the classes at the school and reads one of her short stories. She electrifies several hundred children with her spirit. Her voice is enchanting; her face is soft.

Eventually the day comes to an end. Sandra re-joins my class for a private pizza party. Everyone is drinking soda and all of our hands are covered in pizza grease. Before Sandra and I leave, she signs books for all my students. She then gives out free hugs and waves goodbye. As we leave in my car, she and I sit in the front seats, and the four children who came with us earlier are again with us now.

As we pull out of the school parking lot, Sandra looks at the four kids in the back seat. "Let's go for some Mexican food," she says enthusiastically. "Where do you all like to go? Let's think of somewhere special."

"Let's go to Burro's," says Victor. "We never been there."

I think it's a good enough idea. It's a mediocre Mexican restaurant on Central that's overpriced and overrun with people who don't live nearby. Apparently, Bill Clinton ate there last year while he was visiting America's poorest and most forgotten neighborhoods, which unfortunately included ours.

At Burro's, Sandra buys margaritas for herself and me to celebrate. The kids tell her about our adventures in the classroom. They tell her about listening to Tupac's "Changes" and about watching me pour Dr. Pepper over Corn Flakes and being grossed out when I ate them.

Victor, who's been embarrassingly and uncharacteristically reserved all day, decides to talk. "It's great being famous. It looks like you like it."

"Sometimes I do. It's nice that people listen to me, but it can be difficult to know who my friends are."

Victor asks, "How'd you know that you got famous? I mean, when did you find out?"

"I'll tell you the truth, Victor," she says. "I first found out at K-mart."

"K-mart?" he's surprised.

"I've always gone shopping at K-mart, and I never thought I was famous at all. But one day, when I was on my way out, I had to show my credit card to the check-out girl. 'Sandra Cisneros?' The check-out girl asked. 'You wrote a book about a street,' she went on to tell me. 'We read it in school,' she explained. The girl then asked me for my autograph. She was very nice and helped me bag all of my things. After I thanked her, she said to me just as I was leaving, 'I have one other question, Miss Cisneros. Why do you shop at K-mart? Aren't you famous?'" Victor nods as Sandra continues. "I guess famous people aren't supposed to shop at K-mart. I never knew that." Sandra smiles. "And that's how I found out I was famous."

Once our food arrives, the kids dig in. Victor pummels his enchiladas as if he hasn't eaten in days. Within seconds, there is cheese dripping from his chin. Vanessa has menudo, a beef tripe soup. She asks the waitress to bring her a stack of corn tortillas so she can eat her soup the way she does at home. Beside Vanessa sits Adrianna, who is not very talkative and does not bring up the poem that she loved so much. Nayeli also sits at the booth, but on both feet, bending forward across the table to be as close as she can to Sandra.

I listen as the four kids and Sandra talk about the difficulties of being an immigrant, moving to a new school, a new country, a new neighborhood, and using a new language. Even though what Sandra says doesn't match the Villanueva experience, Vanessa and Victor are taken by her point of view.

"Do you like being Mexican?" Vanessa asks. "Doesn't it make it hard for you, or embarrassing sometimes, for how the Mexicans act, running across the border late at night, sneaking over here and everything?"

"To begin with, Vanessa, I'm an American and I'm a Mexican. I'm both. Like you. I'm not just one, and I'm not just the other. And no, I'm proud to be Mexican," Sandra says. "You know, when I read the paper and hear about twenty-two illegales stuffed into the back of a truck, I know why they were in that truck to come to the United States, and I know about the sacrifices they made and about the families who are suffering because they've lost their loved ones."

Vanessa doesn't give up. "But on the news we always sound so dumb. And they say it. They show pictures where we look all pathetic, like we don't care about ourselves."

"We have to try to understand the news man and not be angry about it," Sandra answers. "Maybe the man who reports the story says they shouldn't be crossing the desert, but, Vanessa, you and I understand why they're crossing. So, we have to explain it to people. That's why I write. I want to tell their stories."

Vanessa eats slowly, holding the corn tortillas by the tips of her fingers. She tells Sandra about her mother, how hard her mother is on her, how she doesn't listen, and how her mother still hits her on occasion. The other kids talk about their families too, and Sandra listens. We all eat slowly, but still, the hour passes quickly, and soon it's time to leave. Sandra has a plane to catch. When we leave Burro's, we drive all the kids back to the Villanueva house. When they get out of the car, Sandra does as well. She gives Vanessa a hug goodbye.

"I know it's hard, but find a way to get along with your mom," she tells Vanessa. "She's trying to love you." She then shakes Victor's hand. "It was good to meet you," she says. He smiles. She hugs Adrianna and Nayeli as well and tells them to keep after their dreams.

We then hurry off to the airport; we're running late. With all of my nervous energy, I accidentally run a stop sign just as a car is flying through the intersection. The car is coming straight at Sandra. She shrieks and jerks at the steering wheel, and I hit the brakes. We're okay. Crap. We sit for a moment in silence while I try to shake it off. What a way to end the day. I wonder if Sandra will remember this, if she'll ever let me drive her again. Luckily, no one is hurt.

As we drive on, I don't let the near accident impede the conversation I've been waiting all year for. I ask Sandra about her love life. She's not married, she tells me.

"I think I'll be married by the time I'm fifty," she says. "That will be the right time. I think by then I will have found the right love." The right love. I hear the words over and over. I say nothing.

"Maybe we can stay in touch," I say hesitantly.

"Sure," she replies with a pleasant smile, as she writes her email and home address on the back of her card.

I tell her I'm going to send her my class's book of stories. I also mention, in passing, that maybe we'll meet up again sometime in San Antonio. "Next time the margaritas are on me," I say pointlessly.

"That would be great," she smiles, as she hands me her card and gets out of the car. "Goodbye and good luck." I jump out of the car to hug her goodbye.

"Take care," I say. "This has been an amazing day. Thank you." She nods and then she leaves.

■ ■ ■ ■ ■ ■ ■ ■ ■ ■ ■

Leaving Mexico, Part 5
By Celia

Two years later, my dad called my mom because he wanted to live with her again. But when he found her, he got mad at my mom and was yelling at her, and she got pissed off and started throwing his things out of the house.

My mom's brothers came over, and they pushed my dad into the stove. His back caught on fire, and everybody got scared. That's why he had to stay in the house a few more days.

That's when my dad got my mom pregnant again. Then my dad was gone for eight or nine months. When my mom had Tommy, my dad came back because he wanted to see Tommy. Then he left again.

Then he came back again because now she was pregnant with his baby, Elizabeth. He came back to visit her when Elizabeth was born.

She got pregnant again that year. That's when she had Jackson. Then my dad stayed for like two years before going to Utah, and he got to know all his kids, including Victor, who was in first or second grade by then.

Mexican Dream

It's a Saturday in late January, it's dark out, and I've been grading papers in my classroom since early afternoon. Because of Sandra's visit, I fell behind in correcting the children's school work. I've been in my classroom for hours trying to catch up.

On my way home, I decide to stop at Victor's house. I have a little more than an hour before I'm supposed to be meeting my friends at an Irish bar in Tempe. I park by the curb and step out of the car. Jackson runs out of the house and jumps onto my back.

As we approach the door, I see it's not just Elizabeth and Celia tonight. There are some twenty Mexican men crowded into the front room. I put Jackson down, and he runs in.

"Come on, JT," he says. I hesitate in the doorway. The room is dark and nearly silent, although it's filled with people. I don't know what to tell Jackson. Then I hear Victor's voice behind me.

"Hey, JT, wanna sit down out here?" he asks. He is outside fiddling with an old bike. "Let's just be out here," he says as if he's saving me.

"Sure," I reply. I am happy to stay outside. Victor brings two patio chairs to the driveway. I think to myself how relaxed I feel now that Victor and I have grown comfortable with each other. I can just drop by, as if his family is my own.

"Who are all those guys in your house?" I ask. This does not feel like family.

"They're people from Mexico. My mom brought them over this morning."

The kids have told me on various occasions that their mother is a coyote, someone who smuggles people from Mexico into the U.S. But this is the first time I've actually seen men in her house.

"How long are they going to be here?" I ask.

"They're leaving tomorrow. She gets paid for each person. She's got a lot of cash."

"Isn't she afraid of getting caught?"

"My mom likes to take risks," Victor says quickly.

"But if she gets caught by the police," I say, as Jackson comes back outside and climbs onto my lap, "won't she be—"

"Shh. Don't talk so loud," Victor says, "Those are my uncles. From Guadalajara."

"Oh." I pause. "You've got a lot of family." I'm not sure if Victor wants to keep his mom's new business a secret from Jackson, or if he's not supposed to be talking about it openly. He and his mother know that I know a little.

I ask him if he likes having all these people at his house. He says he doesn't. His mother woke him up at six o'clock this morning and told him to clean his room. And he and Tommy had to push their beds together.

"Where are you going to sleep tonight?" I ask.

"On the floor. I hate having all these people here."

"Why can't somebody else house them, instead of your mom?"

"'Cause that's why she gets paid. Almost a thousand dollars for every person who sleeps here."

"If you give up your bed, you should get a cut of that."

"I know, but she don't give me nothing."

It seems like I'm joking around with Victor the way I joke around with my friends. "Damn, I'd be like, 'Hey, Mom, you can use my bed, but I want a big juicy cut.' Shit, for a thousand dollars, I'd give up my own bed. That'd pay for a month of rent."

"Huh! You want to? That's a lot a money."

"I know it. But nah, it's not a good idea. My roommate would kill me. We could get in big trouble for that."

"So? We've got all these guys here, and nobody knows nothing."

"But what if somebody finds out?"

"La Migra would send them all back. They'd probably send back my mom and me, too."

"I don't know what they'd do to you. I'm not even sure what they'd do to me. They'd have nowhere to send me back to."

"I know." Victor laughs.

Suddenly, Victor and I hear something outside. A lot of people. Sharp noises. It's too dark in front of the house to see a thing. We sit silently on the patio, frozen. We wait for a few seconds until the noise stops.

"I remember one time when all these people came running down the street," Victor tells me. "There was a drive-by a few houses away."

"Let's go inside." Jackson tilts his head.

"We can stay here," Victor says. "I don't want to go inside."

I'm nervous out here, but I want to keep talking. "Doesn't that scare you?" I ask.

"I mean, there was a drive-by near here." I have forgotten about all the Mexican men inside.

"Not really. I'm not scared of that."

"Can we go inside?" Jackson pleads.

"Are you scared, Jackson?" I ask.

"Yes," he replies.

"Jackson, you're fine. As long as I'm holding you, nothing's going to happen." An odd thing for me to say. Too fatherly. Too much of a lie. And so I decide to tell the truth. "I think I'd have trouble sleeping if people got shot near my house. Do you ever have trouble sleeping, Jackson?"

"Yes."

Victor says more. "Sometimes Jackson wakes up in the middle of the night and jumps on the bed crying. He has scary dreams a lot. He's always having dreams about the devil. It's 'cause he cusses too much."

I look at Jackson. He has tears in his eyes. "Jackson, I want you to promise me that you're going to have a good dream, okay? Maybe you could dream about flying." I say this as if Jackson can control his dreams.

This is something I dream on occasion. For me, flying is peaceful and makes me feel whole. Still, I realize that any advice probably wouldn't have helped me much when I was six, if I had lived in a neighborhood that had drive-by shootings.

"JT, you're a good role model." Victor surprises me.

"Really, Victor? Why do you say that?" I am flattered. I hope he'll say more.

"Just 'cause you're always nice to us and bringing us places. You're Jackson's hero. Huh, Jackson? Who's your hero, Jackson?"

"Mr. Tucker."

"That's really nice of you. You guys are my heroes as well."

"Jackson, what do you want to be when you grow up?" Victor is still making his point.

"A teacher."

"That really means a lot to me," I say. "I hope someday, when you're a teacher, you'll find a couple of nice kids and bring them to lots of different places. Will you do that for me?"

"Yes."

I rub Jackson's head and hold him by his belly.

Victor now looks at me seriously. "One time while I was asleep, I felt like there was somebody lying down next to me."

"Was there?" I ask.

"No, nobody. Have you felt that before?"

"I don't know. What do you mean?" I try hard to remember if I've ever had that feeling. It sounds familiar.

"You feel like somebody lies down by you, and you feel it, right? And you wake up and look, and nobody's there."

"Are you afraid of the person?"

"No, but when you look up and don't see nobody, you're like, 'Damn, dude, I gotta get up and turn on the light.' Sometimes I go to my mom's room."

"I get into my mom's bed," Jackson says.

"Tommy used to wake up crying, and she would get up and kick our ass, dude. He'd be all kicking and stuff. And now Jackson wakes up crying, jumping up and down, like Tommy did."

"What about you, Victor? Did you wake up like that when you were Jackson's age?"

"Yeah, all the time, dude," Victor answers fast. Then he tells about something else, "Hey, JT, sometimes I get this weird feeling like a lizard is crawling under my skin."

"What do you mean?"

"Sometimes, like in the middle of the day, I'll just be sitting there, and then all of a sudden I feel some kind of a lizard under my skin. It starts around my neck and then goes down to my stomach and then back up to my shoulders and then around over here and then over there. And then that's it."

"I had a dream once about a huge war in Houston with everybody carrying sacks and walking along Braeswood, one of the main streets there," I remember it vividly. "I had to hide under a water pipe at a friend's house, and I couldn't move, because if I moved then a soldier would see me and shoot me. I woke up in the middle of the night, and the dream was over, but I was so scared that my body was frozen still."

"I remember the day I saw a man get shot. This guy came to the alley. When they shot him, his money fell out of his pocket. He dropped all his money. I ran and grabbed it. Before the cops got there, I grabbed all his money, dude. That night, when I got in bed, I started to see all the presidents' faces everywhere. I was frozen too." I already knew about Victor's seeing a man get shot. What I didn't know is anything about this dream or the frozen feeling afterward.

"How did you know what the presidents looked like?" I ask, wondering how exactly Victor was able to imagine their faces.

"They looked like the people on the dollar bills, but it was just the faces, and they were white."

"Maybe you felt bad about having the money."

"Yeah, because then, after that night, I imagined the guy was dead, and the money was flying around my head with all the presidents' faces on it. I couldn't sleep. I stayed up every single night. I used to be scared every night."

A car with dim headlights has stopped in front of the house. Victor stands up. I pick up Jackson and follow Victor behind the house. Victor backs up, pushing us farther into the shadows. I'm afraid. What if we have to hide in the laundry room closet outside? I think of my student Jairo, who told me last year that one time his mother had to grab her three babies and run into the bathroom in the middle of the house during a drive-by shooting. Apparently, there were bullet holes in every wall of the house except the four walls of that bathroom.

A minute later, the car in front of Victor's house drives away.

"It's a good thing you're here, Victor, because without you I wouldn't even know what was dangerous or what to do."

"I know what's dangerous, huh?" Victor smiles.

"You really do. How can you tell?"

"I don't know. I just know."

Jackson speaks up. "JT, I want to go in."

"Maybe we should go ahead inside," I say.

"But there are all those guys in there. They'll probably feel uncomfortable if a gringo walks in." Victor is being honest.

"I know. But they'll be fine. Trust me—if I were going to tell someone about them, I would have done it already. I've known about this for a long while."

So we go inside. The Mexican men are sprawled on the floor like a wall-to-wall carpet. Most of them lie on the ground, the rest on the couches. Only Victor's mom is sitting in a chair. She sits beside the kitchen table. Meanwhile, Victor's oldest sister, Celia, is cleaning the stove.

"How are you, Celia?" I ask in a low voice.

"Tired. I been cooking for the Mexicans all day," she whispers.

I wish I didn't, but I feel myself keeping a little distance from these men. Victor and Jackson seem to do the same. The men are silent and hard to see because they are dark and the room has no lights on.

The television is on Univisión. A fat man is hosting several bikini-clad young women. The show is Sabado Gigante, a loud and gaudy spectacle, but the men on the floor aren't watching it. Many of them face their heads toward the ground although their eyes remain open. I notice how sun-burned they look, and I'm surprised that there are so many of them. I wonder how long these men will be in Victor's house, what kinds of jobs they've come for, and what kinds of jobs they'll get. I wonder what made them decide to leave their homes and whether they'll ever see their families again. I wonder what kinds of dreams they have.

■■■■■■■■■■■■■

As Waves Make Towards the Pebbled Shore

We are in Victor's home. He is studying his hands.

"How long do you want to live, JT?" he asks.

"You mean until I die? Maybe ninety."

"I want to live for five hundred years. I bet dying hurts."

"Why do you think it hurts?"

"It hurts a little when you get a little scratch, right? So dying probably hurts a whole lot." Victor has told me this before.

"It might. I don't know."

"Dude, I don't want to die. I'm afraid of dying."

"I guess I'm afraid of dying too," I say. "There's too much I want to do."

"Everybody dies somehow, except old people. They die in their sleep."

Unfortunately, that's not true in a hospital. 'Old' isn't acceptable as a cause of death. I look down at the cement driveway. I tell Victor about my aunt's sister, Cheryl. I tell him that she died last week in a car accident. She may have been drinking, I add, and her neck snapped.

"She died 'cause she had too much beer?" Victor asks.

"It was because she decided to drive when she was drunk," I say. "It used to be a problem for her, but the last time I saw her, she had quit drinking completely."

"Maybe she crashed her car."

"She did, and that's what made her spinal cord snap. Plus I think her heart stopped. She died right away."

"Your spinal cord is kind of like a vein," Victor says.

"Well, sort of, but it's not filled with blood. It's how your brain tells your body what to do. I'm really sad she died." I think about Cheryl and her silly frisbee play with her Golden Retriever.

I feel weird telling Victor about Cheryl. The last time I saw her was the day before I found out that Harvard Medical School had accepted me. I was in California, so my girlfriend checked my mail for me. Cheryl took me to the Pacific Ocean and told me about Alcoholics Anonymous. She then took me back to her house and showed me her favorite Shakespearean sonnet about time and change.

I look at my watch and realize that I won't be home in time to go to a bar. I'm not really in the mood, anyway.

"Tell some good stories," I hear.

Cheryl's death is not a "good story." I wish I could tell Victor more about Cheryl's sonnet than her spinal cord. I wish I could remember which sonnet it was; I think it was number sixty. I wish I could remember the beautiful way she talked about how she had grown and changed as a member of Alcoholics Anonymous and how she had learned that we can't find true acceptance in bottles any more than we can in admission letters. I remember feeling very nervous that day waiting to hear from Harvard, and she knew it. She would have liked Victor, I think. With all their enthusiasm for the craziness of life, they would have gotten along well.

■ ■ ■ ■ ■ ■ ■ ■ ■ ■ ■ ■ ■

White

Victor, Vanessa, Tommy, Elizabeth, Jackson, and I make our usual trip to the Burger King on Baseline just down the street from their house. We spent the day bowling, so we decide to end it with our traditional dinner. As we enter, Victor seems uncomfortable.

"I'm the only one who isn't white," he says. "You guys are all white." He retreats to a booth at the back and sits alone. The rest of us get in line. I wonder what he means when he calls his siblings "white."

When it's our turn to order, Jackson climbs onto the counter, Elizabeth stands beside me debating her options, and Tommy runs back and forth between us and Victor trying to relay messages.

"What you getting, JT?" Jackson asks. "I'm getting a burger."

"I prefer the chicken sandwich," I say.

"That's what I'm getting, JT, a chicken sandwich," Jackson says. "I always get the chicken."

Vanessa and I sit with Tommy at one table while Victor, Jackson, and Elizabeth sit at the other.

"You're different, JT. You know that?" Vanessa says, as she unwraps her own chicken sandwich.

"What do you mean? Because I'm a teacher?" I ask, taking my first bite. Some lettuce falls onto the wrapper.

"Maybe because you're white. You think about good and bad. Like today, 'Let's go out bowling.' Mexican people don't do that."

"Mexican people don't do what?"

"They wouldn't sit down and say 'Let's go do something fun. Let's go bowling.' What they would say is 'Let's go play soccer. Let's go to the park.' That's it. The park to the house, the house to the park. You'll never find a Mexican guy say that."

'Let's go get food.' It's a different attitude."

"Really?" I ask. I wonder if the people she's thinking of are too busy.

"Also, no Mexican people would go out to the mountains and just walk around, like we did one time. You would find a Mexican guy go and eat at the mountains. Go take chips and eat, have a picnic at the mountains and let the kids play. But you won't find a Mexican walking all around. They will, but not that much."

Vanessa never had heard of hiking. The day I suggested it, she was confused.

"And a Mexican will have Mexican boots, a shirt tucked in, and a sombrero," she adds.

"If I ever see you in a sombrero, I'll laugh pretty hard," I smile. These kids dress urban, not cowboy.

"When I was little, I wanted one," she says.

"I used to wear lots of hats when I was little too," I say. "You know, Vanessa, if we're really so different, then why do we get along?"

"'Cause we understand each other," she says without pausing. Vanessa and I both have taken off about half the lettuce strips from our sandwiches. "The difference you have is I don't see the teachers be friends with the Mexicans."

I don't know what to say. "You know, even though I'm a teacher, and even though I'm white, I'm also Jewish. Jews and Mexicans have a lot in common." I turn to Tommy. "The KKK hates us both."

Tommy has never heard of the KKK. "What do the KKK do?"

he asks.

"They'd like to kill all the Mexicans and Jews and blacks and Asians," I tell him. "They'd kill everyone in this whole restaurant if they could."

"But I'm white like you," Tommy responds.

"You're not white, Tommy," I say.

"I'm not Mexican. I'm Chicano."

"Well, that doesn't help. They think that people like you are the reason America has gone downhill." I stare at Tommy. "They'd want to kill you for sure. They'd want to kill me, too, since I'm Jewish."

"How would they know you're Jewish?" Tommy asks. "You look like you're white."

"True, they wouldn't know right away with me like they would with Victor since his skin is more brown," I say. "But they'd find out. Maybe they'd see me going to synagogue." I can't think of a better answer.

"What's a sinny god?" Tommy asks.

"A synagogue is where Jewish people get together to pray. It's kind of like church."

"Can I go to a sinny god?" he asks earnestly. I imagine bringing Tommy to Beth Israel, my family's synagogue back home in Houston, and how kind people would be to him, how comfortable they'd make him feel. I'd love to introduce him to everyone. I'd feel proud of Tommy and proud of Judaism at the same time.

"Sure, you could go. Anyone is welcome."

"Even though I'm not Jewish?"

"Sure. You could go anytime you'd like. It's fun to sit with everybody. People would be happy to have you visit."

Tommy takes his last bite of cheeseburger and then looks back at me.

"Everybody's singing and jumping a lot," he says.

"Well, there is a lot of singing. Not that much jumping, though."

■ ■ ■ ■ ■ ■ ■ ■ ■ ■ ■ ■ ■

Muscle Shirts

I've been taking drawing classes at the Phoenix Center Monday and Wednesday nights as well as Saturday mornings since last year. Dr. Marans thought it'd be good for me. On my way to class one night, I stop by Victor's house. It's been a while since I've seen him. When I arrive, he is folding laundry. He shows me his new pants and muscle shirts.

"I don't understand the difference between when you wear muscle shirts and undershirts," I say.

"When the undershirt has sleeves, it's for dress-up," he explains. "Muscle-shirts are athletic."

"It seems like it's mostly the big guys on TV who wear those."

"Like me," he answers.

"You wish! Why do you wear one kind of shirt instead of the other, anyway?"

"You can move better in muscle shirts. And they feel better. Don't you wear them?"

"Not really. Maybe I'll get one." What Victor calls 'muscle-shirts,' my friends in college used to refer to as 'wife-beaters.'

"I'm going to take this to my room, but I'll put my clothes away later." Victor carries the basket of mostly white, now folded laundry to his room. I am amazed by his capacity to keep his clothes clean and unwrinkled.

As he returns to the living room, someone knocks at the door. He steps outside for a few minutes. When he comes back in, I ask him who it was.

"Just my friends."

"Oh. Was it Miguel?" I always thought his friend Miguel was a good guy.

"No, it wasn't Miguel or his brother. I don't really hang with them anymore.

That was my new friends. They're gangsters in W21—West 21st Street Gang. That's Doble."

"That'd be kind of weird if they came in while I was here."

"Yeah, it wouldn't be good."

"What do you think they'd think of me?"

"They wouldn't like you. They don't like white people. They'd probably be talking stuff about you."

"That's really sad."

"Don't worry. I got your back," Victor says. "They're cool, though. I like talking to them. I don't like hanging around with little kids anymore." I remember that when I was his age, I hated when adults referred to me as a "kid." It seemed condescending. But for me growing up was far different from what it is for Victor.

"What do you guys do?" I am worried about Victor's new friends in W21.

"We just kick it. They're cool, dude. We party and stuff. That's why I stopped going to soccer practice. I suck at soccer, dude. I can't play no more."

I am surprised to hear Victor say this. I have never heard him say he sucks at anything.

"I'm a scrub. I forgot how to play. I just got too lazy," he explains. "I can't make myself stop being lazy. I haven't gone to practice for two weeks. I don't even have muscles that much anymore. I just watch TV. I can't even run around the field twice. I used to run it eight or nine times, but now after I run two times around, I'm already breathing hard and have to stop."

"Are you smoking?"

"Not really. We just party." I wonder what that means.

"I wish you wouldn't party so much. Can't you wait a few more years? You're too young."

"I'm a teenager. This is the best time. I'm old enough."

"It'll be a lot more fun when you're older and not always thinking about what everyone else is thinking."

"I don't know. I've got a bad attitude. I'm a badass now. No one can control me no more."

"What about your mom?" I ask. "Do you get to see her much?"

"No. She's never home," Victor responds. "She's always in Mexico or California or driving somewhere."

"But you need your mom." I say. "When I was your age, I talked to my mom all the time. It's nice to be able to do that." I still talk to my mom once or twice a week on the phone.

"I don't get along with my mom. I don't like talking to her. We just argue about stuff. She can't control me."

"Why not?"

"Just that whenever somebody talks stuff to me, I get in a fight. I guess I just fight too much," he says. "Like when they call me a wetback bitch or a daddy's girl."

He hears 'wetback' and 'dad' insults more loudly than before. "Is that why you fight too much now?"

"It's all these people that always stay here. I need some space. I hate when my mom brings all these Mexicans here. She'll wake me up real early in the morning, and I have to give them my room. I hate that. I told her that if she brings more of them here, I'm gonna spend the night at my friend's house. I'm not going to stay here no more with all these Mexicans." Victor talks as if he's not Mexican.

■ ■ ■ ■ ■ ■ ■ ■ ■ ■ ■ ■ ■

Quartet

Today is Victor's day to stay home, so I take out Tommy, Elizabeth, and Jackson. For several weeks now I have been bringing Victor and his siblings on separate outings. Victor says he doesn't like going out with "the kids," although he doesn't mind bringing Tommy, so Tommy usually gets to go both weekend days, with "the kids" one day and with Victor the other.

We start the day by going to my school so the kids can help me finish cleaning out my classroom. It's early June, so the school year has just ended. We plan to go for burgers and ice cream after we finish cleaning. We work for about an hour, and then we decide to take a break and make a video on a camera I've borrowed.

Tommy has a plan for a movie, so he starts the videotape. "This is The Kid's Club," he says proudly. "You're going to see some fine little kids, Elizabeth and Jackson, the movie stars from last night. You shoulda seen 'em. They were breakdancing."

Elizabeth understands the cue. She runs over to Tommy and jumps up and down in front of the camera. "Jackson, Jackson, we have to dance."

Tommy moves out of the way. Elizabeth and Jackson scoot around for a minute. Tommy walks back in front of the camera and continues, "That's all folks. That was a sneak preview of the dancing. Now for a sneak preview of kickboxing. Ready or not!" Tommy moves out of the way again.

First Jackson shows off a few moves. "Hwah, hwah, hwah," he shouts out.

Elizabeth goes next. She steps in front of the camera and talks in a slow voice, as if her audience does not understand English. "First I'm going to do a little kick. And then I'm going to do a little jump." She continues to explain the moves she's going to do. She seems very excited.

Meanwhile, Jackson is jumping into and out of the scene behind her. He opens his mouth wide and contorts his face for the camera each time his body lands after a jump. When he jumps in front of her, she finally says something. "Jackson!" she shouts. I watch.

Tommy decides to take back his movie. He steps in front of the video camera and says, "Move, Elizabeth." Then he changes his voice.

"Now we're going to do some interviews," he explains. He doesn't try to stop the video camera; he looks back at Elizabeth. "You're after Jackson," he tries to whisper, but the whisper comes out as a frustrated whine.

He pulls two chairs around to face each other. One is brown and the other is red.

"I'm going to interview everybody for The Kid's Club," he announces. "The guest sits in the red chair. Jackson, you first." Sitting in the brown chair and facing the red chair, Tommy holds the video camera and aims at his brother, zooming into his face and giggling.

Jackson has a big grin, showing clearly his missing front tooth, while he sits waiting in the red interview chair. "Okay, Jackson," Tommy says, "tell me about your brother Victor."

"He kicks me in the face, so I beat him up. Then he hits me in my stomach, so I hit him in the face. So I get my—José's—gun and I'm gonna shoot him. I found the gun under my bed."

I look at Jackson. "Have you held a real gun before?" I ask, even though my voice is not supposed to be in the movie.

"Yes."

I say nothing.

"Liz! Liz!" Tommy shouts out while I'm still thinking about Jackson's response. Elizabeth runs to the red chair.

"Okay, Elizabeth, tell about Jackson," Tommy says, peeking around the camera, which he still holds steadily facing Elizabeth.

"Oh, he is too bad," she smiles and puts her hands over her mouth. "He says bad words. Sometimes he hits me in my head, and I tell my mama he hit me in my head. She hits him in his booty and then sends him to his room. Sometimes he jumps into the window."

"Okay, tell about your mother," Tommy says next.

"My mother is really nice. Sometimes she takes us to the pizza. Sometimes she takes me to Mexico with her."

"Now tell me about JT," he says.

"Oh, JT is really nice. Sometimes he takes us to the pizza. He takes us everywhere. I wish he could be our dad. That's what I wish," she says. I smile as I listen. I feel embarrassed and happy at the same time.

Tommy seems to have run out of questions, so he suggests more breakdancing. He puts the camera onto a table so it faces him, then he and Elizabeth dance together. They need no music because he raps out his own beat. He grabs Elizabeth by the arms and twirls her around. They twirl and twirl and then fall back and land on the ground. When he gets back up, he keeps the beat with his mouth while moving his legs in small sharp steps, though not in sync with his beat. Sometimes, as he moves, he looks over his shoulder and down. Sometimes he moves his hands in and out, facing flat with his knuckles toward his body. Sometimes he turns.

Elizabeth dances too with large sweeping movements both behind Tommy and in front as she moves from side to side. She lets her arms rise and fall with each step, her fingers point away from her body, and she sings as she goes. She and Tommy don't seem to notice each other at all. Meanwhile, Jackson is playing silently with one of my puzzles in the back corner of the room. After about three minutes of dancing, Tommy and Elizabeth are sweating; they collapse onto the chairs.

After a few moments, I pull up a chair and bring the video camera with me.

"Okay, Tommy, it's your turn. Tell me about Victor," I say.

"He's always hanging around his friend Albert. He's always swimming in the Salido wave pool with the slide and the waves. And he doesn't take me. Sometimes he takes me to eat. Sometimes he fights. That's all I know." Tommy has a big grin, even though he's still panting.

"Tell me about JT," I say.

"His first name is Jermy. His second name is Tucker. His third name is... Tucker. I mean, I don't know." Tommy giggles. "He's really nice. He takes us everywhere. Movies, skating, Fiddlesticks. He gave me a water gun."

Tommy takes the video camera from me. "Now I'll interview you, JT," he says. Elizabeth gets up so that I can sit in the red interview chair. "Where were you born?" he asks.

"In Cleveland, Ohio."

"What year were you born?" he asks.

"1975."

"That's a long time ago," he replies. "How old are you?"

"I'm twenty-four."

Elizabeth comes over and puts another chair next to mine. "And I'm his sister Elizabeth."

"Where are you going to be next year?" Tommy asks, not acknowledging her.

"I'm going to be in Boston to learn how to be a doctor," I say.

"You are? When will you be done?" Tommy's tone of voice is different, less staged sounding.

"In about eight years."

"I'll be sixteen," he replies in a low tone.

Then he has a new idea. He places the video camera onto the table and stands in front of it.

"Newsbreak. Hundreds of people are dying in Flagstaff. Floods everywhere. It is a bad time. And there was people saying some stuff. Here are some people from our family who were in the flood."

Sitting beside me, Elizabeth says in an exaggerated shaky voice, "I am feeling very bad. Aliens are after us. Aaahh!" Tommy shakes his head. He realizes that she doesn't understand the word 'flood.'

He runs back in front of the camera and says, "I'll tell you more about the people from the flood. The people who are a family are here." Tommy sees Jackson playing with a puzzle. "Jackson, come on, hurry up. We need you." He then runs to get another chair. "Put your chairs like this," he tells us. We line up our chairs as he suggests, and Jackson comes to join us. Tommy points the camera at our line of chairs, and then he squeezes into our group.

Following Tommy's lead, we put our arms around each other's shoulders while we sway and recite words flatly, almost without emotion. "We are family. We are family. We are family. We are family. We are family. We are family. We are family. We are family."

Our voice is singular and haunting. We sound nothing like a panicking family. We are a four-headed alien with a polytonal voice.

■ ■ ■ ■ ■ ■ ■ ■ ■ ■ ■ ■ ■

Badasses

"I hate it here. I can't get along with my mom," Victor tells me as I enter his house one afternoon.

"You and your mom still fight a lot," I say.

"She always be yelling at me. I yell back, dude. I don't care. I'm really bad."

"I used to talk back to my mom when I was your age. I think it's normal."

"You haven't heard what I say to her after she yell at me. I cuss her out bad."

"I guess that's different." I didn't realize that he was swearing at her.

"It's not fair," I often whined to my mom. But I never swore at her.

"I wish I could leave here," Victor says. "I'm gonna move out if she yells at me again. I hate it when she's like that."

"I know you feel that way, but you can't leave your family." My parents wouldn't have let me move out.

"I don't like my family. They're all too much of badasses."

"Badasses?"

"They just be cussing and fighting too much."

"That's no reason to leave them."

"I don't care. I hate it here."

"Victor, they need you. Your brothers and sisters need you."

"No they don't. I'm getting bad. I've changed a lot, JT."

"'Cause of your new friends?"

"Yeah, they're gangsters."

"Are you in a gang now?"

"Nah, I just hang with them."

"How old are these guys?"

"My friends? Like fifteen to eighteen. Eight of us always kick it together."

I think about last year. "Maybe you really have changed. Remember how last year you and Miguel used to ask me about sex all the time and embarrass me."

"We were curious about sex."

I don't answer.

"Sometimes I'm a little concerned about all your new friends' being a bad influence on you."

"They're not. I do what I want," Victor says defensively. Does he think this will become an attack on his social life?

"Maybe you're a bad influence on them," I say.

"I don't tell them what to do."

"Then why do they all act crazy?"

"I don't make 'em act crazy. They just follow me. I'm crazy, dude. I do all kinds of stuff. They like to hang out with me."

"Oh, I guess that's good."

"I don't tell them how to act. They're just bad."

"What have y'all been doing that's so bad?"

"I don't know. Just some different stuff."

"I know you don't want to tell me. But if you tell me, I swear I won't say anything or lecture you. I won't tell you it's bad. I'll just listen and nod. That's it. I'm just curious."

"We been jacking cars," he says. He pauses and I feel relieved. I would have done more than nod if I thought people's lives were at stake. Strange that car-jacking seems okay.

"You're doing that a lot?"

"Yeah, a whole bunch. I learned how to jack cars. We been chased by the cops a few times. Dude, I been through a lot. My friends are badasses."

"Sounds like it."

"I like kicking it with them. But I'm gonna stop. I don't want to be like this. I don't want to go to jail."

"I thought you wanted to be this way." I say. "I wish you wouldn't talk about leaving your house, though."

"I don't want to stay here."

"Your brothers need you."

"I know, but I don't want my brothers to see me like that."

I think of what Victor told me about his father's reason for moving away: "I don't want my kids to see me like that."

I feel as if Victor like his father is also saying, "I don't want me to see me like that."

■ ■ ■ ■ ■ ■ ■ ■ ■ ■ ■ ■

Blind

Victor and I have been planning the road trip that we first talked about last year. We decide it will be Tommy, Joe, my non-singing roommate, Victor, and me. We're leaving tomorrow, and our plan is to camp out at The Grand Canyon, Bryce Canyon, and Zion Canyon, go to Las Vegas, and last camp out on several beaches in southern California. I made our itinerary and reserved campsites for the first few nights. We'll be gone for fourteen days.

Victor, Tommy, and I go to the Arizona Mills Mall the night before our trip to buy sleeping bags and tents. Mrs. Villanueva gave me four crisp one-hundred dollar bills to buy supplies. I feel nervous about where the money came from, nervous about camping, and nervous about taking care of two boys for two weeks. But I feel that this could be a great adventure, so I don't want to let my fears get in the way.

By the time we arrive at the mall, it's just before ten o'clock. The stores will be open for only a few more minutes, and we need to go to two different stores before we leave the next day. So we split up. Victor picks a tent at Oshman's while Tommy and I buy camping clothing at Academy. I give Victor two of the hundred dollar bills and tell him to hurry and not to forget the change. We'll need it for food once we leave the next day. He agrees. Our plan is to meet on the sidewalk outside; we figure the stores will be closed, so we won't be able to meet inside. When Tommy and I finish at Academy, we look around but can't find Victor. We go outside. It's a few minutes after ten.

We wait for about five minutes, but Victor doesn't show up. I start to get nervous. What if he took the money and ran? What if he's done something bad? Was I stupid to trust him enough to send him on his own? Tommy and I search around the main entrance to the mall. I tell Tommy to go back and wait at the front entrance of Academy while I run down the sidewalk to Oshman's to see if Victor's still inside. When I get there, I knock on the glass window. A store clerk sees me and calmly lets me in. Exasperated, I explain to her that I'm looking for a teenage kid wearing a white shirt and baggy jeans. She says that she remembers him and that he purchased an item and left the store several minutes ago, probably right before ten. I thank her and run back over to Academy, figuring somehow we crossed paths, and by now he's with Tommy.

When I get back to the front entrance of Academy, Tommy's not there. Oh God, I think. Where'd he go? Something's happened to him too. He's only eight years old—how could I have left him alone? How could I have lost two kids in one night? How will we survive a canyon?

Frantically, I look inside the store, tapping and knocking and pounding onto the window. Someone inside approaches the window to signal to me that they're closed. I wave my arms around and try to explain what's happened.

"It's an emergency! I've lost two children!" I shout. As I'm trying to communicate with the clerk, my body presses against the glass window. Then I hear a voice behind me.

"Jermy, we're at the car. We're cool." It's Victor. He's calm, subdued even.

I'm not. My adrenaline's running high. "What's happening? Where's Tommy? What are you doing?"

"Everything's cool, Jermy. I was waiting by the car. Tommy's there now."

I look over but cannot see Tommy or my car. My heart is still pounding. I follow Victor into the parking lot. Eventually I see the car, but still no Tommy.

"What's going on?" I say angrily.

"Tommy's waiting on the other side," Victor says with a sad lilt in his voice.

Is Victor playing games with me? I don't notice his somber tone. I run to the car, but I don't see anybody. I am panicking and angry and feel duped and ready to yell out his name. Then I look again. Tommy's sitting on the concrete beside the passenger door on the other side.

"Victor saw me when I went back to Academy. Sorry Jermy," Tommy says.

On the ride home, I try to express my concerns about camping to the kids. When I use words like "safety" and "trust," Victor tells me not to worry. He's really looking forward to going on this road trip, he says. Things haven't been good at home lately. He tells me he was thinking about his problems at home while he was waiting for us at the car.

"This afternoon my mom was talking to me while I was watching TV," he explains. "I wasn't really listening. Then Elizabeth lied and said I called her a bitch and was hitting her, like I was that other time. My mom got so mad. She started beating my ass. Tommy saw the whole thing."

"She got real mad," Tommy says.

"Did she leave marks?" I ask, remembering the school incident.

"Yeah, dude. She hit me with her belt. I want to run away, dude. I wish we could leave tonight."

"You know that what she's doing is called child abuse."

"That's illegal, huh?" Victor asks.

"Yeah, you can't do that to your kids. You can ground them or, if you have to, spank them, but leaving belt marks on your kids' backs and shoulders, that's not okay."

"I know, but what can I do? If we call the police, where would we go? We don't have other relatives here."

"I don't know. I guess calling the police would be even worse. Who knows where they'd send you. One time, I saw her hit Jackson with a belt."

"What'd you do?" He's forgotten. He sat limply beside me during the whole episode with Jackson. Neither of us did anything but watch.

"I just sat there. I smiled at your mom. What could I do? I really shouldn't get involved." I won't be able to help the children if I side against their mother. "I felt real bad, though."

"Probably she could see it in your eyes," Victor says.

"I don't know. I didn't say a thing. There was nothing I could do."

"That's how I feel sometimes, too," he replies.

Not Afraid

After Victor and I drop off Tommy at the house, we decide to eat before we go to sleep. We get Carne Asada burritos from the twenty-four hour drive-through at Ramiro's, a place Victor discovered with his new friends. I think how rushed it feels that tomorrow we're finally going on our road trip.

"Victor, know what's weird, the next time I see you after I leave Phoenix, you're going to be almost fifteen. I hope you'll still talk to me."

"I don't know," he answers honestly.

"I bet you'll be in a gang by the time you turn fifteen," I say.

"Why do you say that?" he asks.

"'Cause you already know so many people who are older."

"What if I never turn fifteen?"

I stop and hold in my upper lip. "Victor, don't say that." His words run through my mind.

"What would you do?" he asks.

"I'd be devastated. I'd cry a lot. Your family would cry a whole lot too."

"I'm not afraid to die," he says.

Victor and I are both liars. I half-lie when I say I think he'll join a gang for sure. Because a part of me still thinks I can save Victor. And he half-lies when he says he isn't afraid. Because a part of him is scared to death.

"Come on, V, you know you're not going to join a gang and get killed. I'm not worried."

"Nah, I was just kidding. I'm not going to die," he says.

Again we're both liars. This time I half-lie when I say I'm not worried. And he half-lies when he says he won't die. The truth is that a part of me is scared to death. And a part of Victor knows he has no control.

■ ■ ■ ■ ■ ■ ■ ■ ■ ■ ■ ■

PART III
what if i never

Dear Dr. Marans,

Our trip starts tomorrow and I'm real nervous. I've never gone camping, never built a tent, never been to a canyon, and for two weeks I'm responsible for an eight year old and a thirteen year old who's not exactly shy. Thank God my roommate, Joe, is coming at first. He'll teach me the ropes of camping and help me endure the canyons.

Last night Victor was looking pretty down in the dumps. I mean, who can blame him? After watching his mother strike her child with her belt, I can more easily imagine what it's been like for him all these years. I am left thinking about Victor's delinquent behavior and poor sense of self.

Lurking in my mind is the question of where his responsibility begins and the fault of his circumstance ends. One could say that he has acted the way he has because his father was killed and because his mother beats and neglects him. And one could say that his mother beats and neglects him because there are too many children in his family and not enough space. And one could also say that there are too many children and not enough space because his father was an alcoholic who beat and raped Victor's mother, time after time, pregnancy after pregnancy.

One might even go so far as to hypothesize that his father himself was an abused and neglected child, taught by his patriarchal surroundings that manliness is defined by displays of power over women and brutality against men. So am I blaming Victor's circumstances for everything? Am I blaming it all on the machismo of his father's father? Where does that leave Victor in terms of his responsibility? Nowhere, it seems. I don't know what's right, but that's not. He makes choices. He's a person and he makes choices.

Our trip ends in two weeks. We'll be heading to three canyons, two cities, and the Pacific Ocean. Joe will be leaving us right after the first week, but by then I'll be able to handle camping, and I'll be ready to have the responsibility of taking care of two boys.

After all, even though one of the boys is a difficult teen, where we'll be, he'll be humbled, small like the rest of us. Sleeping in a tent, using a public bathroom, living by the light of the sun or the campfire, eating sandwiches for every lunch, he'll have to bear witness to his own humanity, his humanness. We all will.

Talk to you on the other side,
Jeremy

Joe and José

Joe, who has become a good friend, is coming with us for the first week of our camping trip. He plans to join us for about half of our hikes and part from us for the others, as he wants some time to himself while he's there with us. He also has to leave after half of our trip, but none of this two-week trip would be possible without him.

Joe has been working at a school that's in a neighborhood with an even higher crime rate than mine. Even though his two-year Teach For America contract is up, he has decided to keep teaching in underserved areas as his career.

When I first met Joe, I never thought we'd become friends at all. His relaxed appearance and his confidence led me to assume he was superficial. I was completely wrong. He is the person I can count on most in Phoenix. He's a tough, strong guy, a Georgetown University Varsity pole-vaulter, and a tri-athlete, plus with a chiseled face and bronzed skin, people who see him think he should become a model, but that's not his kind of thing.

While I've lived with Joe, I've attempted (unsuccessfully) to emulate his healthy lifestyle: regular exercise, lots of fruit, breakfast daily, and rarely a crisis. His wit is sharp and his demeanor calm; he reads a lot and watches TV a little. In terms of life-choices, he's among the most giving people I know. I'm thankful to have him begin this trip with us because he'll be able to help me with the boys and help me keep my emotions in check.

As we head off on our road trip this morning, Mrs. Villanueva is at the house to see her boys off. It is the first time she's ever gone outside to watch her children get into my car. As we pull out of the driveway, she waves goodbye.

"She's shitting," Joe says.

So am I, since this is my first time to go camping.

"Tommy, wave goodbye to your mom," I say. All of us wave and smile as we drive away.

We start off driving on Interstate 17, in heavy traffic, still in Phoenix, feeling as though the road trip hasn't yet begun. You don't really leave Phoenix until you cross the 101. Until then, the lanes are narrow and the cars tail out of habit, even at seventy-five miles per hour. At every exit you wonder if you should get off. But you don't, that is, you wouldn't, unless you were heading to the Grand Canyon to sleep outside when you suddenly realize it gets cold at night, and you have no warm clothes with you. That's how it was for us when Tommy said he forgot his sweatshirt. We decide to exit the freeway at the Metrocenter Mall, even though we don't know exactly which exit to take. We plan to buy some warmer clothes at K-Momo's. Tommy finds a bright red sweatshirt and Victor chooses a blue one with yellow zippers. Joe and I decide to get sweatshirts too.

Finally on our way out of Phoenix, I try to get an interesting conversation going.

"Tommy, what's the longest you've ever been away from home?"

"Three months."

"No, like two days." Victor corrects his brother.

"Really?" I say. "Are you nervous about being away for so long?"

"No, it's more better," he answers. He doesn't seem nervous at all.

"Are a lot of the kids who just finished seventh grade with you getting into gangs these days, Victor?"

"A lot of them are. Roberto was jumped into Doble. They wanted to jump me in a whole lot of times, too, but I said I didn't want to."

"I'm glad. I'm sure it'd be easy for you to get in if you wanted."

"Not really. They beat you up and get you all bloody and shit. Sometimes they break your nose or your chest bone. But you can't cry. If you cry, they just tell you, 'Sorry, we just beat you up for fun.' They want guys who are macho. I remember when José came back all bloody and bruised. He didn't cry. He never does." José is Victor's older brother, who's now eighteen and in Doble.

"Wow."

"Roberto's gang calls him 'Flaco.' It means skinny guy. José's nickname means 'Cactus.' It's 'cause he's slow and stupid."

"Your brother's a touch nuts," I say. "But he's also really funny. Remember that time we went to see the Chucky movie?"

"When we were in the car, I felt guilty, dude. He was boring."

I remember the conversation we had as I was driving Victor and José back to their house. José had me drive in circles around South Phoenix before we went back to his house, just in case we were being followed. He told me lots of details about the color-coding for prisoner uniforms.

After he got out of the car, Victor apologized to me: "He talks too much. Sorry, JT," Victor said after our car-ride. I am surprised Victor still remembers this.

"I didn't think José was boring," I respond. "He told me all about being in jail. The inmate gangs, the open toilets, how the colors for each guy's uniform were based on his behavior. Blue, red, green, and with a point system…it was crazy."

"I don't know. He just talks about himself too much."

"That's true. But he also told me a bunch of crazy stories, like the one about trying to rob different places and setting off alarms and breaking TVs he stole. I thought it was funny, even though I didn't know what he was talking about half the time. That's why I kept looking at you."

"I didn't know either. Nobody can ever understand him. He talks too fast," Victor says.

"He slurs all his words together," I say.

"Maybe he takes too many drugs," Joe interjects.

"Drugs? No, he's not messed up from drugs," Victor says. "He's always been like that."

"I'll bet he has a speech impediment," Joe replies, and I wonder if he's right. Maybe that's why José dropped out of school after eighth grade and why he's so hard to understand. A speech impediment. Hmm.

"José's just crazy, dude," Victor says. "He used to be really bad. He's calmed down a lot. When he was younger, he used to jack cars all the time. And when he was fourteen, he stole his girlfriend."

"'Stole his girlfriend?' What do you mean?" I ask.

"He took her from her house. She stayed with us for like two weeks."

"How old was she?"

"Thirteen."

"Whoa." I hear Joe laugh in disbelief.

"Then he broke up with her and had another. And then about five more. He's already got three babies. And he's just barely eighteen."

"Jesus, that's awful." I have trouble imagining an eighteen year old with three children.

"He don't care."

Joe pipes in again. "It sounds like he's got mental problems, too."

"I feel bad for all his kids," I say. "Where do you think José wants to be in ten years?"

"Sitting on his ass, drunk and shit," Victor says somewhat despondently.

"That's always seemed to be his plan," I say. "I remember when he got out of jail at the beginning of the year, he never did shit. He was always watching TV. When I asked him what he planned to do, he always said he didn't know."

"He didn't get a job for like five months," Victor adds.

"I guess he found something he could do to make money," Joe laughs. "But then he got caught."

"He always doing something illegal," Victor tightens his seatbelt. "Even drive-bys."

■ ■ ■ ■ ■ ■ ■ ■ ■ ■ ■ ■ ■

Flagstaff Gangs

In the summertime, the drive into Flagstaff looks like Christmas shopping. Everything seems speckled, dark green and sharp white. Flagstaff is only two hours north of Phoenix, but to Victor, Flagstaff is barely on earth. To begin with, it's cold. Although it's summer, it's cold enough for jackets and sweaters and pants.

"The air feels different here," Victor says as we get out of the car. "It's not like Phoenix."

"It's a lot colder and less dry," Joe says.

"Why is it colder?"

He explains, "Because we're farther north and at a higher elevation, like when you go up a mountain."

"Speaking of which, you guys should wear your hiking boots tonight to break them in." I pop open the trunk. "Your feet will hurt a lot when you climb up and down the mountains tomorrow if your shoes are still stiff." I sound like my mother.

"Those boots are too ugly," Victor says, taking the boots out of his bag, crushing them with both hands, and then dropping them to the ground. "Look, there. I broke them in."

I remember my mother buying me shoes and begging me to wear them around the house. She was convinced I'd get blisters if I wore them for a whole day without "breaking them in." Usually I lied to her and said I had worn them around the house even when I hadn't.

"Victor, you haven't worn them once," I say. "And they're not ugly. They look like normal hiking boots."

"They're too big."

"Maybe your feet are big," I respond.

"I'll just wear my Nikes tomorrow," Victor says.

"You'll destroy them, Victor." Joe chimes in, "Look, Nikes are like a sports car and hiking boots are like a truck. When you're in the mountains, you need to drive a truck."

"But Nikes are the same as hiking boots. And everyone will look at me if I'm wearing those big 'ole shoes."

"People don't look at people's shoes when they're out hiking," Joe says. "No one will notice."

"I'm just gonna wear my Nikes."

"Fine, you're just being a teenager," I respond. I was expecting more from Victor than this.

For dinner, we decide to go to a pizza restaurant in the college-town section of Flagstaff. After ordering a couple of large pizzas with pepperoni and jalapeños, I bounce out of the booth and lean against the pool table beside us.

"Who wants to play me?" I ask. "Who's my first victim?" I smile as I chalk up my cue.

"I'm playing," Victor says.

"Perfect. This game is for all the shit you gave me over the last two years. Tonight I'm gonna take down your sorry ass. This is our grudge match."

"Fine. Grudge match. Students against teachers. I'm playing for all the students; you're playing for all the teachers. Not you, Joe, but students are smarter than teachers. If I win, students are definitely smarter."

"No chance," I smirk.

We spend more energy talking trash than we do playing the game.

"Who's yo daddy?"

"You suck, bitch."

"Yo mama."

"Yo funky ass."

The game is close, but in the end, I win.

"Now, I forget, who do I represent? The students?" I ask in a loud voice, slowly and with a big grin. I face Victor and then I turn away as if there's an audience behind me. "No, no, that's not it, no, hmm, oh, riig-ghht. I represent the teachers. The teachers. Right. Too bad. We whupped you, didn't we? And what were you? The losers? No, no, that's not it. Oh, I remember, you were the students. Right. Too bad. I guess teachers really are smarter than students. Huh. Makes sense. I got you to come all the way here, didn't I?"

As we tear into our pizza, I think more about my last comment. Did I get Victor to come with me, or did he get me to go with him? Sometimes I wonder who's smarter and who's been outsmarted.

By the time we leave the restaurant, it's already late. The clubs and bars are filling up with college students. As we walk past them, Victor ogles.

"Damn. I want to move here," he says. "This is bad. These girls are fine."

"This is a college town, my friend. This is what people do who go to college," I say. "Work during the day and party at night. And you know how many gangs there are here?"

"A lot?"

"Nope. None. You can walk the streets, and no one will mess with you."

"College is fun. You go out every night. And the girls are loose?"

"Yup, a lot of people hook up in their first year of college."

"When I go to college, I'm going to go here," Victor says. "What's this city called again?"

"Flagstaff," I reply. "You know, when you think about it, fraternities in college give you the same stuff that gangs do. For example, what are the good parts about being in a gang?"

"Girls and partying, I guess."

"All right, and what are you talking about when you say partying?"

"You know, you kick it with your homies, get drunk, smoke some blunts, beat it with the ladies, like that."

"Yeah, well, let me tell you about college. When my dad was in college, he was in this thing called a fraternity. It was like a gang, but no killing at all, and great parties. Him and his friends used to party with lots of beer and girls and shit and everybody'd be hooking up."

"Really? Were the girls college girls?"

"Yup. And then after parties and all the hooking up, the guys would bring the girls back to their sororities, and then they'd stay up the rest of the night playing poker. My dad loved it. They still have frats that do all that same stuff."

"They do?" It sounds unbelievable to him. "Really?"

"Oh yeah, and dude, the frat houses are huge."

"Like mansions?"

"Yup, V. I'm telling you, when you go to college, a frat is just like a gang except even better. It's more fun and nobody uses guns. That kind of crap doesn't happen."

"I wanna go to college," Victor says, looking around gleefully.

I don't mention to Victor that I never had any interest in joining a fraternity myself.

After we cross the main street, Victor turns around. "Hey, did you hear that?"

"No, hear what? What are you talking about?" I heard nothing to speak of.

"That guy yelled at me out of his car, 'Die punk.'"

"Really? I seriously doubt it. Why would he have said that? He doesn't even know you."

"He probably thinks I'm in Doble."

"They don't even have that here," I say. "He's probably never heard of Doble. This is a little town. I don't think he was yelling at you. You're just paranoid."

"I'm what?"

"Paranoid. You know, you think everybody is yelling stuff at you. You're too nervous."

"A thousand people get killed here every year, huh?"

"Here? A thousand? I'd be surprised if a thousand got killed in ten years. This is a very safe place. Probably if even one person got killed here, it'd be a big surprise because it doesn't happen very often. Probably not even one per week."

"In the whole city?" Victor needs numbers. "I bet somebody's killed here every day."

I wonder how many people per day are killed in Phoenix and how many in Flagstaff. I know people would argue about boundaries, but, still, I wish I knew the numbers. Or at least a range or an estimate or something.

■ ■ ■ ■ ■ ■ ■ ■ ■ ■ ■ ■

The Grand Canyon

The next morning, we wake up early to leave Flagstaff. No one talks much, so I watch the roads. The drive feels long. When we get to a sign on the highway that says Grand Canyon Junction, it feels like we've arrived. "We made it," and "It's gonna be big, Jermy," replace the "Are we almost there?" and "Victor, quit it, quit it!". When we exit the freeway, however, we find ourselves on a small, slow going road, what we should have expected in our approach to something grand, like a slow line before a big roller coaster at the state fair. The road keeps going and going. And when I look around, there doesn't seem to be anything unusual around us. I wonder if I've been duped, if this whole thing is a hoax.

The road to the Grand Canyon is probably like the road to every canyon, long, uneventful, and mostly disappointing. It's as if I think I'm about to get big news, and then for some reason, I don't until the next day. It's that kind of disappointment. I didn't head to the Grand Canyon late, but it doesn't hurry up for me either.

The first hint that we're closing in on something more interesting than trees is the slow-growing blue sky behind the green and gray trees, but I don't really think about it. That is, not until we pass through the national park gate. That's when I first see it, the trees in the background have thinned a lot. And then the trees in the foreground thin as well until our entire right side has changed from dark thick green to cotton candy blue. No one says a word as the road twists on.

And then suddenly there's a parking lot.

"Jermy, Jermy, Jermy," I hear from the back seat.

"I'm pulling over," I reply. When I turn off the engine, four doors pop open.

Everyone jumps and everyone hurries and everyone runs. Joe and I want to see what's in the clearing too, but we don't run quite as fast as Victor and Tommy do. And when we get to the edge, lined by rocks and wooden fences and metal bars, we look. We look and we look and we look. And about then is when I stop breathing and start blinking fast.

"My God" is all that comes out of my mouth.

"Jermy, I'm going down" is the first thing Victor says, pointing to the sign that says Bright Angel Trail.

"Hold up, we'll all go in a minute," I reply, and then add, "Victor, don't get too close to the edge."

I know full well I'm not in charge. The canyon will take whomever it wants, how it wants, when it wants. I don't want to tell Victor and Tommy's mom back in Phoenix that I tried to stop them but…I'm so sorry… fell over the edge…I don't really know.

I think of the last time these sorts of thoughts came into my mind. I was standing with Victor in Phoenix beside Baseline. Almost exactly one year ago today. Now, after several long minutes of gazing at the earth and thinking about God, we go back to my car to get our backpacks from the trunk, and then we head down the Bright Angel Trail into the Grand Canyon.

"Tommy," I say as we start to walk, "always walk by the back edge beside the mountain. That way even if you slip, you'll be okay."

"Why, Jermy?" Tommy asks.

"It's because there are no rails, so there's no guarantee you won't fall a hundred feet or more. This isn't a ride at an amusement park, and there're no rangers around to save you. So I think it would be better if you don't go near the edge."

"You'd die if you fall over the edge, huh Jermy," Victor says. "I bet that happened a lot before."

As we walk, Tommy starts singing the song 'Just the Two of Us,' which is about a man and his son. Tommy has changed the lyrics, though, and sings the chorus to himself over and over.

Just the four of us,
we can make it if we try,
Just the four of us,
you and I.
Just the three of us,
we threw Victor off the cliff,
Just the three of us,
you and I.

"Tommy, shut up!" Victor yells.

"Just ignore him, Victor." I say.

"Everybody's looking at us," he grumbles.

"So what if they are? Let them. Tommy's funny," I answer unsympathetically.

"This hike's going to be easy," Victor says loudly. Why is he saying this? Does he feel arrogant or does he want Tommy, Joe, and me to think he feels arrogant?

"Keep drinking your water," I tell him.

"What if we don't make it?" Victor asks me in a low tone.

I then take a moment to look at the canyon. "Just look around, Victor," I say quietly. "We've already made it."

Thick rainbows of rock go on forever. To me the canyon is one of God's life drawings. With all the curves and shadows, shapes are wonderfully unpredictable. The distant trees that color the plateaus far below us look like the dots of a Georges Seurat painting. What's most surprising to me about the landscape is that in a deep canyon, famous for its vertical drop, it is the horizontal lines that stand out. They begin as layered yellow on tan and then switch to brown on red. Then they become smooth sloping fans, spotty green and layered, ripples across an ocean. The sloping fans suddenly stop, and that's all I can see. But it is enough.

The trail down starts off smooth. I get to thinking I don't have to watch each step I take. As the trail winds, on one side is the canyon wall, and on the other are trees and branch tops, beside which lies a mighty fall. Even so, it's not until the first time my foot slides across a rock, buried beneath a thin layer of dirt, that I realize I can't afford not to look down.

After ten or fifteen minutes of walking with my head down, fears of falling are replaced by fears of what I might step in. Hoof marks filled with excrement and urine remind me that humans are not the only creatures climbing in and out of this canyon. And as my legs grow weary at the knees, I begin to ask myself how I, too, could be among the horse-carried, as ignoble as that may seem. When a line of horses approaches, I stand with my back pressed hard to the canyon wall to let the giant creatures pass. They are magnificent from afar, flatulent up close.

The trail continues to morph, changing from dirt steps separated by rock to even landings separated by wood, where each level is its own concave dish filled with water, mud, and, as always, urine. Either I can walk on the trail's wooden siding, or I can hop from wooden dam to wooden dam, hoping to avoid the muck between.

I pause on an unusually large siding to drink some water, and then I realize how consumed I have been by my constant decision to look down. Because the first time I look up, I see the most spectacular scene I've ever witnessed. I take out my camera to capture the view for what feels like my own personal eternity. Again, I drink some more water, and continue to watch my steps as I make my way down.

But a few minutes later, when I stop for more water and happen to look up again, the scene is even more spectacular. I photograph this one, too, take another sip of my water, and then continue, again watching the trail. This same scenario repeats itself until eventually, maybe an hour later, perhaps another mile into the canyon, I realize why it is that every time I look up, I see something breathtaking. It's no coincidence. Everything is breathtaking. I need to watch the trail, I realize, but I also want to watch the canyon walls, to see where I've come from and to see where I'm going and to see the breathtaking view.

When we reach the three mile point, we eat lunch. Joe and I made peanut butter and jelly sandwiches this morning before we left Flagstaff, two sandwiches per person. We also packed fruits, nuts, power bars, and about fifteen bottles of water. As we eat our crushed and mostly misshapen sandwiches, we sit on rocks overlooking the inner earth of the canyon. I feel as though I'm flying even as I sit. As we finish eating, we wander off, each of us in our own direction, to prepare ourselves for the hike back to the top. Victor walks forward, climbing over rocks, until he finds one that stands out, one which appears to be the tallest. He climbs to sit on top of it, removes his Nike shoes, shakes them out, and then re-laces them on his feet. He sits alone for a while. Meanwhile, I refill everyone's water bottles, and Tommy sits beneath a tree and plays with a few pebbles.

On our way back up, Victor sprints ahead with Joe while I walk with Tommy. "You need to eat some trail mix and then finish all this water over the next thirty minutes," I tell him.

"I'm not thirsty," he says.

"That's why I'm making you drink it. Your body isn't smart enough. It needs a lot more water than it thinks," I explain. Tommy doesn't fight me.

We each finish three bottles of water as we ascend the canyon wall. I am relatively quiet while Tommy talks to himself almost the whole way. "You can do it, you can do it, all… night… long," he says, over and over, amused by his newly discovered accent and expression.

"Tommy, do you think you'd ever join a gang?" I ask him while we walk.

"No. Too much death."

"What if all your friends get in a gang?"

"I'd just get some new friends," Tommy replies casually. Good, I think. I'm quick to believe him.

We make it to the top of the canyon in two hours, even though the park ranger says it will take us four.

"You're amazing," I tell Tommy.

"I'm amazing," he replies.

"You know how many eight year olds have hiked six miles into and out of the Grand Canyon in the middle of the summer without complaining once?" I ask, smiling.

"Just one, me. I'm the best."

"Yes, you are. Definitely amazing."

■ ■ ■ ■ ■ ■ ■ ■ ■ ■ ■ ■

Talking to an Astronomer

It is evening. We have finished setting up our tent and have already cooked and eaten our nightly black beans and eggs with Tapatio sauce. Tommy, Victor, Joe, and I have taken the car to sit by the rim of the canyon and await the sunset. Victor has the video camera and is filming the sky as well as the people all around us, who are also watching the sky change. The sun seems to be setting in spurts so that westward facing walls light up in various formations as the sun catches them on its way down.

At the precise moment when the sun slips entirely below the horizon, Tommy notices that Victor has the camera facing toward people on the canyon ledge and away from the changing sky. "Look, Victor, it already went down," Tommy calls out desperately.

Victor turns the camera quickly. "Don't worry. This is the best part, right here, just after it's down," he replies as if he's done this many times. The clouds are orange and black and the mountains, a deep gray. We all sit quietly and continue to watch. Once the clouds turn from red to black, Victor asks if he can bring the camera to the parking lot behind us where an amateur astronomers' convention is taking place. I say yes and tell him that we'll meet him there soon. After he walks off, I wonder how the astronomers can see stars early in the evening, since, to me, the sky looks plain.

By the time the rest of us walk down to the parking lot, it's entirely dark out. Thirty or forty giant telescopes surround us in a maze, and hundreds of people are walking around and looking through them. While I'm wandering among the telescopes, I spot Victor. He's chatting with one of the astronomers, asking questions about the rotating binary stars that fill the view. The man lets Victor maneuver the telescope, so he can explore the sky himself. The man then brings him to a computerized screen under a canopy. He shows him what different buttons do and explains how each one helps in seeing the sky. Victor seems to have charmed the astronomer.

After a while, Victor thanks the astronomer. Then he sees me. He scurries over with a huge smile. "This is bad, dude," he says. "Would you come with me and hold the camera while I interview people?" he asks. "I already got pictures of Mars and Venus. But I want to make a tape of me talking to an astronomer." He shows me how to work the focus and the sound.

Victor approaches a middle-aged astronomer who's wearing tan khakis and a yellow Izod shirt. The man is standing beneath a canopy toying with a control board.

"Hi, my name is Victor Villanueva, and I'm going to be an eighth grade student in Phoenix, Arizona, and I was wondering if I could ask you some questions."

The astronomer agrees enthusiastically—he seems to enjoy talking about his work. As the interview begins, I fumble with the spotlight button, leaving the first few seconds of the interview in the dark. Victor asks the man under the canopy questions about himself and his equipment, where he got it, how much it cost him, and how often he uses it. He then asks about the stars the man's able to see, and the telescope he's using, and how the telescope can see so far.

"You're a professional?" Victor asks. The man says he's not. "Oh, it's your hobby," Victor replies. The man shows him several of the planets and stars. After about ten minutes of discussing the positions of the stars relative to the earth and the sun, Victor shakes the man's hand, thanks him, and signals to me to turn off the machine.

For another hour or so Victor carries the video camera with him, putting it up to telescope eyepieces and interviewing several more people. One has a rotating seat attached to his telescope. Another uses a headset. As I watch Victor wander through the crowd, I'm impressed by his charisma and surprised by his interest.

"That was great, Jermy," Victor says to me as we leave the parking lot later in the evening. "I talked to a lot of people. That's why I got to look through their telescopes 'cause I know how to talk to people. Look, I got invisible stars on my video. It was real fun. I was like a news reporter."

Later that night, Victor shows me the video he made. He is most excited about the still shots of the different planets and stars he saw through the telescope lenses. What to me is a bright dot on a video screen he sees as a new universe, a new possibility for life, both extraterrestrial and his own.

■ ■ ■ ■ ■ ■ ■ ■ ■ ■ ■ ■ ■

The Acrobat

Although I enjoyed the boys' and Joe's company at the sunset last night, tonight I am planning to watch it alone. I want to experience a sunset at the Grand Canyon on my own, with no distractions. After dinner, when I tell everyone that I'm heading off, Victor asks to join me, even though he saw the sunset the night before, even though I tell him it won't be any different. I'm not sure why he wants to go. I'm also not sure I want him to go. But I decide to let him. Tommy stays with Joe.

Victor and I take a shuttle bus to the western wall of the canyon, to the Hopi lookout point. I bring my journal, and he brings the video camera.

"It looks like the moon," I say.

"I'll wait for the sun," he says.

"It's going down fast."

"The other was better."

"Look at the red letters."

"You're going to write?"

"And draw them here too."

"That girl there is crying."

"It's maybe her first."

"Maybe she's never seen one."

"Maybe she's never looked."

"Look at her face."

"I wonder why she's sad."

"It's probably for memories."

"I wouldn't cry here."

"I kind of want to tape it."

"It's sort of embarrassing."

"Not to me. Not like that."

"Not to you?"

"Not at all."

Our dialogue ceases.

I write; he films.

The sunset is colder than I expect, and less momentous, too. Although there is a particular moment when the sun passes through the horizon, at least in a misty, cloudy sky, it is not this singular moment that defines the sunset. When the sun first sets, the sky is still blue—even the horizon offers little red or yellow. Ten minutes later, though, the color is striking—the sky's the light red of watermelon, the deep pink of papaya, and the almost orange of grapefruit.

The sun comes out from the clouds and fades into gray blue behind the mountains. The mountains in the foreground turn gray too, but a darker gray, a night time ocean gray, and the closer they are, the darker they appear. As the sun lowers, the sky directly above turns a shade of blue, an unmistakably sundown blue. It's unnoticeable, though. It makes me think it's not really night-time. Even as the mountains darken into dim monochrome, their textured lines remain as number and letter formations. Clouds overtake the canyon walls as orange becomes the last remnant of light. Carlight appears far away, and the sky becomes an outline filled with dark marker. Everything's a shade of black except the river.

The river at the bottom of the canyon glows. The canyon walls blur, and the daylight escapes, but still the river's curves continue to shine. The river is the last reflection of light, the last glimpse of the canyon at sundown. From the Hopi lookout point, the river is an open "c," an acrobat's body in forward motion. And as I wait for the last bus to bring us back to the car, the acrobat swings through the air. In front of me. As if I already know him.

Our bus pulls away from Hopi point. I whisper to Victor, "Did you get a good video of the sunset and all the people watching? Like those girls?"

He doesn't look at me. "I cry like that sometimes," he says. He knows which girls I mean.

"You've hugged your friend crying?"

"I hugged Vanessa crying."

"I did that once, too," I don't want to, but I need to talk about it.

"I did that a bunch." He isn't bragging.

"But never in front of other people," I say. My reasons don't make sense, but Victor doesn't seem to sense my discomfort. That's partially because I keep talking after we get on the bus. "One time I was hugging my old girlfriend and crying because she was leaving for Uruguay the next day. I wasn't going to see her again for more than a year."

"Were you making out?"

"Not really. We hugged and cried until three in the morning. It was the end of our relationship. It was the end of four years." I need to share a couple of hard moments in my life with Victor if I hope he'll share his with me. "We played songs for each other and talked about what they meant and how they traced our time together. Then I had to leave her. I had to teach the next day. That was two summers ago in Houston."

"I didn't know you had a job there."

"It was teacher training. I worked at a summer school."

"Why did you come to Phoenix?" Victor seems skeptical.

"I was placed there. Teach For America put me in Phoenix. That's the teacher group I'm in. Phoenix wasn't my first choice. I'd never been there before."

"Where did you want to go?"

"San Francisco or Oakland. I thought that would be the most fun: lots of young people, coffee houses, night clubs, poetry slams, stuff like that. Plus living near the ocean."

"You didn't really want to go to Phoenix?"

"I was a little disappointed," I admit. "I didn't even know how to spell Phoenix. But it turns out I've liked it a lot."

"That time with the girl was the only time you cried with somebody?" Victor wants to know more.

"There was another time, actually, when I was hugging a friend back in college. We got in a big fight."

"Did you try to knock him out?"

"No, not that kind of fight. Just mostly talking through problems."

"Like an argument."

"Exactly. But a really bad argument. It hurt a lot."

"What were you arguing about?"

"He started to criticize me all the time for everything that was wrong with me, mostly that I was forgetful and irresponsible sometimes. Finally I got mad and told him, 'I don't criticize you all the time. I don't need you doing that to me.' I didn't like being judged for the things I screwed up, as if forgetting printer paper and towels meant something bigger than forgetting printer paper and towels. I had memory problems. I still have memory problems. His mom told me she knew I was like a brother to him. She was right. I would have done anything for him. That's why it all hurt me so bad."

"How long did you argue?"

"The whole argument was off and on for a week, but the last part went for about twelve straight hours, 8 PM to 8 AM. In the end, we worked things out and hugged and cried. We felt tired and happy and sorry all at once." The bus stops. We're back in the parking lot. We exit the bus.

I stop talking and turn around. I rub my eyes and look to see the canyon again. That's when I realize what a small acrobat I was watching, as no trace of river remains. Daylight has been vanquished, and night-time reigns.

We find the car. "How about you?" I ask, returning to our conversation. "When were you crying?"

"When me and Vanessa heard about my dad, we were crying all the time. We would look at his picture sometimes, but that just made it worse. I was crying so much. I was crying like a girl."

"I don't like it when you say 'cry like a girl,'" I say as we pull off. "You've said it before, too. But it's not what you mean. When you cry because you don't get your way, that's weak, very weak, not girly or woman-like. It's not a girl thing; it's a weak thing. Girls don't do that. Weak people do. Weak people feel sorry for themselves after they get caught. Like you'd cry if your teacher caught you stealing. Or your principal caught you with drugs."

"Like if you cry because you have to go to jail?"

"Yeah, exactly, weak," I say. "But when something bad happens that nobody wanted…what you were doing is not weak."

"Me and Vanessa?"

"No, that's not weak at all. He was your father, for God's sake. Crying's not weak. It's love." I pause to think. "You know, you've never cried in front of me." Victor covered his face when he got back to school after his mother had hit him for wearing the wrong pants. I hope he's not still afraid of what I'd think.

"I know," Victor answers as if he's noticed too. "The night before our trip, I was crying a lot. I couldn't stop. I kept thinking about my dad."

"What made you think of your dad that night?"

"I don't know. I just kept arguing with my mom. She was using her belt. Whenever I fight with her, I start thinking about my dad, and how he could help me. I wish I could go with him and get out of my mom's house."

We sit in my car silently for a moment. I realize that Victor has told me something very important about himself, but first he needed to feel an equality with me. His father's death was not only the death of his father, but it was also the death of his fantasy, his way to escape his mother and the abuse. "You know, I never told you, but one of the main reasons I didn't like Ms. Immaho was that she said mean stuff about you and your dad that made me really mad. Do you want to know what it was?"

"Let's just listen to the music now. Tell me at our campsite."

"Okay."

"No, never mind. Just tell me now."

"You sure? I can wait."

"No, that's okay."

"Well, after your father died, I was really upset and worried about you. But you didn't seem sad at all. It was like nothing happened. So I went to talk to Ms. Immaho about it. I wanted to help you, and I thought she could give me some advice. I told her that you didn't seem sad, and I didn't know what to do. She said probably he doesn't really care, since this kind of stuff happens around Hatfield all the time. I guess I couldn't respect her after she said you probably didn't care. I realized she and I would never see eye to eye. Plus I didn't really like her to begin with."

"I had a really bad attitude after my dad died," Victor says, not too interested in his former teacher.

"At first you didn't seem upset," I say.

"I was just being really quiet and thinking about him all the time. But then, after a couple weeks, I started getting angry, dude. I'd get angry at anybody who said anything to me at all."

Victor turns up the volume on my car radio, and we listen to music without speaking much for a while. As I'm driving and listening to Victor's tape, I notice that he starts dabbing his eye with a towel. He says that he cut himself, but I don't see any blood. For the rest of the drive, we stay quiet.

Outside

After the sunset at Hopi Point, Victor and I meet Joe and Tommy at a Navajo woman's talk about Native Americans at the Grand Canyon. I find the talk fairly boring and almost suggest walking out. But I don't, so we stay for the whole thing.

"That was great," Victor says afterward. "Let's go to the Navajo Plateau she was talking about. The road we're taking tomorrow goes there."

For the second night in a row, I'm shocked by Victor's sincere interest in things outside of himself. Telescopes, now Native Americans. Am I being close-minded about a talk because it isn't exciting enough for me?

"Okay. That would be fun." I say.

"The white people gave the Indians money to move," he says.

"I doubt they were that nice. They probably came with guns and—"

"—started warring against the Indians," Victor says.

"Yes," I say. I like how Victor has turned war into a verb.

Later at our campsite, Joe has gone to bed, and Victor, Tommy, and I play a game called "Burro Castigado." It's basically a dare game with cards. I get to dump a bottle of warm cola over Victor's head when I win the first time. He gets to pour a bowl of soggy cornflakes over me when I lose the second time. Somehow Tommy stays dry.

After we quit playing, I walk over to the community bathroom to clean up, and Victor comes with me. It is already eleven at night, and most people at the campsite are asleep. While I'm using the toilet, Victor starts shouting at the top of his lungs.

"Jermy's got diarrhea! Ew, it smells so bad. Jermy, stop farting. Jermy, you're nasty."

"Victor, stop embarrassing me. People are trying to sleep."

Unfortunately, there is nothing I can do. I'm sitting on the john, in the men's bathroom, living out one of my worst fears as a child, that I would have to use a public bathroom and that something like this would happen to me. "I never would have been friends with you when I was a kid, Victor," I say as we walk back to our campsite.

"I would've been a bully and beaten you up," he replies.

"I would've hidden in my teacher's classroom at lunchtime," I retort.

"I would've still found you later." Victor laughs and pats me on the back.

"What if I stayed there? What if I never went outside?" I say triumphantly.

■■■■■■■■■■■■

Bryce Canyon

On our way to Bryce Canyon the next day, we drive by a little Native American stand on the side of the road. Victor wants to stop to look at what they're selling.

"Do you think this is real?" he asks although he has already decided. "Look, this is real deer skin in the arrow. This is real."

Joe and I decide that after all the super-positive reviews we've been told about Bryce Canyon, we shouldn't linger too much on our drive. We want to get there before the sun sets. The approach to Bryce Canyon is unimpressive, though. Even worse than the approach to the Grand Canyon, it looks like nothing's there. "This is it?" the kids ask as we drive.

I don't know what to say—it looks like a bunch of trees and a couple of mountains. I'm not sure why my friends said it's even better than the Grand Canyon. After driving along the strangely monotonous road and paying an entrance fee to the park, we finally arrive at a small parking lot and see lots of people looking into the distance. We can't see much of anything special from where we're sitting. Nothing huge and gaping like the Grand Canyon. It seems like a small emptiness on the other side of the fence.

"Come on, guys, let's go see what all these people look so damn excited about," I say, worried that we spent a full day driving to see trees. Tommy jumps out of the car and runs ahead to a lookout point. Victor walks behind him, and Joe and I dawdle. We're tired of driving, tired of sitting in the car listening to the two kids bicker, and wonder why we rushed to get here.

And then we see it. We get close to the fence and we finally see it. It's like there's magic inside this canyon. Orange and red rock gods watch us watch them.

"That's tight," says Tommy. "The mountains are black and the clouds are red." He is looking at the distant mountains in the horizon.

I look again. He is right. Broad red brush strokes paint the foreground with black shadows shooting up sharply behind them. Before this moment, there was no hint of anything wonderful. Now there is.

Victor comes running over to me. "Can I hike in? Can I hike in?" he asks.

"It's already late," I say.

"Just for ten minutes; it's not that hard," he begs. I tell him to go ahead. Joe and I will sit and watch the sun. About fifteen minutes later, Victor comes running back out. "Jermy, Jermy, can I borrow your camera? There was some real Indian writing back there."

"Yes, but hurry before it gets dark." Victor runs back inside the canyon with Tommy. He's found something else that's real.

That night we stay at a campsite with teepees, since it's too late to set up a tent of our own. "Dude, this tent is big. Indians have real big tents," Victor is impressed. He doesn't mention the amenities of a house. He never does. "I'm glad we're all sleeping in one tent tonight," he says. "It'll be great."

While Joe and I cook, Victor takes over the job of making the campfire. After dinner, we sit on rocks and roast marshmallows before we go to sleep.

■ ■ ■ ■ ■ ■ ■ ■ ■ ■ ■ ■ ■

Following Victor

Today we hike into the Bryce Canyon kingdom of fortresses and sandstone castles. Joe decides to go on his own while I hike with the two boys.

We are walking along the bottom of the canyon when Victor begins to climb up a sand hill on the side of the trail. As his feet push him up, I watch a pile of sandstones fall down.

Victor calls out to me to join him. I am nervous about getting injured, but then I decide to do something that normally I would not: I follow Victor.

My clumsiness gives Victor a good laugh. "Jermy, look on that side. It's a different path," he calls down to me. I'm unable to climb as high as he does, but I can see a new Bryce over these orange walls, which don't allow entrance from the marked trail. Even though I yell "fuck" about fifty times during the experience, I feel exhilarated. A great adrenaline rush. I can almost understand why Victor loves physical challenges like this. He never knows what he'll see. I wonder if he ever feels nervous as he embarks on these sorts of journeys, or if he simply doesn't think about everything that could go wrong.

"Do you ever feel afraid when you do crazy things like this?" I ask after climbing to the top.

"Yeah, sometimes I get all worried, like, what if this, what if that, but really I don't think about it much. I just do it. I got to. I mean, what if I stayed on the trail? What if I didn't do dangers or climb so high? What if I never saw so much or saw so different?"

I hear Victor. I stop moving. Victor's words change my vision. I am seeing something new. Then, suddenly, I slip, and roll back down the hill.

During one of our breaks that afternoon, Tommy and Victor make up a game, throwing little rocks at larger ones.

"We nuked 'em, huh?" Victor says afterward as we return to the trail.

"I guess you did," I agree.

Victor is wearing a brown-brimmed hat that looks like something goofy my dad would wear.

"I wish you, me, and Tommy were immortal warriors and we could fight against evil, but most of the time we would blend in, like Hulk Hogan," Victor says.

"I'd be an old bearded wizard who can make mountains explode." I point my arm and make laser-beam noises, imagining myself as a cross between Mickey's wise wizard boss in Fantasia and the crazy wizard who makes mountains explode in Monty Python and the Holy Grail. Tommy gets very excited and starts pointing his arm and making strange, cartoon-ish noises too.

"I wish we could really do that," Victor says. "If I had magical powers that could blow up mountains, I would get rid of all the guns and bomb the factories that make them. And I would tell everybody that there would be no more wars."

Me too, I think to myself.

"But what if two countries started fighting?" I decide to play devil's advocate.

"I'd tell them to stop, and if one of them didn't, I'd bomb all their armies."

"How about the war between the Mexicans and the blacks in South Phoenix? What would you do about that?"

"I'd just kill all the damn niggers."

"Some God you'd be. Someone like you shouldn't get to play God."

"No, I wouldn't kill 'em. I'd just send them all back to their own countries. The white people would stay in America, the Mexicans would go to Mexico, and the blacks would go to Africa. Everybody in their own place."

"You know, most black people's families have lived in this country longer than my family. And we're white. White Jews. That doesn't seem fair that my family stays and their families have to leave."

"Well, your family could go back to Jewishland."

"We're not from a place called Jewishland. There isn't one. And we're not from Israel either."

"Where is your family from?"

"My family came from Russia and Poland and Germany, mostly. They left because everybody wanted to kill them there."

"Well, they could go back there."

"But most white people's families came from other places. Italy, England, Ireland, all over."

Victor remains calm even though I'm constantly messing with his ideas. "I don't know," he says. "Maybe all the countries could have a mix of everybody. But I'd make Mexico the strongest."

"I guess you like Mexico the best," I say.

We are walking through mazes now. The trail is flat, the rock figures are uncanny, and our eyes are fixed upward. Victor, who is at the front of the line, looks back at me. "What if all these giant rocks were gods and the little rocks were people?"

"That'd be a lot of gods and people."

"What if I was one of the gods? You know what I would do. I would take away people's babies and train them to be my warriors," he says. "I'd teach them how to fight and then they could go and do what I tell them." We stop for a sip of water. The trail has turned sharply and I've lost track of where we are.

"What if one of them rebelled against you?" I ask.

"I'd just kill him."

"But what if a lot of them worked together?"

"I'd just give them numbers. I'd be like number fifty-two, die!" Victor grabs Tommy as he shouts this out. Tommy giggles. Our miniature line turns into a clump. Victor, Tommy, and I are now walking beside each other.

"It'd be more like, number two-three-six-eight, prepare to die." I say this as if I'm the insane bad guy in a James Bond movie, with a Russian Spy accent and a rolled "r." Tommy is pointing at rocks and making cartoon noises. He's still blowing things up.

"Maybe I'd get two people and they would have lots of babies, and then those people would have even more babies," Victor continues. "That's like the first man and woman in real life?"

"You mean Adam and Eve?"

"Yeah, Adam and Eve. They were the first people before all the rest. Do you believe in that?"

"Not really. I believe in evolution."

"Evolution? What's that?" Victor asks as our trail brings us beneath an arch.

I stop in the shade. "Evolution. That's where over many millions of years monkeys who were smarter survived more often so they had more babies and that meant there were more of the smart monkeys. Eventually, a whole race of monkeys with much bigger brains came about, called humans." I know I haven't really explained evolution, but I hope he's learned about it before, and my bit is just a reminder. "Do you believe in evolution?" I ask.

"Yeah, I think so," he says and then starts walking again. "I don't know. Because what about The Bible and all?"

"You could have both. What if evolution was God's big plan? Anyway, Victor, do you believe in God?"

"I don't know. I do believe in angels though. I think all babies are angels."

Victor speaks in a hushed tone, as if he's telling me a secret.

"Why do you think that?" I ask.

"I don't know. The way their eyes stare at you," he faces me and touches my arm. "It's like they know you." He looks out across the red and yellow gods of Bryce. "Like I always used to hold Celia's baby, Clarissa, in my arms. She would stop crying when I held her. She liked me. Sometimes I'd hold her for a long time. She liked to sleep on my arm."

"When do you think a baby stops being an angel?" I ask, slowing my pace to match Victor's.

"When it learns right from wrong," he answers. "Babies don't know right from wrong. That's why they're angels." After that, nobody says a word. We walk among red and yellow gods. Sammy follows me. I follow Victor.

■ ■ ■ ■ ■ ■ ■ ■ ■ ■ ■ ■

Zion Canyon

Today is Day Six of our trip. We left Bryce Canyon this morning after riding a horse along Peek-a-Boo Trail. The horse ride was beautiful but a bit too expensive for me. Right now, I am wishing the kids had at least thanked me, especially after how much they begged to do it. I was feeling happy and generous when I decided to spend the money, but hours later as we are driving, I am feeling unappreciated and sore.

A few minutes after paying the entrance fee to Zion National Park, I overhear Tommy say, "I hate Zion." I haven't heard the rest of the conversation, so "I hate Zion" means nothing to me. I don't know if he's kidding or complaining or babbling, but I feel tired and irritable, and so I tell Tommy that I'm angry at him for saying he hates Zion, since he hasn't even seen it yet, and that I don't want to hear another word out of his mouth until we get to the campsite.

"From here until we find our spot, every word out of your mouth is one minute of time out at the campsite. Understand me? I want silence. I'm in a really bad mood."

A few minutes later, Victor says something to Tommy, and Tommy responds. During their brief exchange, I count Tommy's words. "That's nine words, Tommy. You've now got nine minutes of time-out."

When we get to our site, I say, "Okay, Tommy. Nine minutes. Here's your tree. Make sure you stare at the tree. I'll tell you when your nine minutes are up." I'm in teacher-mode.

Victor gets really angry. He thinks I'm being unfair, since Tommy was only responding to his questions. He starts to mock me.

"I hate Zion, I hate Zion," he says.

I growl at him, "Fine, you stand against a tree too." He refuses. I start shouting. I'm losing it.

"Tucker, take it easy," I hear Joe say. In friend mode, he calls me Tucker.

But I won't take it easy. I'm not letting Victor take advantage of me this time after all I've done, especially after I took him and his brother horseback riding this morning and for burgers and milkshakes this afternoon. When Victor starts going at me with his "whatchu gonna do, bitch?" antics, I get even angrier. I scream my head off, and then my arms take over my voice and my voice takes over my mind, and I'm ready to go, ready to fight, and about then is when I want to destroy, and then I shove him. Hard.

That's when everything freezes. "What have I done" and "This is my end" go through my head. Victor doesn't move. I don't move. He stares at me and looks in my eyes, and then he goes to the trunk of the car, which is still open, and gets out his bag and Tommy's.

"This is what you get for being a dick," he says. "Come on, Tommy, let's go."

My God, I think. This is the first time I've ever laid my hands onto a child. Have I lost control? Have I become like Victor's mother?

I stand in front of Tommy. "I can't let Tommy go," I tell Victor as I begin to regain my composure. "I promised your mom I'd take care of him."

"Tommy, let's go," Victor shouts, trying to get around me.

"Tommy, stay right there against the tree," I keep shifting my position so that I stay between Tommy and Victor.

Victor stands in front of me, but he won't look me in the face. "Tommy!" he shouts, but it does him no good. Tommy shrinks into the tree. Victor turns around and walks off without saying another word. No threats. No swearing. He drops Tommy's stuff beside the car and takes off with only his bag.

I pretend to ignore Victor as he walks off our camp site and down the dirt road. This is what my parents used to do with me when I'd lose my temper as a child: they would ignore me. I remember how much I hated this, so I decide to do it now. It seems like a good strategy.

I don't want to show Tommy any more signs of weakness. I slow down my speech and speak softly, "Tommy, you have nine minutes." I then sit down beside Joe and act like everything's under control.

Except it's not. Not for me and Victor. I've created a crisis.

I look at Joe apologetically. "What should I do?" I ask. "Should I follow him?" I wonder if my parents had discussions like this about me.

"No, just let him go. He'll come back," Joe says. I try to feel calm. I don't want to show any signs of weakness. Nine minutes later, after Tommy's time is up, I can't help myself. I feel nervous about Victor.

"What do you think Victor will do?" I ask Joe.

"He'll call home," Joe says.

I'm not so sure. "What if he tries to hitchhike? He's very resourceful."

"He can't get far. He's got no money, and he's got no food."

Joe is right, but I fear that Victor could steal or make new friends and then try to leave the park.

After a few minutes more, I decide to change my approach; I am going to search for Victor. As I drive down the main street at Zion, I ask everyone who works at the park if he or she has seen a thirteen-year-old Mexican boy walking alone with a purple sports bag. No one has seen anything. I call his home in Phoenix to see if they've heard from him. Victor hasn't called, and now I can see why. His mom tells me to call the cops if he doesn't return.

As I'm going back to our campsite, after finding nothing and feeling bad, I see Victor walking along the road to the camp grounds, but not to-ward our site. Still, I feel relieved. He's okay, probably very angry at me, but here. I've learned my lesson, though. I'm not letting him go again. And no more angry hands next time.

While I watch where he goes, I slowly bring the car back to the campsite. He doesn't see me as he enters the campground bathroom. I watch Tommy follow. So I walk over to the bathroom that he and Tommy have just entered, and I listen from the outside. I can hear Victor plotting with Tommy how they can get home. I stand outside and say nothing. After a few minutes, Tommy peeks his head around the door. He sees me and then quickly pulls his head back inside.

"Victor, Jermy's standing outside. He's listening to us." Tommy's body is positioned beside the door. He leans into it, pokes his head outside, and looks at me.

"Tell Victor I said to come outside," I say.

Tommy retreats inside. "Jermy said you should go out," I can hear him say.

"Tell Jermy I won't," I can hear Victor.

"Jermy," Tommy says desperately as he leans back across the door, "Victor says he won't."

I pause and then say, "Tell him to come back to the campsite so we can work things out over there."

Tommy again pulls inside. "Jermy said you better."

"Tell Jermy forget it," Victor says loudly.

Looking somewhat dismayed, Tommy pokes his head back out. "Jermy, Victor says no."

I'm not sure what else to say. "Okay Tommy, tell Victor I already called your house, and your mom said I should tell him that he has to go back to the campsite and if he doesn't that I should call the cops."

Tommy looks surprised. He then goes back inside the bathroom to repeat my message, but after a second of silence, I only hear a grunt from Victor's voice, even though I can't make out what he's saying.

After about a minute, Tommy comes back out. "Jermy, Victor says he doesn't care."

"Well, then tell him you don't like being in the middle," I say instinctively, "and that he should come out here and talk to me face to face like a man."

After a few more seconds, where I hear Tommy whine Victor's name several times, Tommy sticks his head back out and says, "He won't." Tommy then whispers to me, "Jermy, maybe you should go inside and talk to him."

Tommy is right. I'm embarrassed that as a "sensitive" twenty-four year old, I need an eight year old to tell me the right thing to do. Here I am, so stuck on proving to myself that I'm an adult, and a child will not take advantage of me, that I need another child to suggest to me how to bring this debacle to a close.

I gather my thoughts, take a deep breath, and go into the bathroom.

I'm nervous, and I don't know what to say. Staring into a mirror, I stand silently. I can see Victor's reflection. He is sitting on the bathroom tile floor, his back against the wall beside the sink. He also says nothing. I remember what my mother used to say to me when I would lose my temper as a child: "Jeremy, don't turn a molehill into a mountain. Get over it." Her words always seemed cruel to me, but, unfortunately, they also made sense.

Finally I break the silence. "I hope you come back soon, Victor. It'd be too bad to turn what could be a little problem into a big huge problem. I'm not angry at Tommy anymore. This whole thing really could be over with already. No one's in trouble."

Victor doesn't respond.

As I look at him in the mirror, I think about what I always used to hope my mom would say to me when I ran away from home or hid in my room. So I add, "If it makes you feel good, you might as well know that I searched all over the park for you. I asked lots of people about you, described what you look like, told them you had a purple bag and said anything else I thought would help." After a couple of seconds of silence, someone camping near our site comes into the bathroom.

Leaning against the far wall, Victor still sits on the floor. "This isn't a good place to talk," I say, and then I leave. As I walk back to our site, I glance back at the bathroom door every couple of seconds to make sure Victor doesn't try to sneak away. I'm not taking any more chances.

A few minutes later, I watch him exit the bathroom. He walks back toward our camp site.

He doesn't speak to me. He spends the rest of the afternoon lying in his tent listening to his walkman. That night around nine o'clock when I'm going on a food run, Victor suddenly comes up to me and asks if he can join. Seconds after pulling out, he says, "I'm sorry for running away, Jermy. And I'm sorry for being rude. I just got really mad when you pushed me."

"I know," I say. "I shouldn't have done that. I'm sorry too."

"You lucky I didn't beat you up. I coulda beaten your ass."

"Come on, you wouldn't have done that," I say. He laughs.

At the store, we buy chips, soda, beans, and marshmallows.

■ ■ ■ ■ ■ ■ ■ ■ ■ ■ ■ ■ ■

Frogs, Wolves, and the Wind

It is Day Seven of our trip, our first full day at Zion. In the morning, Joe and I go on a hike and let the kids sleep in. Irresponsibly, we leave the kids by themselves. I am still processing yesterday. I'm also thinking about Victor's mother, how her role in his life is very different from mine, and I think about Victor as a victim of her indefensible behavior. I'm no Mother Teresa, but with kids I'm a fairly relaxed person. If he makes me this angry this fast, his mom must go berserk. But for her, that's no excuse; she's his mother. She should love him unconditionally. She should never ignore or strike him.

While Joe goes on a different hike by himself that afternoon, I take the boys river rafting. Holding our tubes together in a line and flipping each other upside down, the boys and I have a great time playing in the river.

Unfortunately, when we get out of the river, I realize the key to my car has fallen out of my swimsuit somewhere in the river. We have to find someone to give us a ride back to our campsite. Luckily, I had given Joe an extra key to the car. After getting his key and walking a couple of miles back to retrieve the car, I rejoin the group to eat our regular dinner: black beans, eggs, ham, and Tapatio hot sauce.

Victor surprises me again by asking enthusiastically to go onto a late after-dinner hike. I can't say no, so I take the boys to Emerald Pond for a short hike. Because it's getting dark out, many of the little animals come out onto the trail. I'm not sure what gets into Victor, but while we're doing the hike he's requested, he starts chasing little frogs and squashing them. It's disgusting, but he's deaf to my protests. So I decide to run ahead of him to scatter the frogs from the trail. Victor acts as if this were a game.

The slow frogs don't survive. Victor steps onto them with his feet. I feel as though he's murdering them. "Go frogs, save yourselves. Please, go," I shout out. I don't understand his aggression, and I don't like it.

When we return to my car and drive back to our camp site, he goes on and on about all the frogs he killed. Partially because his behavior was reprehensible and partially because he continues to exaggerate, I am getting increasingly angry. Was murdering the frogs supposed to be an easy way for Victor to release his emotions? He doesn't seem to understand that the purposeless killing of innocent animals is ugly and wrong.

Instead, he thinks it's fun and a little funny. He makes up a song about himself "pounding them nigga frogs" to fit the tune of the Montell Jordan song on the radio, "This Is How We Do It." It's ironically a song I know well and really like. But I never listened to the lyrics closely. The song is about young men in a gang in south central L.A. celebrating the drive-by shooting of a rival gang. Victor is celebrating the mass murder of frogs. Montell Jordan also says "the guys are in denial" in his song, but he does so in such low tones and with so little emphasis that this meaningful, uneasy line is barely intelligible to anyone, let alone Victor.

When the song ends, and Victor finally stops singing, I ask Tommy what he thinks about how Victor killed all these frogs.

"It was tight, but gross," says Tommy.

"I'll probably dream about frogs tonight," Victor tells us, talking in a less "gangster" tone. I suppose a part of him did know he was being cruel. I wonder why he wouldn't stop.

"I hate death" is all I can say.

"I learned a lot this past year," Victor says out of nowhere. "That's 'cause I paid more attention in school. Remember a couple years ago how we were playing that algebra game to see who could make the bigger problem?" Victor has switched out of his gangster persona entirely.

When we get to the campsite, Victor's gangster persona returns briefly. He brags to Joe about how many frogs he killed, and how skillful he was at killing them.

"That's because the frogs in a national park don't know they're being attacked," Joe says this in an unimpressed, sarcastic tone. "National parks try to preserve wildlife animals, not kill them." Joe doesn't want to tell me how to do my job, but I think he would have liked me to hold back Victor physically from this killing spree. I probably should have.

Later in the night, all four of us play poker for a while. Once Joe is ready to turn in for the night, I decide to go to sleep as well, since he and I share one tent, and the boys share the other.

As I am about to say goodnight, Victor says, "Come on, Jermy, let's kick it by the fire."

I think for a moment. We've had a couple of rough days lately, so I figure it'd be nice to keep things cool between us. "Yeah, all right, I'll stay up for a little bit longer." I'm really not that tired.

"How much longer you wanna stay up?" Victor asks. His enthusiasm is charming to me.

"I don't know. Let's roast some marshmallows."

"I know how to make a fire good, huh?" Victor has been in charge of building and maintaining our campfires each night. He needs twenty or thirty matches to get it started, but the fires he's been making have been big and last the whole evening.

"I'm in the mood to go see mountains," Victor says in a whisper. He doesn't care which ones or what they're called. "I want to see them at night. I wonder what they look like. Come on, Jermy, let's go. Let's hike into them." Victor seems particularly interested in mountains. Since practically the first day I met him, he's been talking about and writing about mountains.

"You want to hike now?" I hate to say no, but it seems unsafe to me. "It's really late."

"Come on, dude. The mountains are bad at night."

"All right, I'll walk for a little bit to check them out." I'm also curious to see these mountains in darkness. "Not a big hike, though."

"Nah, just a little bit," Victor agrees. Tommy wants to come too.

"I heard wolves howling last night, dude. I was scared," Victor confesses as we begin our walk. I wonder if there's a family myth about wolves. Celia mentioned wolves in Mexico when she told me about her family's immigration day.

"You sure you weren't dreaming or mishearing."

"I swear on my mother's life."

"I don't think wolves would come to a campsite," I try to sound confident.

"I heard them walking, dude. Tommy woke up when he heard them too. I thought it was you or Joe, so I called out 'Jermy!' Then I yelled 'Joe!' Joe yelled back 'What?' We went outside and put all the food away. That's why all the wolves came."

"Huh." I don't remember this at all, and Joe didn't mention it. I wonder if it's true. Tommy says he doesn't remember last night anymore.

After walking in darkness for a few minutes to see mountains that are too dark to see, we decide to go back to our campsite. The three of us sit around the fire and drink hot chocolate.

"Sleep in our tent tonight," Victor suggests. I'm surprised. "There's a lot of wind, dude. It makes me nervous 'cause our tent's not that strong."

I smile. "I'd like to; it's just that you snore really loud, V." Victor laughs. "I do? Okay, if I snore tonight, just sock me. I'll wait for you guys to fall asleep."

"All right. I'll try, but if I can't sleep, I'm gonna move."

"Just sock me, dude. I don't mind." I take Victor at his word. When he starts to snore during the night, I punch him in the arm. Somehow it works.

"Hey, Jermy, did you lock your car?" Victor asks me not long after I'm asleep.

"What Victor?" I say groggily.

"I don't think we locked the car door, Jermy."

"Shit, I forgot." Victor reminded me earlier that we needed to clean up our campsite and put away our lantern. But I completely forgot about locking up the car. Victor is right: it's not safe for me to leave the car unlocked while we're all sleeping. I get up to find my keys and flashlight.

"You want me to go with you?" Victor asks, probably noticing that I'm having trouble finding my shoes and keys and getting myself together.

"Sure. That'd be great."

"It's better with you in the tent. It makes it warmer," Victor tells me while he's helping me at the car. Even though it's the middle of the night and I'm barely conscious, I get the feeling Victor's thanking me.

A few hours later, I hear Victor whispering my name, "Jermy."

"What?" I was sound asleep.

"I don't think we're gonna make it." While I've been sleeping, the wind has been blowing hard against our tent. I suppose it's getting worse.

"Have any of the corners come out of the ground?" I ask.

"No."

"Then I think we'll be all right," I say, more lazy than sure.

Victor's afraid of the wind, I realize as I'm drifting back to sleep. He's human—his personae, his beliefs, and now his fears: he's actually afraid. I quickly fall asleep.

■ ■ ■ ■ ■ ■ ■ ■ ■ ■ ■ ■ ■

Close Together

This is our second morning at Zion National Park. The hiking trail we're on is called "The Narrows." We walk upstream through a river between two giant cliffs. This is the most sublime and incredible hike of my life. As we go, the walls beside the river get closer and closer, and the river depth increases little by little. I walk behind the boys.

Victor holds Tommy's hand to help him navigate the river's rocky bottom. With my camera in one hand, it's hard keeping up. I have difficulty maintaining my balance with only one hand, but I want to hold my camera in the other so that I can take pictures of the boys together as they struggle to walk upstream. Even though I realize that walking through water while I'm holding my camera is risky, I want to be ready to capture a moment which may exist for only a second.

Tommy's a lot shorter than Victor, so more of his body than Victor's is submerged in the river. This means he must push a larger portion of himself against the river's flow. This upstream hike is harder for Tommy than I realized, but Victor holds onto him and helps him with every step. Victor finds rocks on the river floor that are steady for Tommy to stand on, and he looks for areas in the river that are less deep, where it will be easier for Tommy to walk through the river as it keeps getting deeper and deeper as its walls get closer and closer together.

The boys navigate the river. They push hard against the river current, holding hands, searching for stable ground on an unstable floor. Even with my longer legs and heavier body, I have a hard time keeping my balance too. But I know I am witnessing something remarkable, even divine, in these brothers, so I struggle to keep up, to stay close enough behind that I can see.

Eventually we reach an island of sand where the boys decide to rest. Victor has carried Tommy's water and his food for the better part of our hike. At times during our hike, Tommy had to tread water; he couldn't carry anything more than himself. Victor tells Tommy to drink and gives him a few handfuls of raisins and peanuts to eat.

While he is sitting beside his brother and taking care of him, a bright yellow butterfly lands on his shoulder.

"Look, Tommy, on my shoulder. Don't move, Tommy," he whispers. Victor reaches out his finger and convinces the butterfly to climb on. He then turns to me slowly with his yellow butterfly and a huge grin. He points his eyes to my camera and I know what he wants. I hurry to take the picture. It's the first butterfly he's ever held, he tells me. "It trusted me because I was sitting so still," he says. In guessing why the butterfly trusted Victor, I don't think it was his motionlessness, it was something else, but I do think that it was unbelievable, incredible.

After the butterfly leaves us, Victor rips off his shirt and dives into the water.

"Tommy, Jermy, come on, let's swim!" he shouts. Tommy and I follow behind.

While we're in the water, another yellow butterfly gently lands on Victor's head.

■ ■ ■ ■ ■ ■ ■ ■ ■ ■ ■ ■ ■

Good Times in Vegas

We leave Zion that same afternoon, day eight, and go to Las Vegas. We take Joe to the airport and say goodbye—he has to return to Phoenix to pack his things and move a week earlier than I do. Even though I'm sad to have Joe leave, I am no longer nervous to be traveling alone with the two boys. We get the cheapest room we can find at a hotel called Circus Circus. That night we decide to go to Old Vegas. I borrow Victor's pants because both of mine are dirty. Even though I'm half a foot taller and ten years older, his pants fit me well. "You want to be like me?" Victor asks, smiling. I think of what he said the night before while we were staying at Zion, "You wish you were my brother, don't you, JT?"

Once we're dressed and ready to leave, Victor looks me over and flattens out the pants I'm wearing. "You actually look pretty good," he says. I laugh. I realize I have to wear his clothes to get his approval on my appearance. I doubt it will ever happen again.

After a nice evening in Old Vegas, the parking lot security guard stops us, "Hey there, what business have you got here?"

After I talk to him in my Ivy League voice and tell him what we've been doing, he lets us go.

"You know why he stopped us, don't you?" I say afterward. I want to discuss what's just happened. I want Victor to understand.

"Why?"

"Because of how we look, dressed all baggy."

"He thought we were gangsters," Victor says.

"And you know why he believed us after I talked to him?"

"'Cause you're older," Tommy interjects.

"Partially. But also because of how I speak, because of my voice, and because I'm white."

"I hate that cop," Victor says.

They say you can't judge a man until you've walked a mile in his shoes, but after tonight, I'm not so sure I'd say that even walking a mile in his pants is enough.

The next afternoon, Victor does everyone's laundry while I drive around doing errands. I find him working when I get back. "I know how to wash clothes good." It has taken him three hours.

Meanwhile, Tommy has become friends with another kid. The boy gives him money to play video games. After Victor and I interrupt and then enlist Tommy to help us bring the dried clothes to our room, we go back outside to swim in the pool. We play Marco Polo.

When we enter the main game room at Circus Circus, I decide to give ten dollars to each boy to spend as he chooses. Tommy doesn't win anything, but Victor gives him all his stuffed animal winnings. I remember how well Victor did at the state fair game, too.

At the end of the evening, we watch the circus performance. Unprompted by me, Victor stands with a small blond girl and what appear to be her two parents. I sit with Tommy on one side of the stage; Victor is on the other. He remains in my eyesight at all times. He claps with the little girl and laughs at the clowns.

He later tells me he was talking to the young child and her parents. I think about Victor talking to this family and imagine he's great at it. I then think about Victor talking to his own family. It wouldn't go too well, I imagine.

After the circus routine, we decide to walk down the street to see some of the other hotels. We watch an outdoor show at the Treasure Island Hotel, where Tommy sits on a fence-like structure in front of a group of young adults and blocks their view, but still he strikes up a conversation with them and manages to charm them with his good humor, outgoing nature, and enthusiasm. I feel bad about where he's sitting, but they keep saying they don't mind.

On the way back to our hotel, Victor asks me what kind of doctor I want to be. I tell him I want to be the kind that helps kids who've been abused or neglected and have to deal with psychological trauma and physical trauma. I try to explain to Victor what trauma means.

"Oh, I had that before," he responds. "I couldn't sleep for a year. I was seeing presidents in the air." I recall some of the nightmares Victor has told me about, including this one.

I have one bed, and the boys share the other. They are very enthusiastic about our room. Sharing the bed in our hotel room, they appear to be as happy as they've been anywhere else on our trip. Their bed is a grand canyon.

Pacific

Today starts the tenth day of our trip. We sleep late, and then we leave for California. We drive through grasslands and mountains, past trees and over rivers. It is slow going, and it takes until the afternoon to make it to the ocean, and it's cold.

When Victor first sees the beach from the car, he says quietly, "This is bad." Soon I pull off the road, and we all get out of the car. As he approaches the ocean, he pauses and kneels. He looks like he has that feeling you get when you know you're looking at something bigger than you, and you wonder what brought it to you and you to it and you try to make sense of it all.

After staring at the ocean for a minute or two, Victor throws off his shoes and runs out to the shore to join his brother, who's teasing the indifferent tide and letting waves chase him in.

The water here is too cold to get all the way in, but it feels good on my feet. So I stand in the shallow water. I also walk a little, but mostly I just stand. I sink my feet into the soft sand and try to think deeply about this ocean and pacific oceans. But instead I find myself meditating on beans.

So we replenish our food supply. Tommy sits in the cart as we start off on the aisle with beans. Our aisle first brings us to fifty kinds of coffee beans. We have no interest in coffee beans, except that we are impressed that there are so many kinds.

Then, unfortunately, our "beans" pathway goes to candy. Tommy climbs out of the cart to look around. Several hundred, get-it-yourself bins of candy with clear plastic shovels are an irresistible Pandora's box for me. The store signs encourage candy sampling. There are twenty dark chocolate candies and another twenty milk chocolate ones. In addition, there are fifty jelly bellies and another fifty jelly worms, sour and tropical. And I'm just starting a candy inventory. There are a gazillion other candies, too. The candy gets me; I have no control, no control of myself. In the candy section, I buy nothing but taste almost everything.

I feel a little sick when we get to the beans section, where we pick four cans of regular refried beans and four cans of spicy refried beans. Beans are good with breakfast and with dinner.

"We have to find cheese." I tell Victor the time and how long we have until sundown.

He knows he should hurry because he likes sunlight better than head-light for setting up a tent. I do too, but I'm not nearly as good with a tent as he is, so I don't usually do much. He asks the first person we see. "Where the cheese at, sir?" This person is not an employee, unbeknownst to Victor, but Victor is very polite. His words slur, though; so he's hard for the customer to understand, even hard for me.

"Do you happen to know where the cheese is?" I ask. The man is friendly and points at something large. "There are about fifty kinds of cheese over there. I do recommend the sample. It is quite good."

I thank him and we walk off. "I meant to ask 'where is the cheese?' not 'where cheese at?'" Victor tells us. "I sounded like a Mexican who doesn't know English."

"Where cheese at?" Tommy giggles. "Where cheese?"

As we walk toward the cheese, Victor whispers to me, "That was embarrassing, dude."

"Don't worry about it, bro," I pat him on the back. "Don't worry about it."

We find the cheese kiosk. "Don't they have normal cheese?" Victor mutters.

"This is normal cheese," I laugh. "It just hasn't been cut yet." He won't find pre-sliced, processed, wrapped cheese here. No Kraft.

After the boys bicker for a moment, they finally choose a nice-looking and well-priced cheese. Although Tommy and I don't dawdle, the cart moves slowly to the other items on our list. My ache is now gone, but Victor runs around the store quickly, finding items, scouting out prices and quantities. He, for example, finds the lowest priced eggs, but returns to ask me if we should get twelve or twenty-four. Then he runs back to get them. He probably cuts our total shopping time in half.

On our way out, I realize we have no marshmallows, a favorite for all of us at campfires. I punch playfully at Tommy, so he'll turn around. "We need marshmallows for me to burn."

"You're gonna burn Martians, JT?" Tommy asks.

Victor drags the cart and goes straight to the nearest red uniform. "I'm looking for marshmallows, sir," he says properly and politely. He grins at me.

I smile and nod. The man points.

Victor speaks out, "Thank you, sir." After we walk off, Victor looks up to me, "He really likes me, huh Jermy?"

After we leave, we find the campsite where we planned to stay. Victor sets up the tent while Tommy and I unpack the trunk. Because the site is deserted and the ground won't hold the tent stakes well, with little debate, we decide to find another site. When we leave, Victor growls, "I'm sleeping in the car, dude. No clean-up, no packing. Easy."

But once we get to the closest site in a town called San Clemente, Victor loves it.

"College girls everywhere," he says. A couple of hours after arriving at San Clemente, he asks if we can stay a second night. I think what he likes best are the large crowds of people who talk to him. The college students at the bonfire beside us have really taken to Victor, and he likes talking to them. He's quite extroverted. After a day at an ocean, a grocery store, and two campsites, he seems truly at peace.

■ ■ ■ ■ ■ ■ ■ ■ ■ ■ ■ ■ ■

Body and Soul

On the tenth and eleventh night, we camped at San Clemente. On Day Ten, we first saw the Pacific Ocean. On Day Eleven, we went to the small town Oceanside and played at the beach. Day Twelve, today, we drove to San Diego to a city beach to spend a few hours there. Tomorrow, Day Thirteen, we will go to the San Diego Zoo, and the day after that, Day Fourteen, we'll be driving back to Phoenix.

At this city beach on Day Twelve, I'm nourishing me, not the kids. I want to re-energize. The beach is well-peopled and the boys are body-boarding. Victor will take good care of Tommy.

I therefore trust that the boys have enough support and entertainment on their own, so I take personal advantage of the time, don't watch the boys body board, and walk along the ocean with my journal, car keys, and cash.

Without thinking about the boys' safety, I make a selfish—and probably poor—decision.

That evening in San Diego, we find a campsite where we can spend our last two nights. Victor goes to use the phone while Tommy and I get ready for bed. We have already fallen asleep by the time Victor comes back to the tent. He climbs in and asks solemnly, "Jermy, can we go back to Phoenix tomorrow?"

"What?" I mumble. Tommy's sleeping deeply.

"Can we go back tomorrow?"

"When? Tomorrow?" I wake up. "Tomorrow? One day early?" I 'm confused.

"How come?"

"Vanessa's pregnant."

"Oh my God. Jesus."

"She hasn't been home for a few days, and I'm the only one who knows where her friends live."

"How did you find out about her?"

"I called some of her home girls, and they told me she was pregnant. That's why she isn't going home." Vanessa's sixteen.

"Your mom must be really worried."

"She's furious. She's talked to Vanessa about waiting until she's married a lot of times."

Tommy's still asleep.

"Why did Vanessa have to go and do this? She's so smart and could have such a good future."

"All her friends are even more messed up than she is. One of her home-girls just moved to New York with her boyfriend."

"How old is that friend?"

"Same age as Vanessa, fifteen. Another one of her friends left home and is living on the streets and with different friends just to stay away from her parents."

"Wow." I pause. "I remember once Vanessa went for Chinese food with us, and she was talking about hating how she had to stay home to clean and take care of her mom's kids. Even though a big part of her has no desire to change, another big part of her wants to change. She said she wished she could be independent and go to college and lead her own life. I think she really could have done that."

"I'm gonna tell my mom that she said all that." Victor stops talking. "Jermy, what's an abortion?"

"Abortion. Hmm." I'm in my sleeping bag in the dark, and it's a complicated issue. So I can only define it a little. "It's hard to understand, but an abortion means taking certain cells out of a woman's body."

"You mean taking out the baby's cells and blood?" he asks.

"Sort of."

"She wouldn't do an abortion. She thinks it's not right."

"I know. I'm worried about her, and upset, too."

"Me too. She's too young to have a baby," Victor replies.

"I wonder if Vanessa is ready to raise a child," I say.

"I'll talk to her about it. That's why I need to go home. Probably no one else can find her. I need to talk to her boyfriend as well."

"I don't get it. She said he was so great. If he was really all that, I don't think this would've happened."

"I know him. He's cool. He knew better. Vanessa did this to herself." Victor speaks very quietly. He seems upset.

"I just don't get it," I say. But I sort of do. Vanessa had told me that having another man's baby would be the only way she could get out of her house. She would have to go to his.

"Let's talk about it later," Victor says. "I want to go to sleep." I don't think he's ever ended a conversation this way before.

It's dark in our tent, and no one is talking, but it feels like no one is sleeping either. I'm crying a little. I want to find Vanessa and shake her and hug her and tell her that her baby's soul isn't ready to come out, that it needs a few more years to become whole. Or maybe it's Vanessa's soul that needs a few more years.

■ ■ ■ ■ ■ ■ ■ ■ ■ ■ ■ ■ ■

Cats

Today is the last day of our trip. It's Day Thirteen. Tomorrow we drive back to Phoenix. After Victor makes several calls, and we have a fairly long discussion, he decides not to cancel today. I agree. Finding Vanessa one day earlier won't make a difference for her and may not give her the space she now needs. Even though I don't like secrets of this sort, Victor isn't ready to tell Tommy, and I prefer for him to decide a family matter like this. So we don't talk about Vanessa all day. We shift our moods for the day. We focus on ourselves, our trip, and the zoo. We enjoy the incredible animals and laugh at Victor's antics.

Victor dons his G attire today, trying to look like a gangster, even though he's at a zoo and the only people he's with are Tommy and me. His pants are black denim and baggy, his shoes are orange and Nike, and his shirt is white and sleeveless, a muscle shirt. His pants sag well below his waist line, exposing his boxers, drawing attention to him in a way that might be appropriate at a dance club, but to me that's odd at a zoo. I think he looks ridiculous, and I don't hesitate to tell him so.

It's also ninety degrees and sunny outside, so to me it's also odd to wear black denim pants. But Victor insists that Mexicans don't wear shorts. As we walk around, I specifically point out Mexican-looking men, nearly all of whom are wearing shorts. According to Victor, they're Chicano like Tommy, not Mexican like him.

We look at the different animals in the zoo. We imitate the giraffe face, we giggle at the monkey antics, and we sneak around the reptiles. Eventually we get to the African Safari section of the zoo where we get to see our favorite animals.

We are particularly drawn to the lion. It's a massive creature, an amazing creation, a breathing grand canyon. No wonder Tommy loves the lion. He wishes he could be as massive and strong as a lion. He hopes it will crawl out of its shaded slumber so he can get a better view of royalty. I inform Tommy that kings like this would rather be talked about than seen. But then we get lucky; the lion crawls out.

The king decides to approach. "Hey, what's up fool? Wassup G?" Victor says, addressing the king. The lion peers at us between the metal bars. Tommy giggles as Victor keeps going. "What you looking at me for?

I'll barbecue you. I'll eat you alive. I'll feed you to the tigers." Victor likes making Tommy laugh.

That is clearly his goal this afternoon.

Tommy starts to list the names of different kinds of cats, "Tiger, jaguar, bobcat, lion—"

"Put 'em all in there." Victor suggests.

"They'd fight," says Tommy.

"I wonder what would happen," I say.

"That'd mess them up," Victor replies.

"Jermy, Jermy–" Tommy is getting excited.

Victor looks at Tommy. "Who do you think would win?" he asks.

"The lion!" Tommy shouts. Tommy's no revolutionary. His loyalty to the lion is strong.

I ponder out loud, "Lion, tiger, bobcat, jaguar, cheetah, leopard... hmm."

"What about pan...thers?" Victor stumbles on the word while he talks.

I don't hear panthers. "Pandas?" I ask. I'm puzzled.

Tommy giggles, "pandas."

I look at both kids. "If that panda's smart, he'll climb in a tree and get his butt outa there," I say. Both kids laugh.

"I think the jaguar," Victor says thoughtfully.

"Yeah, maybe the jaguar would win," I agree, thinking about the car more than the animal.

"Jaguar, 'cause they just walk around," Victor says.

"The lion, I think. Who would kill the lion?" Tommy asks almost rhetorically. He stays faithful.

"I'll jump the lion," Victor replies. "The lion is barbecue." He stares at the lion in the cage in front of us and growls.

"Maybe they'd all start out trying to kill the lion first and then go for each other," I suggest.

"No!" shouts Tommy. He's attached to this lion.

"They couldn't try the lion on their own," Victor says. "So they could get together, gang up on the lion."

"But they're not that smart," Tommy responds.

I have no answer. Tommy's right; the lion is safe. No one could hurt him.

■ ■ ■ ■ ■ ■ ■ ■ ■ ■ ■ ■

A Final Sunset

I am alone. I am traveling back to Houston. I'll be moving to Boston in another month. My car is tightly packed with my belongings. On my way home, I decide to stop for one last sunset at White Sands National Monument in New Mexico.

I spend so long searching for the right place to sit at White Sands that by the time I find it, the sun is already gone. "Already" is the wrong word, though, because I don't mean the sun 'already' set behind the mountains and that I am late. I didn't come late, but the sun left the sky early. It 'already' set behind clouds in the horizon, earlier than I expected, leaving behind only shade. My last days in Phoenix before returning to Houston were like this too.

I had hoped for a final sunset, a sunset with colleagues at my school, a sunset with friends in Teach For America, and most important, a sunset with Victor and his family. But it didn't happen like that. I wasn't walking on a sunset trail, and I wasn't sitting at a sunset point. It was more of an early sunset. The final moments weren't supposed to be final. Sunsets happened while I was still figuring out where to sit.

Maybe the final sunset happened the day Sandra Cisneros came to my class, and my students asked her hard questions about her book, and I brought her and a few of my former students out for Mexican food, and she and I toasted the kids with our margaritas.

Maybe the final sunset was the second-to-last day of school at Garcia, the day I wore a suit and tie, and my students asked me why I was wearing special clothes, and I told them because this was a special day, our last day together with me as their teacher and them as my students.

Or maybe the final sunset was the videotape I made with Tommy, Elizabeth, and Jackson, the video in which we in unison chanted, "We are family, we are family, we are family, we are family..." I remember that as we said those words, I only heard how they sounded, monotone, haunting, like a four-headed alien, certainly strange. I didn't hear the words themselves.

But then, the last day I saw the kids, the day before I left Phoenix, I watched the video with them. I listened to how they talked about the end of our movie. I realized that to them it wasn't the sound of the words that mattered, but the meaning. These words were not just an ending to an hour-long home video, but also an ending to our two years of outings, adventures, and conversations. "We are family."

But what about Victor? When was the sunset with Victor? It wasn't when the kids made the video—Victor wasn't even there for that. It wasn't my anticlimactic yelling episode on Day Fourteen when we drove from San Diego back to Phoenix. At that point, we were tired of traveling and tired of each other. And it wasn't my goodbye handshake with Victor or our slightly awkward final picture together.

Was it when Victor was telling his brothers and sisters about his video of the stars when we got back? Was it when he said to his mom, "Look, that's the sunset at the Grand Canyon. Look how beautiful it is..."? Or was it the last time Victor and I talked in his driveway, our brief conversation about my quick visit with Vanessa, and my passing along to him how much she missed him during our two week trip?

No, none of that. I think the sunset for us came the very last time we talked in Phoenix, on the phone, unplanned and unemotional, the night of Day Fourteen when in the afternoon we were at his house. I forgot the road trip videotape there that last afternoon. I called his house as soon as I got to my apartment, but it was already late, and he was going to bed.

"Hey, Victor, it's me. I think I left two of the videotapes in your house. Can you check?"

"Sure, but I don't see them. I don't think you left them here."

"Look again. Look by the couch where I was sitting while we were watching the videos."

"I'm looking around. I don't see them."

"Try under the seat, or behind the cushions."

"Oh," he said after a pause, "I found them. They were stuck under the cushion. You want to pick them up tomorrow?"

"I'd rather get them out of your mailbox right away. I'm going to leave for Houston really early tomorrow, and I don't want to bother anyone. I'd like to go get them tonight."

"You want me to put them out there now?"

"Yeah, do you mind?"

"No, it's okay."

"Thanks. By the way, you don't have my phone number in Houston, do you?"

"No. That's why I told you to call me first."

"Oh, okay. I'll call you first. Goodnight, Victor. Take care."

"You too. Bye-bye."

But even that wasn't the sunset. The sunset, the actual moment of day passing to night, the moment which marked a conclusion for me and Victor, a transition for Victor and me, was when I got to his house and opened up the mailbox. The two tapes were there. Just as Victor had promised.

Our sunset wasn't really a conclusion. It was a transition. A transition for Victor and me.

■■■■■■■■■■■■

Dear Dr. Marans,

I got back to Phoenix from our road trip. We ended our trip by talking about money issues, and the kids slept a lot. It was uneventful. During my drive I got to thinking that maybe I'm missing something with Victor in terms of limitations and personal responsibility. Maybe that's not what this experience is really about, anyway. Circumstance and blame and limitations are parts of his background that I need to appreciate in order to appreciate him.

This experience, my experience, is not seeing about his background: it's about seeing him. First I have to be sensitive to his circumstances. Then, and only then, can I assign blame. Blame and responsibility and limitations. And finally, from what I think are his limitations and assets, I can try to make out the canyon in Victor.

To begin with, Victor had nothing to do with his circumstances. But as a thirteen-year-old child, he sure has endured a lot of pain from day to day—just as I would have had my father been killed, had my mother beaten me all of my life, and had I been afraid of stray bullets killing me at night while I was sleeping. When I was thirteen, I had trouble sleeping when the closet door was open, and I lived in a well-fortified, well-alarmed house in the Houston suburbs. I can not imagine the nightly difficulties I would have had in a thinly walled house in a neighborhood infamous for its drive-by shootings. For Victor not to have made many of the bad decisions he's made as a teenager would have required enormous strength. For me not to recognize his circumstances would be extremely insensitive.

Had I been in Victor's shoes, had I grown up with those circumstances, I probably would have been responsible for behaving very much the same way he has. Maybe that's why I find him compelling. I see something in Victor that I have fought off in myself: a certain weakness of self, an irrationality in action, a self-destructiveness in purpose and in consequence. Had I been in Victor's shoes, probably I, too, would be to blame for many of the reckless decisions he's made along the way. Maybe only the strongest two or three people I know could have been in his shoes and not become brutal or sadistic at some point.

But then, in my mind, that's the point—it may be very hard, but it's not impossible. It would be condescending to say he's entirely limited by his limitations. He didn't have to use the anger and fear beaten into him to propel him toward a life of violence, to weaken him into a person with no capacity to postpone gratification, and to leave him with no persistent sense of self. He possesses kindness and curiosity and spirit, too; that was obvious during most of our trip and even before our trip. He didn't have to make so many poor decisions in his life. He didn't have to be uncaring and selfish. He's a loving, giving person.

Now, don't get me wrong: if I were a betting man, I'd certainly give Victor bad odds, but that doesn't mean his failures are inevitable, predestined. His life wasn't entirely predetermined before he was born, but it certainly didn't give him a fair chance either. He needs an incredible kind of strength to be able to maintain a sturdy sense of self and an acceptable aura of dignity at the same time. And even though he doesn't have it yet, I think it's learnable or findable, that strength. I've caught glimpses of it inside Victor.

That's enough philosophizing for now. I'll tell you details of the trip another time.

Very Warmly,

Jeremy

P.S. I mean to say I don't feel sorry for Victor, but I do feel sorry about all the obstacles in his life. Still, Victor has been blessed with good health, good humor, good nourishment, and the capacity to think and to feel. I think, overall, he's a lucky person.

PART IV
doble ve

The Same

It's weird being back in Phoenix a year later. As a first year medical school student, I have two months off this summer, so I'm spending a week in Arizona. The streets still seem fast and the traffic mean. One thing that's apparent to me now, more than ever before, is the lack of diversity. Everywhere I go with the kids, whether it's to movie theaters or driving ranges, all the people are either white or Mexican. On occasion we see someone who's black, but not very often. And I'm not sure how a third of the people on the planet can be Chinese or Indian, yet none outside the restaurant business have found their way to Phoenix.

Victor looks quite a bit larger to me. He's fourteen years old now, and he's broader around the shoulders since we hiked the canyons last summer. Also, his face is rounder at the cheeks and stronger at the chin, like his mother's. He's not nearly as friendly or enthusiastic as he was the last time I saw him, but it might just be that we haven't warmed up to each other yet. Or it might be that he's a jerk.

The inside of his home is also much larger and nicer than before. His mother built a few additional rooms onto the house, she modernized all the fences, and she bought several bedding units and couches to fill the new rooms.

One thing that hasn't changed this year is that Victor's house is still the place in Phoenix where I feel the most at home. Everyone, except for Victor, has been really warm and inviting. Maybe Victor's the exception, because he knows that I'm not happy with him.

When Victor first told me on the phone that he joined Doble, I decided not to say most of what I thought. I didn't want to tell him this is a terrible decision and he's responsible for making it until I saw him in person, and since I've been in school in Boston, I've had no choice but to wait for many months.

Until now, Victor and I haven't had a few minutes of privacy. Even though we aren't talking much now, I still think that now may be the best time for me to tell him how I feel about his gang.

Kids join his gang Doble at about thirteen years old. The gang name is Wetback Power, WBP, but everyone calls it Doble because the first initial "W" is "doble ve" in Spanish, translated back as 'w' or double 'v' in English.

So Victor's in the gang 'Doble,' his initials are 'doble,' both initials are a "ve," and his personality is 'doble'—there're at least two Victors. That's four reasons that it's fitting he's in a WBP.

"Wassup puto?" he says nicely to me. He sits at a plywood desk tightly squeezed between a narrow white bed and a bare white wall, so even though I haven't seen him for almost a year, I can't really see him now either.

"Nothing," I say. "Things are cool." We sit silently for a few moments. "You know, Victor, you're messing up your life."

He doesn't flinch or stop playing Solitaire for even a second. "What you talking about, homes? I be doing all the same stuff."

"The same stuff?" I ask, feeling my head get warm.

He knows what I mean. "Nah, just how I always kicked it with my older homies. All that happened is now I'm a G. Don't be worried, ese. It just means a few pints and a few bitches more, with a blunt or two in between. Plus now my homies got my back. See, homes, it's basically all the same." Although he's being friendly in tone, he keeps me facing his back.

"Then why'd you wait?" I ask.

"I was scared, fool. I didn't think I could hang wid' it," he says casually, clicking the mouse to pick up a card.

"What makes you think you can 'hang wid it' now?"

"I don't know. I'm not afraid no more. I got muscles, pendejo. When they jumped me in, I fought back, dude. Pah! Pah! Pah!" he says proudly as he demonstrates three punches with one arm while he keeps the other on the keyboard. "I was strong."

I'm still sitting on the side of the bed in the same place.

■■■■■■■■■■■■■

Solitaire

The door to Victor's room opens, and Jackson, who's now seven, peeks inside. Only a sliver of his face is visible, but his eyes are open wide. "I'll be out in a few minutes," I tell him. He says nothing and closes the door.

I don't know what to say to Victor. I feel my heart beat hard and my stomach pull in as I think about Victor in a gang.

"Dude, let's just kick it," he says, clicking on another card. "Let's talk about something different, ese."

I'm angry about this gang nonsense. I want to make Victor angry too. But I'm having trouble getting his attention. "If I were in a gang, I wouldn't want to talk about it either."

"This is my problem, okay? It don't matter, anyway," he says, faltering slightly.

"Don't matter?" I shout. I look away from his back and stare at the ceiling.

"What happened? Why'd you change so much?"

Victor stops. He takes his hands off the keyboard and glances over his shoulder.

"What's your problem?" he says loudly. "It's not that different. I just wanted to be a thug."

He twists his body around and bends his head up. I look hard at his face. He keeps it virtually emotionless. Only his eyebrows seem tight.

"A thug?" I say mockingly. "A thug? You lied to me. You told me you wouldn't join a gang."

"I always wanted to be in a gang, Jermy. Ever since I was a little kid watching them in their low riders, blasting their radio, I always wanted to be in a gang," he says with a crack in his voice.

I squint. As always, his room is impeccably clean. "For what?"

"So all the little kids would see me, and they be like, 'Damn, that nigga's tight.'" His entire body's now turned and he's sitting sideways in his chair, but still he's not looking at me. My hands fall. I feel lost. "Let's just kick it, dude. Chill out."

Jackson opens Victor's door again. I keep the door in my peripheral vision because I'm looking hard at Victor. A small child is at his door. I know it's Jackson, but I don't really look. I'm concentrating. "Jackson, I'll be out in a little bit."

"Stupid fucking—" As Jackson shuts his door, Victor doesn't continue.

I notice a crack in the white wall behind Victor. "What if you get yourself killed?" I try to ask calmly. In a sense, I want to talk about this possibility. I know I have to. I hold a finger over the lid of each eye. I stand.

"I don't want to talk about this no more," He says angrily. "Forget it."
He then turns back to the computer and moves the cursor to the deck.
He draws the king of hearts, appropriately. I wonder if he's ever looked at
that king.

"I don't care what you want," I speak in a low, controlled voice. "You
have to think about it." I've lost control. I feel like pushing Victor off his
stupid chair.

"What?" Victor asks sharply without looking away from his computer.
"You want me to think about it?" He pauses. "There, I thought about it." He
then looks at me briefly and looks back at the game. I'm stunned. "Happy?
Now chill out."

"You and your mother-fucking games. This shit, Solitaire, what next?"
I am starting to shout, I think about what I could break. I spit with each 'f':
"Who the fuck you think you are, telling me to chill the fuck out? Look at
me, goddamn it, and get your face out of that fucking game."

"My mom doesn't even yell at me like this," Victor recoils with a whine.
"Get off my freakin' back." He doesn't swear. "We're not at school anymore.
We're in my room, and you're at my house, so chill out. I don't like being
yelled at."

"You've made me so mad I have to yell." I shout, "Sometimes I don't
think you care about anyone besides yourself."

"My mother and my father."

"Oh, well now, that's great. That's really great. You hate your mother,
and your father's dead. And now you tell me they're the only people you
care about. I'd hate to know how you feel about the people you don't care
about."

I mean to be insensitive about his mother and rude about his father. I
mean to imply he's alone in life. I hope I hit him where it hurts.

"You always getting in everybody's business," he mumbles, keeping his
eyes on the computer. Again, I cannot see his face.

I sit back down onto the edge of his white bed and stare at the brown
carpet. I listen to his hands move across the computer keyboard as he continues to play Solitaire. A few seconds pass.

"I don't get in everybody's business, Victor. Just in yours and mostly
right now." I stutter, "I care about you. That's why I'm getting in your

business and yelling so much. I'm tired of losing my friends."

"You aren't supposed to yell at your friends."

"I know. But sometimes I have to."

As I say this, Jackson opens the door again. He has a tired look on his face. He comes in and sits down beside me on the side of the bed, leans over, and puts his head onto my lap. "Hey Jackson," I speak softly as I pat his head. "This isn't a good time for you to be in here," I try to speak gently. He doesn't move.

"Jackson, I don't want you in here right now. We'll be out in a few minutes." I shift my legs. He gets up and leaves without a word, his head still slouched over his chest.

■ ■ ■ ■ ■ ■ ■ ■ ■ ■ ■ ■ ■

Care

I look toward Victor and say, "I know I'm yelling a lot, but when my friends mess up this bad, I yell at them."

"That's 'cause they're stupid," he replies.

"My friends are stupid? You think my friends are stupid? Who's the stupid one, Victor? Who's in a fucking gang?" I stand up again. I wanna fight.

He pulls his legs around the chair and faces me. "Fine, if you're friends are that way, fine. But I don't like being yelled at." He looks right at me.

"You know why I'm mad?" I respond. "Because you have a choice, you know, a goddamn choice. And all I can think about right now is my friend who had no choice and died of cancer last week. I mean, he had no choice. And here you are, and look what you're choosing to do with your life." I remember sitting in the car with my friend four months ago and telling him about Victor. I'm very sad about losing him.

"You wish I had cancer, huh?" Victor says.

"No, I'm not saying that." I stop. His comment throws me off. I forget what I want to say. I mean to be personal and tell him that I'm afraid of another terrible phone call about someone I care about a lot. Instead, I revert to a lesson; I compare gangs to cancer. "All I'm saying is I wish my friend were as lucky as you. I mean, with all you're doing, you might as well have cancer."

"I wish you'd get cancer," Victor mumbles without looking at me. He's barely loud enough for me to hear.

I imagine Victor in a parking lot in the back of a low rider, sitting between two older guys, who are holding guns and who laugh at him when he jumps at the sound of a shot. "You didn't always act like this, Victor," I say. "I even remember a time when you told me you were afraid of dying."

"I don't want to hear about it, and I don't care what you remember," he says sharply. His body stays frozen. "I just wanna play Solitaire." He pauses as he speaks. His voice is ice.

"Stupid—" I stop myself... His words 'don't care' sock me in the stomach.

"It's not that bad. I'm probably gonna graduate from high school, anyway," he says out of nowhere.

"I remember when you used to talk all the time about going to college," I feel sad, shifting my weight, unsure what to say or how to stand.

"I still might go," he replies. He gets up and looks behind his bed. He seems to be searching for something.

"Sure," I say in a flat voice. I've given up. I can't even make a good case against a gang. I'm pathetic. I sit back down.

"Dude, chill out. You're using that all hushed voice," Victor says. "Let's just kick it. Let's just have a nice time."

■ ■ ■ ■ ■ ■ ■ ■ ■ ■ ■ ■

Vida Pasada

I'm four years into my five-year medical school program, and during my first semester, I've returned to Phoenix for several months of research. I'm doing a research project that involves students and their writing, so I've returned to the second school where I worked in Phoenix. And because I live near the Villanueva family, I get the added benefit of their company.

I haven't seen Victor for two and a half years. The last time I saw him, we argued in his room about his gang. Victor's seventeen years old now. It's been more than three years since our road trip.

"Thanks, homes," Victor says to me as we walk up his driveway and bump fists. He's been on house arrest, since he was caught driving in a stolen car, but his probation officer agreed to let him go out with me.

"No prob, V, I'm glad we finally got to hang out," I say.

"I know, it's the first time since you been here," he replies. I've been in Phoenix for the past two weeks, and I've seen him in passing nearly every night. I've been going over to his house often: to eat dinner with his family, to help his siblings with homework, and to bring them on various errands. But tonight is the first time Victor and I have had a chance to talk one-on-one since he picked me up at the airport when I first arrived.

"It was nice of the P.O. to let you go for dinner with me," I say. I spoke to his probation officer on the phone earlier today.

"It's 'cause you sounded like Harvard," he says, giving me a knowing smile.

When Victor and I return from our Chinese dinner, we decide to talk outside for a while longer. I lean against the brown sedan, which sits in the driveway. I'm facing the silhouette of South Mountain. Victor faces me. He sits on the bumper of his white truck, which is parked behind the brown car. His legs somehow squeeze between the back of one car and the front of the other.

"How's your book about us coming, Jermy? Did you sell it yet?"

"No, I'm working on it, though. Hey, I've been meaning to ask you, what last name should I use for you? I don't want to use the real one. That way you and your family won't get in any trouble."

Victor nods knowingly. "Hey, how about Rivera—that's my father's name and it's my middle name."

"I know, but even that could be too real given your mom's business and all. I had an idea, though. It's not great, but it sounds a little like your real last name. What about Villanueva?"

"Vidanueva," Victor says back, not quite hearing what I said. "I like that idea. Vida nueva. My name would mean new life." I remember, during one of our after-school feasts, when he said, 'maybe life-after-death is starting over in a new life,' and laughed when I asked if it was 'similar to redoing a quiz.'

As Victor and I continue to speak in low tones about family problems and girl problems, Jackson comes running outside and jumps onto the trunk of the brown car. He leans his head against my back. I think back to the last time Victor and I had a long conversation. We were sitting in his room, and he was playing Solitaire. I recall not letting Jackson stay then, but now, I don't mind. Maybe the difference is that tonight we're outside and chatting without any direction, maybe the difference is that Jackson is ten now rather than seven, maybe there's something different about Victor's tone, or maybe there's something different about mine.

Victor looks at me intensely. "I need a counselor, Jermy. I want to learn to control my temper."

I nod but say nothing.

"There a lot of things I want to get off my chest. Sometimes I get real stressed out."

I speak softly, "You're right. We should find you one." I feel Jackson silently lean against me.

"I act terrible sometimes."

"You do," I say.

"When I get mad, I'm a monster. I don't even know what I'm doing. I lose control, Jermy. I become a monster." I understand what Victor means by losing control, his fights at school, his bank card craze in my car on Baseline, the frightening phone incident with Elizabeth, the frog genocide at Zion. But still, I'm surprised and glad to hear him say it.

"Have you been that way recently?" I ask.

"Yeah, last weekend, when I hurt José. He was talking some stuff to me, and I lost it, dude. I started boxing him. I socked him with my fist." I saw the cut on José's eyelid the night after the fight. Knowing I was in medical school, he had asked me to look at it.

"I know, his cut was real bad," I say. At the time I saw it, I didn't think to ask about the cause of the cut.

"That night he kept calling over to me, but I wouldn't open my door. I didn't want to talk to him. The next morning he saw me and tried to apologize, but I wouldn't let him." José had accused Victor of sniffing paint. Victor had claimed it wasn't true, but José had refused to believe him.

"What did you do in the end?"

"I apologized to him. I didn't mean to hurt him like that. I don't know what happened. I felt bad afterwards."

"You've got a terrible temper," I say.

"I want to be calm and be like an adult. Look, I'm a grown person now. I'm seventeen. I'm gonna be on my own soon. I gotta get my life better. I wish I never started WBP and the gangster life."

"You've grown a lot," I say.

"I got to get me out of here. The only way I can get off the streets is getting married. Get me a girlfriend. You know how girls are. Go over here, go over there. I think that'll help."

"It might," I say, "But even if you move into a new house and have a new wife, the problem's still inside you." I think back to Victor's paranoia while we were in Flagstaff. He thought people were flashing gang signs at him and shouting at him, even though it's a small college town with no gangs, hours away from Phoenix, and even though it was the first time in his life that he was there. Plus, he wasn't even in a gang back then.

"It's in my head. It's how I think. Everyone around me are gangsters. It's 'cause I was raised that way, like a G."

He's right. He's finally saying what I've been hoping he would say for years.

He continues, "I grew up with guns, huh Jackson, all my life I grew up with guns."

Jackson has said nothing until this invitation from Victor. Jackson sits up.

"Every day—every month, Victor gets a gun, every month. When he gets money, he's like, 'I'm gonna buy me a strap and strap my shit up,'" Jackson says. "Next day, he comes with his nine millimeter and shit."

Jackson, as a ten year old, has learned how to speak the way Victor does in public and knows how to imitate our quiet tone, but he doesn't really understand what we're talking about. I'm not sure I do either.

"That's why I got a lot of friends in jail 'cause they grew up the same way I did," Victor says.

"I wonder how come your friends all went to jail and you didn't," I say.

"I've always been the smartest," he answers assuredly.

Jackson speaks proudly, "Victor always runs and shit. He always runs."

Victor continues, "Every time the cops come or something, I'm gone. They don't get me. One time we were at some apartments and they caught like five fools, but they didn't catch me. I know how to run good."

"Everybody got caught, but not you?" I ask, unsure if I should feel thankful.

"The only times I got caught was for traffic violations," he says.

"I can't believe everybody has gone to jail but you."

"I been in the hood longer than all my homies. I been in the hood two years longer than all the fools my age, and they still got in jail quicker and sooner than me."

"That's crazy," I say. "They went to jail 'cause they don't know how to run."

I wonder what this means. I wonder if Victor runs faster or if he starts sooner. I wonder if he's more intelligent, more self-protective, or more afraid.

"Did any of them get shot?" I ask.

"I had like two buddies, three buddies that died, four buddies…"

"Jesus."

"…four buddies killed in the past two years." I have never heard Victor use the word 'buddy.'

"That's awful," I say.

"That's why I'm scared to death. 'Cause look, my homies died. I had one homie that died, he was drinking, going down First Avenue by Central. You know how the road splits? He went down the wrong way. Hit a car. Killed him. Killed him and his brother. He was one of my homies from my hood. And his brother died with him too, all 'cause he did that and crashed. And another one of my homies was on Central and Roeser when some fools rolled up on him and shot him with an AK."

"Oh God," I say.

"They killed him right there on the spot."

"Hey Jermy—" Jackson's got a story he wants me to hear, but I am listening intensely to Victor.

"How old was that guy?" I ask Victor in a somber tone.

"He was like sixteen. The other one that died was like eighteen." I shake my head. Victor continues, "I had another homie that died at the apartments on First Street and Broadway, seventeen years old, he was a drug dealer, my age, a big time drug dealer. Made a lot of money. Some guy sold him a motorcycle and my homie bought it for like fifty dollars, a motorcycle, and then he crashed it into a wall and hit his forehead. He died immediately."

"Did you know all their families? Like their mothers?" I ask instinctively.

"Yeah, I did. That's when I be like, 'Man, what if I get killed?'" Victor says.

"You're lucky that you haven't." It feels unreal to be saying this.

Victor shifts his body but continues to look right at me. "They shot me up a couple times. They shot me with an AK in Celia's car, shot it all up. They didn't hit me, though. They thought I was dead, but actually they didn't hit me. And then, they shot me up again with a twelve-gauge. They shot me with an AK. Over there, I was on 7th Street and Roeser, I was at the light. Some fools recognized me and shit, and started dumping at me with a nine millimeter. Shot up the car, but missed me. Lucky. Real lucky. That's why I'm scared to death, fool."

"And then him and—" Jackson starts to say.

"And then I got my homie Chango and my homie Nagarita. My homie Nagarita is sixteen, Chango's nineteen. They murdered some fools on Central. They got, like, one of them got twenty-five years, Nagarita, and Chango got fifteen years. Murderers and everything. I'm always around it."

"Have you ever been in a drive-by?" I ask.

"Yeah, but I didn't do it," he answers, "I didn't do it. But I was in the car. I was drunk. My homie shot a lady in the head. I was there with him. He did it just for the fun of it."

"An old lady?" I ask.

"Not that old. And just for the fun of it."

"Wow," I am overwhelmed.

"I was drunk. I didn't know what I was doing. He was talking shit, and then boom, boom, boom, boom. I don't even know how many people he shot. But I did see a lady get shot, one of them lady gangbangers."

"What did you think?" I ask, not sure what to think myself.

Victor looks at me and answers slowly.

"I'm kicking it with killers," he says, his voice rising. "I got to get used to it. I'm with them all the time."

He pauses.

"I don't want to kill nobody," Victor says, "You know how gang-bangers are. Half of them will shoot you; they don't care. They're bad killers. Then half of them just make drug deals and stuff. There's different types of people. There's the people who like to make the money, the gang bangers, and there's the people who like to kill people, the murderers. My homies, they always go around shooting people. They're murderers."

■■■■■■■■■■■■■

Vida Nueva

A truck pulls up and stops in front of the house. We all turn around. A man gets out; the boys tell me he is their mother's new boyfriend.

"All right there, Frank," Jackson shouts out, greeting the man as he walks up the driveway past us. "That fool comes early in the morning. He comes here and gets some coffee. Early, early! He comes at midnight and then early in the morning. He don't even sleep—I mean, he sleeps like one hour, that's it."

"Frank was a gang banger like me when he was my age, but now he's an OG," Victor explains. "I mean, he changed, he really changed. I'm

gonna be eighteen years old next year, and I'm changing too. I'm changing my life. I'm getting started already. This was just my juvenile life."

"You're lucky you're not in jail or in a coffin," I say needlessly.

"I know," Victor agrees, "But this was just my juvenile life. By the
time I'm twenty-two, I'll be an OG."

"Then you don't have to act like this anymore?"

"Yup, nobody can tell me what to do. I remember when I was just
thirteen, all my homies were bossing me around, all my big homies. 'You
better fucking watch it. You better fucking hold my rifle. You better fucking shoot.' I be like, 'All right, dogs. I got your back. Cool, dogs. All right.'
And then I was fucked."

Victor stops talking. He stares at his home.

He says, "They wanted me to see all the killing. They wanted me to
get used to seeing all the murder and grow up just like them."

"Do you want to?" I ask.

"I don't. That's why I'm gonna change. Watch." Victor says this and
pauses.

I lift my head and look deep into Victor's eyes. "You've got to figure
out what's different about you from all those other guys."

He sits quietly for a moment, still, intense, between the brown sedan
and the white truck. "I think I got a kind heart," he says, looking down.
"Out of all those guys, I think I got a kind heart."

We don't move.

"I feel bad and I just—" he stops himself and looks back up at me.
I give him a strong hug. He holds nothing back. He is breathing hard.
"They don't. They don't care." He crumbles.

No one speaks. Everything is still.

"I'm gonna change my life," he looks deep in my eyes. "I swear, Jermy,
I'm gonna change."

Darkness washes out the Phoenix sky, and the street lamps rise like
stars above us.

afterword

Why I Wrote About Victor

Had I written a book about my experience as a teacher, it wouldn't be about my student Victor Villanueva, nor would it be about the adventures and misadventures I had with him and his family.

Rather, it would be about my student Shamika, who wrote several hundred-page stories filled with palpable dialogue about girls in rap groups, their delinquent boyfriends, and teenage pregnancies, Shamika who wanted to go to Harvard and afterward become a doctor and famous writer.

It would also be about Emanuel and Andrés, who worked together in my classroom each day during lunch for the last two months of the school year to build a Spacewarp marble roller-coaster for an overly ambitious science fair project—Emanuel, who happily obsessed over every curve and angle of the marble track until he made it work to perfection, and Andrés, who was the smallest boy in my class, but wrote his anger as if he were a giant.

And it would be about Arthur, who told me he wanted to run a homeless shelter someday, and his mother, who desperately wanted him to stay in my class and not be switched into Special Education, because she knew better than the test-man what was best for her son.

And finally, it would be about Karina, who had been abandoned by her mother and whose father was in jail, Karina, who seemed to ponder every word she wrote, and who wrote darkly and slowly and always finished her class work last.

That's why, if I were going to write about my experience as a teacher, it wouldn't be about the twelve-year-old Victor I knew as a student, who lied more often than he told the truth, who shrugged off D's and F's, who stole during his favorite class, and who rarely did his best in school. I wouldn't focus on a child who was constantly trying to prove his masculinity, who persistently demonstrated a racist thought-process, and who bragged incessantly about the pain he caused others. I wouldn't choose the Victor I first knew in school as an example of my students. He really wasn't.

Had I written about the community of South Phoenix, I wouldn't use Victor's perspective of that either. Rather, I'd describe the colorful small houses that dot the desert landscape, the brown mountain behind them, and the city pools that by afternoon are always filled with children. I'd describe a two o'clock lunch on Central Avenue at Pete's Fish and Chips with a half-dozen people sitting around me at shaded picnic tables eating grilled chicken and greasy burgers.

And I'd describe the time at Pete's when I saw my student Freddy, who last week at school had explained his single mother's death two weeks earlier. "Life feels like a dream," he had said. "I want to punch God." He had to change schools, teachers, homes, neighborhoods, neighbors, routines, rules, and social worlds, all without his mother. Freddy and I sat at school that morning and cried. Several months later, at Pete's, Freddy was with his brother, Dave, who at twenty-four was just a year older than I was. Dave was Freddy's legal guardian, and Freddy had been living with him ever since their mother had died.

I'd describe a warm Saturday evening in Dave's front yard, sipping beers with him and his construction worker friends, who told me proudly how they managed to raise five thousand dollars to help him pay for his mother's funeral. One of Dave's friends donated a thousand dollars to the fund and gave the brothers a bear hug in front of the bonfire and said to me in a slow, drunken voice with tears streaming from his eyes, "These boys will never be alone. They will be my sons, and I will be their father."

Despite this book's setting in a poverty-stricken neighborhood, it is not a story about poverty. Also, despite the wealth of hope and love and spirit in South Phoenix, the book is not about that either. This book is not about its main setting in South Phoenix at all. It's about a person who lives there. It's about the layers I've been able to see in Victor Villanueva.

To be honest, the main reason I chose Victor is that he chose me. He came to me after school more often than any other student and allowed me to enter his world and to see sides of him that I otherwise could not have seen as his school teacher, and that would not have fit into a newspaper as an article. And I continued to write about Victor because he more than anyone showed me that people don't always say what they mean, and there is often a wide disconnect between one's behavior and one's feelings, between the content and context of one's actions, and between one's persona one moment and his persona the next, and that to understand a person, I have to read between the lines of his words and actions, between and among and through and outside and within.

I no longer think it a coincidence that a child whose behavior was among the worst of his community, who was practically an outsider living inside South Phoenix, who was usual to the newspaper reports of the place, but unusual to the people in the place, would be the one with whom I'd spend the most time. Because the reasons that Victor acted like an outsider are also the reasons that he was interested in talking to me on the patio of his house at eleven o'clock at night. Victor needed a friend. And, as it happened, so did I.

■ ■ ■ ■ ■ ■ ■ ■ ■ ■ ■ ■

Did I save Victor?

At what point can I say one has succeeded or failed in life? When does Victor's story end? Victor as a character in a book has an ending, maybe not closure, but an ending. Victor as a person does not. We cannot evaluate success or saving a person without a time-frame. We ought not even think in those terms.

Would it have been a success for Victor to do well in eighth grade and high school but not get into college? Would it have been enough for Victor to graduate from college but not get a good job? Would it have been enough for Victor to get a good job and make a good living if he hated his life? What does it take for me to label Victor a success?

So, did I save Victor? From what? Being at risk? No, I think not. We're all at risk. We cannot make a statement about life that leaves no room for the passage of time or the ambiguity of success.

■ ■ ■ ■ ■ ■ ■ ■ ■ ■ ■ ■

Cancer

Six years ago, during a summer break from my residency, I was diagnosed with brain cancer and had surgery. I didn't tell Victor what was happening. My symptoms had been minor. I didn't know they'd find extensive cancer and have to do surgery and radiation. The results of the surgery and radiation were not at all minor. Now I have regular appointments with a neuro-oncologist, a wheelchair specialist, a neurologist, an endocrinologist, a urologist, a psychiatrist, a hematologist, an optometrist, an ophthalmologist, an internist, and two rehabilitation therapists.

Every quarterly MRI I've had over the last six years since the cancer indicates that I'm cancer-free. Though eighty percent of us with this cancer do fine in the first five years, only twenty to twenty-five percent do fine the next five years. Not a lot of us luck out totally. But some do, and they're cured. It may very well be that I'll be among the lucky ones. I've always been lucky, even in my misery in the hospital. Through the window of my VIP room in one of the five private hospitals where I received care, I could see the yellow brick wall of the public hospital on the other side of the road.

In a different way, Victor is lucky too. He's lucky to be alive. It's a scary thought, but with all the shootings, at him, near him, in his neighborhood, throughout his world, he's lucky he's alive. He has grown up surrounded by danger. Most rational people would be afraid to enter his world.

I didn't want to call Victor once I was able to. It's not that I minded his knowing about my cancer and disabilities; they explained my long absence. But I did mind having him hear my new voice. I felt it was hard for other people to understand me. I couldn't even understand myself. My new voice embarrassed me. I didn't want Victor to hear me sound like this. I wanted him to remember the way I used to sound. I wanted to be dead to Victor. But finally I called.

I thought exposing my voice was enough. I didn't want my whole new self to be exposed, too. So visiting? Going in person to Phoenix? Forget it. I had a shred of dignity left. Although we had talked about it, Victor could not have known what I looked like now, five years after my surgery. And I didn't want him to know. He, ten years ago, and his father, fifteen years ago, had said, "I don't want them to see me like this." I felt the same way. Maybe it was unwise, but I thought I looked ridiculous. I hated it, and I didn't want to be seen. I wanted to be a memory. Not a person.

But I am a person. I ended up feeling sad about the situation. I felt distant from Victor, where we had been close before. Part of me wished we were neighbors. And now we were far apart. Most of me wanted to sit next to my boy. I wanted to know about him. I wanted him to know about me. I wondered if he still cared.

I didn't expect to visit. I tried to talk my way out of it. He said my limitations didn't matter. There was a part of me that also didn't want them to matter either. Eventually I went. "Don't worry about it, Jermy," he said to me over and over while I was panicking about going. "Mi casa es tu casa," he kept saying. He meant it too.

■ ■ ■ ■ ■ ■ ■ ■ ■ ■ ■ ■ ■

New Life

My ten year reunion with Victor begins with a view from South Mountain. I still know thirteen-year-old Victor's street. That's where he showed his mother videos of himself at the Grand Canyon. But twenty-four-year-old Victor has a new life. I wonder if, ten years later, he still thinks about being a news reporter. I do know, at twenty-four, he likes being a foreman at his construction job because he only has to work six of seven days each week.

"I'm not rich," he often says. But he has four kids, a wife, and a job. He's not in jail and no one's in a hospital. Arizona's immigration policies have been rough on him, but not debilitating. I don't think he's poor. In many respects, he seems like a wealthy man.

"Jermy, grab on up there and then on this thing." I'm transferring from my wheelchair into a borrowed station wagon. "Are you okay?" he asks. He's had to transfer me into this station wagon only once before. "Then there's another thing up there." I try to do what he says. "Hold on.

Grab the other thing. Right there. By the door. I got you. Good," he says, as he fastens my seatbelt. "Are you comfortable, Jermy?" I still like how Victor calls me 'Jermy.'

"I'm good," I say.

Victor sits in back of me, next to his baby in a car seat. His other three kids sit behind him. It's one o'clock and no one's eaten yet. "Are you hungry, J?" he asks. He knows about the problems I have with appetite and food.

"I don't know," I say honestly.

We're leaving South Mountain to go back to Baseline. Victor's wife is driving. He's directing us to a Chinese joint. Three years ago, General Tsao's Chicken was too spicy for me. Now, I eat it and love it. I'm getting better at eating. Even though I can no longer use chopsticks.

When we're leaving South Mountain, we have to pull over to rearrange my belongings. They've fallen onto his children in the back of the station wagon. We pull over on Central before we get onto Baseline, and Victor gets out and goes to the back of the truck to rearrange my things.

He has to take everything out: the folded main wheelchair, the wheelchair cushion, the wheelchair back, the manuscript papers, and my backpack, all beside three of his four kids. When he finishes, he gets back into the car in the seat behind mine and beside his baby daughter.

As we turn from Central onto Baseline, his wife asks me, "Did you have papers? I think some papers were flying off the roof."

"Oh," I breathe in.

Victor realizes that he left the box of manuscript papers on the roof of the car when he was rearranging my things.

The papers fly and they float behind us.

"The papers are all the way back on the ground on Baseline," His wife tells me. I can't tell if she's as surprised as I am about dispersing the pages of my book draft. "You wanna go back and get 'em?" she asks me warmly.

"Yes, that's a good idea." I try to speak clearly. I also try to make my voice loud enough that she and Victor can hear me.

"We can't go backwards. There's too much traffic," Victor says. He seems concerned about my manuscript papers.

I intended to have a nice neat stack of *Before a Canyon* final draft papers to give Victor. I hoped the process would be simple and forgettable, practically invisible and unobtrusive to our time together because I felt uncomfortable about mixing business into an otherwise personal and emotional journey. But so much for the poetry of reunion. My manuscript papers have become a family event.

"So what am I supposed to do?" his wife asks, annoyed.

"Stop," Victor says.

"Huh?" she says. "They're all over the ground."

"Stop."

"Why?" she seems to disagree. "The papers are way over there."

"Right here," says one of the children. It seems the whole family's involved.

"Go around and pick me up on Baseline at Central." Victor tells her.

"You're gonna walk all the way over there?" She pauses. "On Baseline? To there?"

"I'm gonna walk back there," he says as we drive. I don't understand what's going on. I have no idea what he's saying behind me. I can't hear his words, can't see him, and can't figure out exactly where we are. I need a moment to get oriented. I say nothing.

"Pull over here." He jumps out of the car. It's all happening too fast for me. I don't get my moment. Victor's walking on Baseline again. I haven't had a chance to shout, "Hold on. Wait up."

Oh God oh God oh God I should be thinking. But I'm not. I see him walking in a field, jumping a gate or two.

His wife continues, "We're gonna get back there in the car before him. He's walking way, way over there, in this heat," his wife says to me. "He's gonna get run over with all these speeding cars."

"He'll be okay," I say. Victor's always lived by Baseline.

"We have to find a place to U-turn to go back to where we were."

"Mommy, I'm famished."

"I know, Angel."

Did he just say famished?

"Mommy, why are we taking so long to get to the Chinese?"

I wonder if they eat Chinese often and if they use chopsticks.

"We dropped some papers. We went to pick 'em up. It's real complicating."

"There's Dad," says Angel. "Look, the cars all stopped like if there was an accident. Some man is giving papers to Dad."

"Where is he?" she looks around. "Oh, yeah, he got lots of them. We're gonna go get Dad 'cause he was picking up papers." His wife sounds relieved.

I'm relieved too. I don't think authors normally have conspicuous drafts that people gather from busy roads.

Victor gets back in. "You got them all?" she asks.

"Hope so." He's silent for a minute. A gazillion white pages droop from his lap. Many have tire tracks on them. My manuscript looks like a road. "How many were there, Jermy?"

"In total? Two-hundred and twelve." I say. He touches each page as if it's an original photograph of his life.

"All these pages? All about me? You're gonna make me famous?" He puts them in order and checks the page numbers too. Miraculously, they're all there.

We arrive at the Chinese restaurant, and his wife goes in with three of the four children to get food and chopsticks. Victor and I wait in the well air-conditioned station wagon. No reason to do and undo my wheelchair an extra time. Victor's son, Angel, waits with us in the station wagon.

Angel's a tall skinny boy with an impressive vocabulary who looks like his Mom.

"He looks just like me, huh?" Victor asks with a smile.

Angel was only one when I was in Phoenix six years ago right before my brain cancer, but Victor wasn't there and I didn't want to see his baby boy for the first time without him. Seeing his child for the first time in a station wagon isn't what I imagined either.

"Look how smart Angel is."

"Be-fore" Angel bends forward to read the cover.

"A Ca-n-yon," He is quiet and then looks at his dad. "What's that?"

"A real nice place. Someday, in a few years, we'll get to go."

"A story about—" I say. With a soft nudge, Victor cuts me off. I wasn't supposed to read that part. I point at the next word and smile.

"Vi-Vic," Angel starts off slowly.

"Think of your dad." I glow. I'm feeling proud. Victor smiles and holds his finger gently below the word.

"Vict-Victor." Angel looks up. Victor beams.

"You got it," I say. "And 'me' means me." I gesture toward myself. "My book's a story about your dad and me."

■ ■ ■ ■ ■ ■ ■ ■ ■ ■ ■ ■ ■

Home in Houston

I am watching Stephen Colbert and eating leftover pizza when Victor calls. I hurry to put down my food and the remote to free my hands, and then I grab the phone.

"What you doing?" is the first thing he says.

"Victor?" I say.

"I hate your book," he says. "It's making me cry. It's all real stuff, too. Even my girl is crying."

"Yeah," I smile.

"Angel's excited to try to read me the whole thing," he says. "We decided. One page at a time."

acknowledgements

When I was twelve, I thought I was a poor writer. I relayed this to my English teacher, Mrs. Sylvia Bartz, in a journal entry. She found my statement and wrote back, "You're not a bad writer; you're a very good one." She typed my poem that day. It looked fabulous and was thrilling. No one had ever studied or typed my writing before, except me.

So I'd like to thank her first, even though my writing a book was probably not what she had in mind.

You ask me, "When did you start writing your book?" This is a short, straightforward question. Yet the answer is long and convoluted. "I don't know" is the simple truth.

This book, *Before a Canyon*, evolved; it didn't really start. At first I was writing emails. I didn't know I was writing a book. Then I started staying up late to write down the day's crazy dialogues. My college writing tutor told me to take good notes. And I took advantage of my one weird skill: people's voices come into my head. If I can remember what we talked about, I can replay a whole conversation that just occurred. As I look back over my work, I am most surprised by my own dialogue. How did I remember that?

I'd like to thank Shameem Black for encouraging me to write long and self-centered emails. My emails often evolved into stories. I'd also like to thank my Phoenix writing group for telling me which stories were boring and which were good. Meanwhile, Shameem was getting a PhD and a job. She got married, moved often, but she kept reading my drafts. She urged me to write about backgrounds, explain situations, and keep the narrative well-focused. She tried to teach me to show, not to tell. She also helped me understand the experience more deeply so that I could make connections and see ironies.

Two undergraduate professors from Yale have also been extremely supportive of me since I completed college. Bryan Wolf has always encouraged me to write, and Leslie Brisman has treated me like a colleague. Both English professors helped me with a draft and both have gone far beyond the role of professor. I have been blessed by each.

Also, Jan Simpson, my writing tutor at Yale and general tutor in life, was always in my corner. She not only spent many hours helping me with what I wrote, she also helped me choose moments to focus on. She gave me faith in myself at Yale, and more so afterward. She counseled me regularly. She is my "shoulder to cry on." She will love the book, but will despise my "shoulder to cry on" language and will tell me it's trite and inaccurate.

Also three close friends from college, Lara Narcissi, Itzolin Garcia, and Chris Schuck, gave up many, many hours to help me make sense of my manuscript. Lara was most interested in childhood development and was instrumentally helpful in manuscript development, Itzolin was most fascinated by the Latino setting and pushed me to understand a Chicano boy's struggles, and Chris was most concerned about the children's socioeconomic inequalities, and he displays unusual gifts of logic. All of them were very enthusiastic about helping.

Friends in medical school read a draft, and each gave me good honest criticism. I know that's hard, so I'd like to thank Jean Lee, Shruthi Mahalingaiah, Rahul Sakhuja, Suzanne Goh, Jeff Edwards, Luis Castellanos, Eric Rosenthal, and Elizabeth Buzney for doing so with great gusto. They were all people I lived with in a residential building, so they know firsthand about how this book was written.

When I moved to a house, Jeff and Luis were my housemates, so they lived with my book as well as me. Jeff is a very caring and wise person. He said his goal in life is to be "a good father, a good husband, and a good man." When I went to my academic advisor in medical school for advice about a program, she asked me what Jeff thought. She was well aware of his attributes. When I told her his thoughts, she said, "Well then, that's what I think too." Luis is very calm and very calming. He giggles when he laughs, which is often. He is proudly Mexican but is interested in everyone. He is truly non-discriminating. He finds all TV shows, all plays, even all lectures informative. He is interested enough by everything in life never to be bored, always asking questions and engaged.

Another friend, Cal, (aka Calvin Hennig), an art professor at the Boston Museum of Fine Arts, read the manuscript and talked to me about it. He also fell victim to hearing my daily medical school gripes and gave me great advice for this book, for choosing movies, and for life in general.

I'd like to mention another group, the writer dudes from Twenty

Nine Harvard Avenue. They were too sophisticated to have a TV, so they came over to watch ours. We spent many hours together, chilling, eating, and playing on our iMacs, not doing anything medical. They each read my book carefully, not because they were obligated to as fellow writers in medical school, but because they were close friends. Each taught me a different specific lesson: Davin Quinn repaired story beginnings, Alvin Ikoku helped me to make my characters honest, and Harsha Reddy helped me with setting, teaching me how to show canyons without showing off. He did that in life, too, showed me my blessings, plus he made me laugh with his words, his schemes, and his slowness, and he always dragged me to the gym and even got me surfing.

Greg Chang, Nik Udompanyanan, and Scott Damrauer were not writers but were also great supporters of me and my writing efforts. They were great friends for outings, for food, and for talks, like the writer dudes. These three guys, the three writer dudes, and Luis, Jeff, Eric, and I, plus a few others, called ourselves "The Usual Suspects." We hung out together, graduated medical school together, and celebrated holidays together.

When I was diagnosed with cancer, all of "The Usual Suspects" came forward. They mourned my losses. But they also celebrated my life, not as a superhuman, just as a friend. They helped me fight and still do. They are kind to me. In many ways, there would be no book without "The Usual Suspects."

At one point, my former English Professor, Jane Levin, Yale's first lady, gave me great, copious writing criticism. As my first English Professor at Yale, she did that too. She is an extremely careful and thoughtful reader.

Laurie Rosenblatt, a medical school professor, took a special interest in this book too. She helped me through some very tough times in my life, and she helped me immensely with all my writing and opened my eyes to possibilities for me as a serious writer.

Now working as a marketer for PBS, Katie Sigelman as an agent's assistant did so too. She had the uncanny ability to see what wasn't there but should be. She functioned as an editor and helped me strengthen my story even when she didn't have to.

My former agent, Don Gastwirth, wouldn't edit, but loved to love.

Don praised my book so much that he even persuaded me.

Wendy Kopp, the CEO and founder of Teach For America (TFA) supported me through my trials as a TFA teacher. She doesn't edit books: she's busy with the education of all children in our nation (no small task), but she's always been generous with her time. During my years of teaching, she probably had five-thousand other teachers. Yet she spent many hours working with me. She's also given me many leadership roles as a corps member and as an alumnus of her group. Also, I originally met Victor through TFA.

There's one other TFA person I want to thank: Tom Ryan. He was my roommate both years I lived in Phoenix. He has remained a friend, and he helped me with the book. He knows Victor and Victor's family well. In college at Georgetown University, he never planned on being a teacher. Now he's in his fourteenth year. He probably didn't plan to help form the book's title either, but perhaps more than anyone else, he did. And most of all, I think he'd be shocked to know how much he helps me define moderation in human health, how much he guides my attempts at daily living.

My former rabbi, Sam Karff, has become a fantastic friend and mentor to me. He gives me great advice and helps me go down the bumpy road that is my life. He uses powerful words, such as blessing and balance and beauty, he talks with me about both philosophical issues and current movies, and we often discuss both the daily challenges and funny moments of our personal lives, our jobs, and our limits. I've been surprised by Sam's frankness about himself. Hearing Sam describe his daily challenges and imperfections, and then seeing the modestly-described but huge Sam Karff celebrations and events is rejuvenating for me. He's an excellent speaker and an insightful thinker, taking on life's most difficult questions. But most of all, I like Sam, and I care deeply about him.

After my brain cancer and after my agent's life-changing illness, I gave up on my book. But by then Sam had become a good friend, and he got his hands on it, gave it enthusiastically to his friend, Lois Stark, who gave it enthusiastically to her friend, Josephine Smith, who gave it very enthusiastically to my editor, Lucy Chambers, at Bright Sky Press. She loved the story, proudly signed a contract, and published my book.

What's more, I want to thank Lucy not only for her tough love to make my book shine with her own beautiful writing style, but also for her silliness and honesty, for being fun to see, and for caring for me above and beyond her role as editor. She turned me from a writer into an author. She's fought hard for this book. She's put me into an author world. She's helped me see myself differently.

I also want to thank the people who've been taking care of me the last six years. There would be no book if there were no me. So there are many, many people to whom I owe a debt of gratitude: nurses who helped me on toilets and in my bed, therapists who worked with me on walking and talking, pants and food, doctors who helped my shaking, my breathing, my eyes, and my blood, and last, but far from least, my aides, who help me to live from day to day.

Some aides, though, are more than aides. For example, Victory Berry, really just Vic, has become a mother hen to me. When I feel down on myself, she gives me confidence. Whenever there seems to be a problem, she fixes it. With Vic around, there are no problems.

Then there is Tray, Travon Black. I'm with Tray most of the time. I first met Travon Black as an aide, as his patient. But he has become my friend. Many of his friends he calls best friends and Godfathers, his sons and sisters, his nephews and aunts, so I never have clue who's talking to whom about what. I don't mean to brag, but I've graduated to brother-from-another-mother status. My problems are his and his are mine, but more important, my life celebrations are his and his are certainly mine. I get to hang out with his kids and his wife Tanya Clark at Thanksgivings, birthdays, and often for non-holiday holidays. I do need his help often, but regardless, to him, I'm a man. Being disabled makes you feel small. Tray doesn't see me or treat me that way. With him, I stand tall.

My sister, Jennie Tucker, read an early draft of my book while we drove from Ann Arbor to Boston. She was returning my mother's car, which she affectionately named Luigi after the green-panted Mario Brother. She also read and discussed with me each page of my then three-hundred-page drafted manuscript. I remember mostly in New York how she struggled to balance all those pages while reading and talking. This was why I relished her opinions about my book. It's also a small part of the reason why I called her "The Brain" while I was in the hospital and couldn't speak. She figured out that one finger meant yes; two, no; and three, dinner. Jennie's husband, my new brother, Josh Levin, has also been a fabulous support and fun to talk to. Josh and Jennie have both shown great care with my cancer and tremendous excitement about this book.

Betty Tucker, my grandmother, Nanny, as I say, sends me the vocabulary word quiz each month from *Reader's Digest*. We both do the quizzes—she often does better than I do. I love hearing her stories, watching game shows together (Jeopardy), and talking about her husband, Harold, my grandfather, Papa. He taught me about who and whom, when to use subjunctive verbs, how to play gin rummy, and gave me my first taste of Bailey's Irish Cream. But most of all, I love seeing Nanny and getting her hugs.

I'd also like to thank my enthusiastic and fun uncle, Rick Rosen, who introduced me to beautiful Yale at age six, to not-so-beautiful tie-dye at age seven, and to great art at age eight; Aunt Janet (Rosen), who's always loads of fun because of her amazing, youthful energy and enthusiasm; Matt Rosen, who's a real cool guy and is great to hang out with; and Mark Rosen, who's learned from Matt how to be cool but not cold—he's a bit of a firecracker.

Let me return to Phoenix. I want to thank Victor and his family. Victor's wild brothers and sisters have all been very kind to me. Each sibling is fun in his or her own way. Jackson has lots of energy, enjoys virtually everything, and has a fun sense of "fun." Elizabeth is humorously careful and deliberate, and Tommy's a thinker and a doer, not a talker; a watcher and listener, slow to react, but when he does, he's usually right. Vanessa's a rebel, Celia's a care-taker, and José is pure crazy. Victor, well, I care deeply about the guy. He's a good man.

The Villanueva family's front door has always been open to me, the family has been very open with me, and somehow Victor was able to talk about himself honestly, the proud parts and the hard-to-discuss parts, too. Speaking under the title "About Me" turns out to be a daunting task, I now realize, and in a sense that's what he's had to do all along. It's hard enough to be a person. But to show your canyon is not easy at all. And now he's a great guy. He has a wonderful and warm family, and he's someone I'm proud to call a friend. A close friend.'

Finally, I want to thank Margaret Tucker and Jeffrey Tucker, my mom and dad. Although I say their names together, Mom and Dad, it was Mom who wouldn't let me quit my job, and it was Dad who worked hard on my contract with the publisher. It was Dad who traveled to Phoenix because he wanted to help me organize my life well enough that I stopped mixing socks and lesson plans together. It was Mom who traveled to Phoenix to be sure I wouldn't drive to Houston at night alone. Dad taught me how to relate to children. Mom taught me how to think about children. Both Mom and Dad have supported me more than they had to as parents. Both have read and helped my book thoroughly and carefully. Both gave me the guts to write and publish this book. Both have loved me hard.

I apologize to everyone I have left out. Every criticism proved helpful. My book's evolution happened because of a huge team effort. Credit me alone for pig-headed bad decisions. Credit my team for any moment of brilliance. It was probably their idea.

■■■■■■■■■■■■■■